Smart City Infrastructure

Scrivener Publishing
100 Cummings Center, Suite 541J
Beverly, MA 01915-6106

Publishers at Scrivener
Martin Scrivener (martin@scrivenerpublishing.com)
Phillip Carmical (pcarmical@scrivenerpublishing.com)

Smart City Infrastructure

The Blockchain Perspective

Edited by

Vishal Kumar

Department of Computer Science & Engineering, Bipin Tripathi Kumaon Institute of Technology, Dwarahat, India

Vishal Jain

Department of Computer Science & Engineering, Sharda University, Greater Noida, India

Bharti Sharma

School of Computing, Dehradun Institute of Technology, Dehradun, India

Jyotir Moy Chatterjee

Department of Information Technology, Lord Buddha Education Foundation, Kathmandu, Nepal

and

Rakesh Shrestha

Yonsei Institute of Convergence Technology, Yonsei University, South Korea

Scrivener
Publishing

This edition first published 2022 by John Wiley & Sons, Inc., 111 River Street, Hoboken, NJ 07030, USA and Scrivener Publishing LLC, 100 Cummings Center, Suite 541J, Beverly, MA 01915, USA
© 2022 Scrivener Publishing LLC
For more information about Scrivener publications please visit www.scrivenerpublishing.com.

Wiley Global Headquarters
111 River Street, Hoboken, NJ 07030, USA

For details of our global editorial offices, customer services, and more information about Wiley products visit us at www.wiley.com.

Limit of Liability/Disclaimer of Warranty
While the publisher and authors have used their best efforts in preparing this work, they make no representations or warranties with respect to the accuracy or completeness of the contents of this work and specifically disclaim all warranties, including without limitation any implied warranties of merchantability or fitness for a particular purpose. No warranty may be created or extended by sales representatives, written sales materials, or promotional statements for this work. The fact that an organization, website, or product is referred to in this work as a citation and/or potential source of further information does not mean that the publisher and authors endorse the information or services the organization, website, or product may provide or recommendations it may make. This work is sold with the understanding that the publisher is not engaged in rendering professional services. The advice and strategies contained herein may not be suitable for your situation. You should consult with a specialist where appropriate. Neither the publisher nor authors shall be liable for any loss of profit or any other commercial damages, including but not limited to special, incidental, consequential, or other damages. Further, readers should be aware that websites listed in this work may have changed or disappeared between when this work was written and when it is read.

Library of Congress Cataloging-in-Publication Data

ISBN 978-1-119-78538-5

Cover image: Pixabay.Com
Cover design by Russell Richardson

Set in size of 11pt and Minion Pro by Manila Typesetting Company, Makati, Philippines

10 9 8 7 6 5 4 3 2 1

Contents

Preface

The goal of this book is to provide detailed, in-depth information on the state-of-the-art of the architecture and infrastructure used to develop smart cities using the Internet of Things (IoT), Artificial Intelligence (AI) and blockchain security—the key technologies of the Fourth Industrial Revolution. The book outlines the theoretical concepts, experimental studies and various smart city applications that create value for inhabitants of urban areas. Several issues that have arisen with the advent of smart cities and novel solutions to resolve these issues are presented. The IoT along with the integration of blockchain and AI provides efficient, safe, secure, and transparent ways to solve different types of social, governmental, and demographic issues in the dynamic urban environment. A top-down strategy is adopted to introduce the architecture, infrastructure, features, and security. The topics covered include the following:

- Chapter 1 starts with the basics of blockchain technology such as the design of blockchain, its elements, and functionalities. It then takes a deep dive into aspects of blockchain technology such as security, various types of consensus mechanisms, and application of blockchain technology in a smart city. Also discussed are the financial application and citizen-government framework, along with security and privacy issues and the future research direction of blockchain.
- Chapter 2 begins with the emergence and concept of the smart city. It discusses how new technologies such as the IoT can be utilized in the health industry, home automation, agriculture, supermarkets, transportation, etc.; and how they are interconnected to become a smart city. Technical innovations used in the smart city provide support for city management and transform natural resources, infrastructure, and intellectual assets into automation.

- Chapter 3 surveys the integration of blockchain and AI from the perspective of the smart city by presenting an in-depth review of various scientific research studies on the basics of blockchain and real-time applications. It then summarizes the applications and opportunities associated with blockchain, and the challenges involved in its use in smart cities.
- Chapter 4 explores the use of information and communication technologies (ICT) and AI along with the IoT in smart cities. It focuses on the issues facing increasing populations in urban cities around the globe and discusses the impact of implementing AI to change existing cities into the new smart cities of the future. Moreover, it discusses the applications in smart cities that reduce issues related to areas such as smart grid, agriculture, transportation, smart metering, etc.
- Chapter 5 discusses the use of blockchain in vehicle registration to support the smart city based on 5G technology. It presents a vehicle management system called DriveLoop, which is a simple method that allows car manufacturers, owners, repair companies, and insurance agencies to register and add new entries for cars. A detailed architecture view, algorithm, and working scheme for the DriveLoop application system is presented.
- Chapter 6 discusses the solution to the issue of using excessive computer technology in a modern-day smart city. It gives a detailed description of the design of an adaptive chair and desk based on a fuzzy controller system to maintain a correct posture for humans of different physical stature while sitting and using a computer system excessively. The adaptive system adjusts the chair and desk autonomously based on the quality of data collected and provided to the control system.
- Chapter 7 examines how blockchain technology can disrupt the traditional financial practices of the agro sector by drastically minimizing the financial costs in the international commodity exchange. In addition, blockchain helps in transparent commodity exchange settlement, easy tracing of exchanged trading, specified documents formatting for sales contracts, as well as accelerates the settlement process.
- Chapter 8 delivers a complete secure blockchain-based framework for smart farming based on IoT sensors and the use of an interplanetary file system (IPFS) for storing sensitive

information related to farming. Also, blockchain-based smart farming provides farmers with a support system to meet some of their needs.

- Chapter 9 provides a review of different aspects of blockchain technology and highlights its key characteristics, architecture, and taxonomy. Moreover, it also provides insights into the various consensus algorithms and major application areas of blockchain technology.
- Chapter 10 explores the mechanisms that make a city smart as well as explains the different technological dimensions of smart cities. It explains the problem domain along with the various challenges faced during the development of a smart city such as waste management issues, pollution, traffic congestion, outdated homes, huge energy consumption, etc.
- Chapter 11 focuses on the future status of blockchain, which will either revolutionize the digital world and transcend trending technologies, or pose a threat to them becoming obsolete. It explores the keys to making blockchain a debatable benchmark rather than an unfortunate event in the technical podium.
- Chapter 12 provides an overview of blockchain technology along with its detailed architecture and components. It also discusses various types of consensus mechanisms used in blockchain technology.
- Chapter 13 considers the prospects of implementing blockchain technology in the construction industry to help alleviate the current challenges and disruption in supply chain and value chain activities. It also discusses the issues faced by the industry as a result of blockchain still being in its infancy stage and therefore is crippled by limited funding, the unavailability of skilled manpower as well as lack of proper governmental support. It presents strategies for robust, resilient, reliable, less costly, environmentally friendly smart cities by initiating all the stakeholders in private and public sectors to work jointly with the provisional guidelines prescribed by the policy makers.

This book is formatted in such a way as to allow relevant requirements to be analyzed and adopted by the reader. The wide range of topics presented in this book was chosen to provide the reader with a better understanding of smart cities integrated with AI and blockchain and related security issues. We anticipate that the reader will benefit from this approach.

Vishal Kumar
Vishal Jain
Bharti Sharma
Jyotir Moy Chatterjee
Rakesh Shrestha

Acknowledgment

I would like to acknowledge the most important people in my life; my grandfather, the late Shri. Gopal Chatterjee, my grandmother, the late Smt. Subhankori Chatterjee, my father, Shri. Aloke Moy Chatterjee, my late mother Ms. Nomita Chatterjee, and my uncle Shri. Moni Moy Chatterjee. The book has been my long-cherished dream which would not have been turned into reality without the support and love of these amazing people. They have continuously encouraged me despite my failing to give them the proper time and attention. I am also grateful to my friends, who have encouraged and blessed this work with their unconditional love and patience.

Jyotir Moy Chatterjee
Department of IT
Lord Buddha Education Foundation
(Asia Pacific University of Technology & Innovation)
Kathmandu, Nepal

Deep Dive Into Blockchain Technology: Characteristics, Security and Privacy Issues, Challenges, and Future Research Directions

Bhanu Chander

Department of Computer Science and Engineering, Pondicherry University, Pondicherry, India

Abstract

Since the innovation, blockchain technology has exposed ingenious applications in our daily passing life. From the beginning of crypto-currency to the current smart contract, blockchain is practiced in numerous fields like digital forensics, insurance payments, online micro-payments, healthcare records sharing, and supply chain tracking. Through enlarge the blockchain talent to the Internet of Things (IoT), Wireless Sensor Networks (WSNs), and Cyber-Physical Systems (CPS), we can obtain a provable and noticeable record transaction data offline-to-online data verification and optimize existing network performance. The above-mentioned works aimed at expanded safety measures, automatic transaction command, decentralized stands, etc. The incorporation of blockchain technology has modernized the traditional trade due to its distributed ledger characteristic. Every record is secure by rules of cryptography which makes it more secure and impregnable. Therefore, blockchain can modify the way we buy and sell, how we intermingle with the government, and prove the legitimacy of everything from property names to natural fresh vegetables.

In recent times, the rapid expansion in urbanization population causes various cost-effective and environmental issues, influencing people's living circumstances and class of life. The thought of a smart city that developed with the rise of IoT brings the ability to solve urban issues. Information and Communication Technology (ICT), IoTs, and WSNs play a vital part in executing smart cities. Blockchain has several good creations like pseudonymity, trust-free, intelligibility,

Email: gujurothubhanu@mail.com; ORCID: https://orcid.org/0000-0003-0057-7662

Vishal Kumar, Vishal Jain, Bharti Sharma, Jyotir Moy Chatterjee and Rakesh Shrestha (eds.) Smart City Infrastructure: The Blockchain Perspective, (1–32) © 2022 Scrivener Publishing LLC

democratic state, computerization, decentralization, and safety measures. These creations of blockchain useful to progress smart city services then endorse the expansion of smart cities. On the other hand, to use blockchain efficiently, it must consider security and privacy portions.

This chapter presents the exceptional safety as well as privacy sides of blockchain. Mainly, we present a detailed explanation of the background work of blockchain and consensus methods. After that, we shifted focus to blockchain integration with smart city development, challenges, and applications. Further, we review common security attacks on blockchain and security improvement solutions and the directions for future research.

Keywords: Blockchain, smart city, security, privacy, Internet of Things

1.1   Introduction

Blockchain has gained tremendous popularity in recent times because of its fundamental properties and peer-to-peer operations. Blockchain theory was the future of well-known researcher Santoshi Nakamotos in 2008 with Bitcoin crypto-currency innovation. More than 2,500 crypto-currencies exist, but the authentic utilization of Bitcoin is still not explored effusively. Various issues like secure document transferring, anti-money laundering, decentralization, and authorized and unauthorized mining actions are near related to Bitcoin [1–5]. The Bitcoin system model nearly takes 5 to 8 minutes for the mining process and validation of the transaction, which plays a crucial role in numerous appliances such as industry, economics, supply chain management, healthcare, and the Internet of Things (IoT). In present situations, digital information streams from one-end to a new dissimilar end via an unauthorized transmission channel. Where securities models and privacy are the two significant worries in any transaction, blockchain produces a protected peer-to-peer broadcast. Moreover, all the transactions of blockchain publicly accessible for analyzing although none can amend the transaction one time it is recorded [1–6].

Blockchain is a scattered data catalog that monitors an emergent directory of transaction reports with systematizing them into a hierarchical series of blocks because of database management. Coming to safety potential, blockchain builds and maintains with peer-to-peer overlie setup and secured with intellectual, decentralized exploitation of cryptography techniques. Experts forecasted that blockchain-related annual revenue would reach approximately 22 billion dollars at the end of 2030, with an annual growth rate of 29.6%. Numerous distinguished organizations like Accenture, Cisco, Morgan Stanley, Google, Citibank, Ali baba, IBM and IT vendors, financial consultancies, and internet giants designed and developed a high-standard research laboratory to make a capital layout blockchain knowledge [3–6]. Moreover, blockchain with Artificial Intelligence (AI), Machine Learning (ML), and big data are considered the heart of computing skills for the upcoming generation financial inducts. A few governments have released methodological reports along with white papers on blockchain utilization for a positive approach. Some of them like the European Central Bank unconfined credentials on distributed ledger expertise, and the UK government liberated a fresh testimony that illustrates the outlook of distributed ledger technology. The Chinese administration liberated white papers on the blockchain tools besides improvement in China; the USA builds an authorized and authoritarian background for blockchain knowledge development. In academe, several documents are available on blockchain in the earlier period, consist of a dozen of the article, and provide information on safety then secrecy risks of blockchain. Furthermore, most of the safety then secrecy risk–based articles of blockchain-focused on uncovering attacks that suffer blockchain, and some target specific proposals for employing some current countermeasure adjacent to a subset of various attacks. Among these, very few attempts describe a complete investigation of the safety then confidentiality characteristics of blockchain along with different protocol implementation methods [2–8].

1.2   Blockchain Preliminaries

1.2.1   Functioning of Blockchain

Blockchain is a collection of heterogeneous distributed networks. It considers as a unique technology of this century among other famous innovations because of its elements like crypto techniques, consensus algorithms, and public ledger; working procedure of blockchain consists of various styles, among those we mentioned some of them: customer, client, or node who desire to make a transaction will record and broadcasts the data to the appropriate setup, next to the receiver or the node who interest to receive the data validate the genuineness of data received, and after validation stores data in a block inside the network, every node or the customer in the network authorize the transaction through implementing the PoW or else PoS algorithms which need the validation, and finally, the network that utilized the consensus models will be stored into the block and connected to the blockchain list. Then, every single node in the setup acknowledges the relevant block and then enlarges the chain position on block.

1.2.2   Design of Blockchain

The expansion of the blockchain system will make tremendous changes and impact approximately every industrial, educational, and scientific field in the coming days. In particular, financial transactions are progressing in inventive ways, making it exceptionally important for one and all to understand the blockchain mechanism's architecture and working style. Blockchain blocks are continuously enhance, secure with crypto techniques [6–10]. Here, each block holds a crypto-based hash value of the preceding block, a timestamp, along with transaction info.

In the design of blockchain, information or records are professional along with a related listing of transaction blocks well-maintained in a balanced catalog in the pattern of smooth files. Each block, linked with the preceding block, the initial block entitled the source block. The blockchain database visualized as a good stack, blocks mounded on the peak of one another, finished as the initial block as the stack's base. Every block of blockchain authorized with cryptography has a function by implementing the SHA-256 algorithm and stored in the block's header. One parent block can hold multiple children block; every child block encloses some parent hash value. The characteristics of child blocks purely depend on the parent block's identity and properties. This procedure prolongs until getting each grandchild blocks [6–12]. The cascade consequences confirm that, just once a block has several productions, it cannot interfere with all the successive blocks' forceful recalculations. For more understanding, we mentioned some ingredients with more explanations [4–16].

    i. **Data:** In blockchain, data stored in the database mostly depend on the respective services and applications, like recording the transmission particulars and banking with IoT. They were storing if data performed peer-to-peer, cloud formation, etc.

   ii. **Hash:** In the hash function, we can give any length message as input, but it produces unique predetermined length output. If any assailant made changes in the message, then the output comes out entirely differently. For example, if anyone client makes an effort to modify the info kept in a block, then afterward, the block shows an entirely different hash value. To avoid this kind of situation, there must be an assurance that minors of the network must have the knowledge prepared by revising the ledger replicate of total abusers. This will surely boost the reliability of info kept in the blockchain.

iii. **Timestamp:** For every transaction, it is compulsory to note the time once the block is shaped. Timestamping is a technique employed to trail or to follow the formation or else adapt the period of a certificate in a safe mode. This kind of procedure turns into a vital tool in the corporate business world. Moreover, blockchain authorizes only the concerned parties to recognize the source and then accessibility of a certificate/file on a specific day and occasion.

iv. Moreover, the data contains nonce and digital signatures; each customer holds both public/private keys. Digital signature restrains both keys for signing (private key reserved, sign-on, transaction data) and verification (public key for validation and decrypt the data) phase. Nonce value with 4-byte strength utilized for message authentication.

1.2.3   Blockchain Elements

Blockchain collects different techniques like mathematical methods, algorithms, cryptography protocols, and economic standards. It merges every part of end-to-end networking plus distributed consensus algorithm to resolve the management issues from a long-established scattered database. As we mentioned earlier, blockchain contains numerous elements; out of them here, we discussed some important points below [4–10, 12–18].

i. **Decentralization:** Decentralization can distribute functions and controls from a centralized authority to every entity that is associated. In the blockchain, each blockchain client provides a replica of the transaction record; moreover, a new block is implanted for the justification of transaction by the clients who are part of the blockchain structure.

ii. **Consensus model:** The inclusion of consensus models supports maintaining the purity of data recorded on the blockchain. In general, a consensus protocol contains three possessions; depend on applicability and good organization. Those are fault tolerance—a consensus procedure offers resilience while reviving to a failure not contributing to consensus. Safety—It must be safe and sound, reliable, and every node must produce a similar output legally binding under the protocol regulations; Liveness—Protocol must assure every non-faulty node to yield a value.

iii. *Transparent:* For explicit transactions, a blockchain scheme after a specific time (depend on application) verifies itself to make self-audit the eco-system of a digital price that resolves communications that occur in specifically mentioned time breaks. In a blockchain, the collected works of these transactions are acknowledged as block. As a result, it shows the intelligibility and incapability of frauds are engendered.

iv. *Open source:* As a decentralized structure blockchain kind, closed-source appliance trust that the appliance is purely working as decentralized then data not be contacted from a central basis. Blockchain-based locked appliances act as a hurdle to approval by customers. However, revulsion to a locked network was not traceable when the appliance plan to collect, hold and transmit customer endowments. Open-sourcing, a distributed appliance, alters the formation of business performances who utilized to support the Internet as the general denominator.

v. *Identity and access:* In any network, identity and access are the two central pillars to succeed. Like in a blockchain, identity and access are associated with three major public, private, and consortium standards. A public or permission less blockchain proposed to eliminate the middleman at the same time maintains the security high. Private or permission blockchain restricts the customers from holding authority and justification of blockchain restrictions while creating smart contracts. The proposal designed for private blockchain endows with the effectiveness and seclusion of transactions. Last, consortium blockchain, moderately private, also allows a few determined discriminating nodes to have complete control.

vi. *Autonomy:* The central part of a blockchain is to exchange the trust from one authority to another authority exclusive of any indication. Every entity of the blockchain arrangement securely updates and transmits information. The transaction trace plus smart contract particulars are kept as blocks in the blockchain.

vii. ***Immutability:*** In any financial transaction, immutability is one of the major elements, which means unchanged over time. Just once, any kind of info noted in a block of the blockchain never alters after record. This will extremely helpful for data auditing, easily prove that the data is safe and sound, proficient, and not interfere or distorted. Moreover, in the recipient end, data is confident, genuine, and untouched.

viii. ***Anonymity:*** Anonymity is an entity in the blockchain address of a miner that is indispensable for this aspect, and no other aspect is requisite; consequential in anonymity determine trust-related concerns. In a communication structure, the anonymity set can be alienated into two sets: the dispatcher then the receiver.

1.3   Key Technologies of Blockchain

Time moves blockchain, gaining more and more attention from various domains. In general, blockchain associates with blocks scattered more than several peer nodes and then employed in an unnamed location. Here, every block is enclosed with transaction data, preceding blocks hash values along with its hash. In a blockchain, the element distributed ledger is acknowledged as a blockchain that accumulates data designed in tamper-proof formation. An authorized network makes an equivalent carbon copy of the ledger that executes all blockchain transactions without any additional influence.

Additionally, a smart contract program is a design that runs inside the blockchain platform and executes definite roles. Cryptography models are employed to make sure the reliability of data. Another element of system management endows with function creation modification and monitoring mechanisms in the scheme. At last, the ingredient of scheme mixing is utilized to incorporate the blockchain scheme through outside parties.

Here, we discussed some of the vital technologies that influence blockchain utilization in the near future [2–8, 11–18].

1.3.1   Distributed Ledger

It works as data storage space of collected data from different nodes across the peer-to-peer setup, and every participated node holds a carbon copy of identical data. Blockchain is a decentralized structure, so there are no federal supervisors; hence the data reliability is maintained with the consensus models to ensure the data duplications' truthfulness on every dependent node. Several nodes must execute through a consensus model to accomplish an agreement to commit to the order of transactions. In particular, a distributed ledger is an appended-only data storeroom, plus the transaction modernizes actions traced at every entity node in an ungraceful approach.

1.3.2   Cryptography

In any decentralized structure data, reliability is a fundamental constraint; blockchain is one of the decentralized techniques designed and planned in an untrusted atmosphere. Cryptography models are the essential explanations to ensure the integrity and detection of tamper-proofs—distinct varieties of cryptography models like symmetric, asymmetric, and zero-knowledge testimonies extensively utilized in blockchain technology. The data truthfulness sheltered through the hash tree with hash indicators. In blockchain structures, only the existing worldwide status is preserved, and long-ago states' records can only attain via walking throughout the block transaction records. Hash or Merkel trees permit well-organized and safe, and sound authentication of the distributed ledger. To make sure a block cannot be tainted once it is attached to the ledger, any block modification will affect all subsequent blocks' termination.

1.3.3   Consensus

As we mentioned, earlier blockchain technology works exclusive of any federal controller. Hence, to keep the distributed ledger's reliability, blockchain desires to approach a consensus on the block transaction records. The consensus is a self-motivated mode of achievement and concord in a set. In PoW procedure, a cryptanalytic enigma has to decipher to append a block to the blockchain. This involves a massive quantity of energy plus computational handling. Hence, guarantees evade the Byzantine attack. Ethereum is a special kind of consensus algorithm, which changes the algorithm for a proficient protocol. Coming to PoS practice, if a node needs to insert a block to the chain, it will authorize the block through employing a stake on it. In the PoW procedure, every node continuously working on the longer chain since it is only a squander of computation power employed on the shorter chain. BitShare is an enhanced edition of PoS; DPoS consensus trusts on the authority of validator with more proficient and elastic evaluates with PoS. Paxos is a group of consensus practices that build a variety of trade-offs among hypotheses regarding the processors, contributors, and messages in a particular scheme.

1.3.4   Smart Contracts

Smart contracts (SM) are generated with computer codes then store simulated in the blockchain scheme; furthermore, it could be useful in ledger procedures like money transmit and service delivery. Mostly, smart contracts effectively assist in translucent, conflict-free, incontrovertible, and quicker automatic secure transactions without any arbitrator. A few blockchain proposals only afford an imperfect set of patterns to mark contract drafts like Bitcoin. Several other proposals maintain a more ample set of codes. Ethereum presents a Turing machine with total code for identifying uninformed computation. A few proposals permit SM codes to run in their inhabitant runtimes, whereas further proposals generate virtual machines for implementing agreement-type codes.

1.3.5   Benchmarks

The efficient performance of blockchain is one of the critical characteristics of the blockchain platform. There are no authenticated universal tools with principles, which present performance estimation for different blockchain results. The hyperledger cluster prepares frequent attempts in defining the performance scale of blockchain. Hyperledger caliper describes the most crucial performance signs like transaction latency and resource exploitation.

1.4   Consensus Algorithms of Blockchain

In the blockchain, consensus algorithms implement as a group-based set of rules for a group's dynamic agreement. Usually, in group models, we go for a voting majority for a mutual agreement. This consensus emphasizes the entire group, for the intention to everyone benefit and realize a consensus [8–14]. However, the difficulty is actively making or receiving a consensus in grouping relies on the group's synchronization. Such synchronized consensus may be tamper in the attendance of malevolent actors as well as flawed processes. For instance, awful actors covertly form contradictory messages to formulate group members who are unsuccessful in agreeing, which breaks down the group's value to synchronize its trials.

Below we mentioned some well-known consensus algorithms for reader understanding [4–12, 22–28, 36–42, 46–50].

1.4.1   Proof of Work (PoW)

PoW-based consensus algorithms are a kind of fiscal measure to deject the outbreaks of DoS, spams that increase the computing process time. In the blockchain, high priority node will elect to record the transactions by selecting random users or nodes, leading to various vulnerable attacks. Also, nodes wish to publish a block with transaction details, which needs vast computational energy for selection, validation of random users, or nodes. In PoW, nodes that estimate hash principles described as miners. Each node in the setup analyzes the hash rate of the block header, which holds a nonce. Then, miners utilize these values to create distinct hash values; just once the target value is reached by a node, it distributes the calculated block to other nodes to verify the hash value's precision. If a block is legitimate, then added nodes include this newest authorized block to their blockchain. The procedure of scheming the hash standards is acknowledged as mining. In PoW, the longest chain is considered trustworthy and accurate, but to build that longest chain will cost high computational power; hence, to overcome this problem, some consensus employs other models to preserve the energy resources.

From the literature, PoW has two excellent characteristics: It must be complicated and time-consuming in favor of every entity to make a testimony that convenes particular necessities. It should be quick plus straightforward for others to validate the testimony in terms of its precision. For a block to be legitimate in the blockchain, a miner must calculate the hash-value, which is fewer than or equivalent to the existing objective, then extant its explanation to the setup for authentication through additional nodes. The twin assets of PoW guarantee that it is though then time-intense to discover the correct nonce for the suitable hash objective; so far, it is effortless besides straightforward to legalize the hash product no tamper happened.

1.4.2   Proof of Stake (PoS)

PoSs are broadly applied consensus algorithms in blockchain appliances; it states that an abuser or client can mine or else authorize transactions in a block, depend on the number of abusers or clients. Protocol believes that clients who have more cash are less likely to outburst the setup. Here, blockchain trails on various clients or miners if they hold high crypto-currency named a validator. All validated applicants then carry the procedure of generating and authenticating a new block. The PoS algorithm has numerous tangs, depend on the ways the rewards are consigned. Some of them are chain-based PoS—where a validator is preferred at a random method and a time slot for a new block is created by the authority. Hence, based on time, many blocks unite to a solitary emergent chain. Previous editions of chain-based PoS models build with naïve technique since rewards are utilized to produce blocks with no penalties, pushing them to endure nothing at stake issues. In BFT-style PoS, miners are arbitrarily legalized to advise an original block's design, but block's approval made by the multi-round voting method. The PoS characterizes different kinds of distributed consensus protocols for undertaking the confidentiality, accessibility, and privacy properties of public blockchain models.

1.4.3   BFT-Based Consensus Algorithms

The major reason behind the BFT algorithm's innovation was its tolerance potentiality of a system in opposition to the BGP. For a more detailed explanation, consider a group of nodes where each node grasps a unique initial value. Here, every node must follow the same mind behavior by accepting a consensus procedure's solitary cost. In such a scheme, an agreement will reach with bulk nodes that consider truthful nodes that thoroughly follow the protocol instructions; still, some nodes molest, deviate from the protocol. This situation is acknowledged as Byzantine fault-tolerant (BFT). We know that long-established distributed computing arrangement controls central authorities, and they conclude what step has to be taken when Byzantine failure arises. The blockchain is a decentralized scheme maintained with a distributed ledger where every node holds the chain or block's replica. For every applicant block, the authentication is prepared by having the system harmony via the digital signatures of an adequate amount of nodes. Only those applicant blocks the system confirms those can be linked to the blockchain. To avoid Byzantine faults, blockchain must apply PoW and PoS consensus models to approve transactions, which turns blockchain more powerful and efficient. However, PoW or PoS is not always a perfect key to deal with BFT issues. Identifying the working procedure of BFT will play a key role in applying blockchain with efficient appliance results. Also, open consensus algorithms and protocols planned on behalf of the Byzantine fault trouble might not be sufficient when functional to additional blockchain appliances.

In 1982, well-known persons like Lamport, Pease, and Shostak introduced the leading solution to resolve BFT misconceptions and prevent associated mistakes. Miguel Castro and Barbara Liskov anticipated the PBFT model for realistic BFT in 1999 for the Byzantine state mechanism's high-performance reproduction. AlgoRAND and Honey Badger BFT are two exceptional works that describe various concepts of BFT.

1.4.4   Practical Byzantine Fault Tolerance (PBFT)

PBFT is a simulated version shaped to continue Byzantine faults. Specifically, to tolerate the Byzantine fault, we must realize the working style of Byzantine issues illustrated as an agreement issue. Byzantine trouble gets even more composite by continuing unfaithful nodes which might cast a take part in an election for a trivial stratagem. In PBFT protocol, each node recognized by additional nodes in the setup can inquiry with remained. Delegated BFT (dBFT) is a consensus model similar to PBFT, but, in dBFT, a cluster of specialized nodes nominated to sign dealings as different to arbitrary nodes. The justification of a transmission operation can be done in three steps: In the first step, validators specify the reason for transmission of a block when it gains 2/3 votes from the setup. In the second step or pre-commit phase, validators decide to pre-commit on block and transaction deal. Just once, block obtains 2/3 votes for the pre-commit stride when it come in the assigned phase, which is the third step. Here, a node legalizes a block or transaction plus transmits a consign for it.

1.4.5   Sleepy Consensus

The sleepy consensus model builds on the sleepy model concept, where participate or nodes swing in both ways online (awake) and offline (sleep) in the protocol implementation. It is demonstrated to be flexible when the truthful contributors are the mainstream. This algorithm's most important initiative is to recognize the Bitcoin. But sleepy consensus cannot endure effort in the box when an unfair online group of actors is mainstream.

1.4.6   Proof of Elapsed Time (PoET)

PoET brings low computation with justification, designed by intel via leveraging SGX, a trusted computing policy. In this algorithm, each node waits for the threshold period; here, the node which finishes the threshold time is allowed to generate a new block. The PoET consensus is required to guarantee two key features: First, the joining nodes legitimately decide on a time that is sure arbitrary plus not a shorter interval. Second, the frontrunner concluded the waiting time. However, the issue is SGX is not a reliable, trusted computing skill. Two features proposed to overcome this issue: varying the probability distribution and executing statistical analysis to refuse a few blocks engender by a specific portion of nodes.

1.4.7   Proof of Authority (PoA)

Compare to other mentioned consensus algorithms, PoA sustains fast transactions. The main objective of PoA was that barely validators have the fundamental right to commend the contracts along with new-fangled blocks. A node becomes a validator only when the node receives a high reputation score. Compared to other PoS and Pow, PoA is more vigorous because validators authenticate every transaction or contract with high integrity. If not, nodes are attached with negative status. More importantly, a solitary validator cannot grant any two successive blocks, preventing confidence from being central.

1.4.8   Proof of Reputation (PoR)

PoR considers as an expansion of PoA, which is newly promoted by various research communities. In PoR, reputation is calculated with pre-arranged rules; moreover, different variations and constraints are fine-tuned for its best performances. Once the node establishes a reputation with reliable verification, it turns to an authoritative node.

1.4.9   Deputized Proof of Stake (DPoS)

DPoS is an extension of PoS, aimed to accomplish a distributed consensus in a crypto-currency scheme. It is different from PoS script; valuators of the crypto scheme vote for allot to authenticate then practice a deal in revisit for transaction charges, which is entirely dissimilar PoS where stakeholders authenticate then perform a contract to produce recompenses along with transaction charges. Compared to other algorithms, the DPoS is the quickest, prolific, proficient, decentralized, and adaptable consensus replica. Deterministic collection of block producers' permits contacts will be complete typically in one second. DPoS procedure engages the utilization of trusted sub-networks inside a superior system in which the nodes can be separated into a server or the customer.

1.4.10   SCP Design

SCP is technically reliable Byzantine consensus practice for blockchain and its respective contracts with a contract or blocks in terms of epochs, here, every epoch makes a target then decision based on available rules. The principle idea of SCP efficiently utilizes the existing computational power. It separates existed computational powers into sub-groups, where every group works on an existing algorithm to agree on a solitary result. In SCP designed algorithm, the processor completes five phases in every epoch; in the first step, with the help of the local computation virtual committee identifies a processor. In the second step, processors try to recognize remained processors implicated; in the third step, processors execute on an authenticated procedure to consent on a value. In the fourth step, final consensus algorithm validation and ending value from each spread. In the fifth step, distribute random generation for virtually independent random assessment.

1.5   Internet of Things and Blockchain

1.5.1   Internet of Things

The invention of the IoT impacts promotes our daily life than ever before. In the coming years, kitchen applications, utility materials, thermostats, televisions, cars, smart phones, intra-body sensors, and approximately everything connects with the internet then reachable from anytime, anywhere on the globe. The rising ease that IoT brought to the 19th century is unmatchable and uncomparable. Moreover, it continuously improvising every human segment, manufacturing starts from healthcare, smart home, e-healthcare, along with smart city to surveillance, data mining, intelligent transport, and manufacturing [6–8]. Scientists and researchers highly focused on addressing IoTs computation and communication scalability concerns from the past few years. Undoubtedly these two concerns are most important for the success of IoTs and should carefully explore. Both IoT safety and confidentiality are vital research actions to be conquered [10–16].

Up-to-date IoT systems are implemented with a central-based architecture and client-server-based access model. IoT dealings like data, documents, and instructions among IoT entities assigned to monumental, federal service providers. However, eventually, IoT is vulnerable to various privacy as well as security problems. In particular, federal and centralized service providers use IoT data intelligently; some of the centralized data gathering systems can rendering the method of hacking by malevolent activities, with awful consequences for citizens [18–28]. One more dispute is the authentication of IoT units, which is mostly employed naturally with limited supervision. If these issues not appropriately answered, there was a chance to create hard active and passive attacks.

The amalgamation of blockchain along with IoT has disruptive potential and assists the IoT's development into our culture through providing subsequent essential rewards:

i. ***Anonymity:*** An IoT entity with the inclusion of blockchain with various secure keys, but it does not expose entities real characteristics and individuality.

ii. ***Decentralization:*** Long-established centralized methods need each operation must be legalized from end to end with a centralized model, which unavoidably transforms into a performance block. In opposition, third-party confirmation is not required in the blockchain because consensus processes preserve data reliability.

iii. ***Non-repudiation:*** It guarantees that the dealings can be authorized then illogical dealings not confessed—it is almost intolerable to remove any transactions once integrated into the blockchain.

While the blockchain might appear as per a solution to the IoT's safety as well as privacy problems, but still numerous researches detect various challenges while employing IoT into the real-world. Greatest part of the research works states blockchain as an undeniable, incontestable data composition from literature. Still, it is theoretically unfocused to describe it as indisputable or not able to be forfeited. If truth be told, then there are patterns where the blockchain entries have been altering after attacks or misconduct of the system/network. As mentioned in the introduction section, blockchain technology has been broadly employed in various services like digital forensics, online micro-payments and insurance payments, supply chain management, and health-management documentation sharing [6–16]. By enlarging the blockchain skill to the IoTs, we can get a certifiable and distinguishable IoT system. Promising research studies in IoT appliances take advantage of blockchain skill to testimony transaction data, optimize existing method performance, and assemble next-generation structures, moreover, giving additional safety, regular transaction supervision, decentralized proposals, offline-to-online data confirmation, and many more.

IoT networks allocate direct communications as well as interaction among devices over the internet. At the end of 2025, the number of IoT (smart mobiles, vehicles, smart city, home applications, and various indoor and outdoor sensors) devices will reach above 25 billion. With numerous devices, conventional IoT appliances face contests in several points like information security, confidentiality, and healthiness. Blockchain affords a handy, well-located explanation to deal with many limits of conventional IoT appliances. Here, blockchain guarantees IoT data integrity, not including any third-party, and saves bandwidth and computational supremacy of IoT objects. Furthermore, blockchain can endow with a safe and sound outline aimed at IoT setup to send sensitive raw data without any centralized server [12–18].

1.5.2   IoT Blockchain

IoT with blockchain inclusion systems personalized and optimized to allocate IoT appliances. As we discussed earlier sections, IoT is employed in various real-time applications, but most of them prone to various attacks and issues. To moderate these tricky things, blockchain can be utilized to offer superior security along with reliability for time-honored IoT functions. Furthermore, the inclusion of blockchain into IoT is not an easy task because limitations of IoT devices, some of them are power consumption, task scheduling, and computational capabilities. To handle these concerns, many stabs to assume blockchain in IoT appliance [2–8].

Blockchain assumes various IoT appliances; however, there is a particular focus on digital payments, data storage, and smart contracts. Digital payment is the utmost applicable domain for blockchain. Although it primarily works on a scattered system maintained in high-performance machineries, superior optimization is now maintained by significant blockchains like Bitcoin and Ethereum, which are applied for objects/things with inconsequential computation energy like smart phones, tabs, and pocket PCs.

1.5.3   Up-to-Date Tendency in IoT Blockchain Progress

Recent developments in various technologies boost the progression of IoT and blockchain and its continuous revolution. The recent trend is principally revealed in four characteristics: popularity, range of applications, development of underlying technology, and business models [4–14].

i. *Popularity:* From the last few years, the incorporation of IoT with blockchain appliances proliferating. In the early days, IoT applied to specific domains like industrial manufacturing and transportations. However, as time passes, many emergent businesses converted to the movement of IoT like digitalization, smart home, E-healthcare, and then smart city. Dissimilar brands of consensus processes offered, and then, basic upgrading has planned for IoT blockchains.

ii. *Range of Applications:* From the invention, blockchain was continuously employed in various domains; at the start, blockchain applied for decentralized currency structures. Bitcoin was foremost considered to make a decentralized currency scheme exclusive of any administration. With the expansion of blockchain expertise, smart contracts in Ethereum have facilitated a more comprehensive range of appliances other than economic use. The merger of IoT into blockchain schemes affords extra capacities for appliances. Logistics businesses spotlight employing blockchain to execute product tracking: Computer hardware and power-driven manufactured goods trades exploit blockchain to improve the interface among humans with IoT devices. Power industries exploit blockchain to execute power distribution then power transaction dealings.

iii. *Expansion of Basic Technology:* The immediate progression of several principal technologies speedy development of IoT and Blockchain. IoT device connectivity, communiqué expertise like LoRa, LoWPRA, NB-IoT, and 5G communications with IoT devices improved quickly. To meet different blockchain appliance requirements, recently designed structures must be outfitted with optimization techniques. Public chains like IOTA and EOS with digital signatures resolve the low transaction rate difficulty in long-established accomplishments.

iv. *Business Models:* Many academic, industrial, insurance, and science-based companies are searching for possible chances for integrating blockchain practices in their business models to boost business turnover. But, the blockchain structure performance might rigorously distress the sustained companies' productions, e.g., how much rapidly the consensus procedure legalizes dealings, which justify further concentration when manipulative industrialized appliances.

v. *Resource Limitations:* Usually, blockchain consumes high computational power, channel frequency with little delay. Extreme part of IoT smart devices outfitted with uncomplicated hardware setups with deficient processing, computational power. So, it is not an easy task for IoT strategies to execute various mining jobs of blockchain. Besides, most blockchain appliances employ PoW as their basic consensus algorithm, which requires high computation energy. On the other hand, blockchain is required to regularly present data encryption, but the encryption rate plus time will be dissimilar since dissimilar IoT strategies have dissimilar computational energy.

vi. Furthermore, other progressions, constancy models, and then regular testing need massive processing power, which excesses IoT devices' low power ability. Furthermore, blockchain's consensus practice involves the transformations of information among nodes regularly to reach an agreement to preserve blockchain's accuracy and create novel blocks. This practice needs high bandwidth with little latency.

1.6   Applications of Blockchain in Smart City

1.6.1   Digital Identity

Over the past decades, humankind continuously touches on accepting blockchain (BC) technology allocating for the association, and getting in touch with a high altitude of consistency and precision. Moreover, blockchain avoids arbitrators in financial transactions. In the same way, smart cities were also efficiently utilizing the characteristics of blockchain. Estonia is one of the famed cities that employed contemporary knowledge in its real-time appliances. The original motivations that force us to employ the BC in the appliance of digital identity are BC's uniqueness like incorporation, security, and inscrutability without the need for an arbitrator. Millions of people worldwide cannot respond to an easy issue if a particular administration body requests them, "Who are you, and what are your credentials?" because they cannot prove their individuality with real facts. Famous companies start their business with digital identity by employing the internet. These kinds of operations will successfully influence smart city appliances and improvement. Forecasting city inhabitant's development helps to observe cities' growth.

With recent advances in blockchain characteristics, the government can re-evaluate the actual transactions to validate citizens' personalities. Finally, blockchain skills make transactions more transparent, democratic, and decentralized, with no need for an arbitrator. There is a potential tendency for the utilization of BC in transactions involving the administration besides its citizens to elevate the phase of assurance besides transparency in transaction deals.

1.6.2   Security of Private Information

With the rising population, the entire globe faces enormous urban development since most of the population concentrated on settling in large cities for a better life. However, the problem is how to utilize available resources although preserve the high protection in the transmission of data records. When employing information tools, we should keep safety measures in the transmission of information and employ secure knowledge like IoT, edge and cloud computing, and other ground-breaking solutions to assist citizens and the government. In some situations, there is a chance for criminals can access individual personality information while information is transmitting among devices by employing unofficial methods. Long-established security techniques are not so successful in securing transmissions in smart city environments. Most smart city appliances utilize different transmission techniques like 2G, 3G, 4G, Bluetooth, 6LoWPAN, infra-red, and various radiofrequencies. To provide safety measures and confidentiality while transmitting, blockchain is accountable for every transaction, it stores every record, and distributed ledgers behave like a decentralized database. Besides, digital signature and timestamp are incorporated with every record in the ledger.

1.6.3   Data Storing, Energy Ingesting, Hybrid Development

As the population expanded in urban lives, the number of smart electronic device usage also increased. Moreover, there is a requirement for optimal structures to preserve the power addicted by these devices. It is a fact that the incoming day's numerous electronic devices will join the internet, and the number will continuously enhance; these devices create a massive quantity of data that wish to be stored, performed, and planned. For that reason, a smart city structure should fabricate a flexible approach and acknowledge this quantity of data. While designing, we must care about various individualities in the smart city construction like reliability, flexibility, compliance, performance plus consistency, privacy and defense, competence, and simplicity of deployment and lifespan. Every controller in the network is linked with blockchain, where every controller outfits with open-security replica. Statistical-based ECHA techniques are mostly used to select the most excellent controller. The inclusion of blockchain tools led to enlarge throughput, response time, and shrink continuous delay to assist the requisite services' condition.

1.6.4   Citizens Plus Government Frame

Smart city applications give a chance to strengthen the relationship among government with citizens; this will increase citizen's inclusion in the government environment where they live. In smart city, the atmosphere numerous actions take part simultaneously, which will allow citizens to offer a safe and sound existence for citizens. Recent advances in modern technologies like IoT and cloud computing might help execute this affiliation involving government plus citizens. The real-time data composed by the sensors can be utilized to enhance citizen-government involvement, as a consequence to accomplish sustainable advance. The government will be accountable for evaluating data records presented by abusers through mobile appliances to construe consumer implications and requirements.

1.6.5   Vehicle-Oriented Blockchain Appliances in Smart Cities

If any kind of traffic accident occurs, then the person accountable for the accident mostly gives to the person who was in driving. In earlier times, vehicles equipped with ad hoc–based conventional technologies are not efficient in the present circumstances. Advanced kind vehicles self-controlled; an accident may occur with inbuilt mistakes, manufacturer defects, and vehicle software malpractices—moreover, vehicles are outfitted with special sensors that collect real-time information, including the driver's behavior. High-profile companies build vehicles with numerous technical parts like Auto-manufacturer—it receives information accumulated from different sensors evaluates, forward updates, and, if possible, corrects bugs in software. Autonomous vehicles (AV) store collected information in a secure place. Witnesses (Wi) store vehicles drawn in similar accidents; insurance company ingredient gathers all the available facts cause of the accident. To avoid the inclusion of blockchain skills restricts various issues that are not solved by mentioned issues. In the blockchain, once the transaction is reordered successfully, it cannot be modified. This skill helps collect reliable indications means the person cannot contradict his actions after the record. There is no central administrative, as all entities that have witnessed the occasion will play a part in the ultimate judgment. For reliable data, public key and hash-based are deployed. Actually, in improving the smart city highest part taken by IoTs, incorporation of

IoT with blockchain allows us to automate dealings at lesser charge plus difficulty than in a central-based computing atmosphere.

1.6.6   Financial Applications

The fundamental nature of blockchain application is economical and fiscal transactions, which reduces the time exhausted in tracking transactions, shrinks the financial hazards, and decreases the data's recurrence rate. The intention of smart cities means to construct an intellectual society proficient in spending a variety of forms of modern technology like blockchain and 5G knowledge. All parties concerned in the procedure can observe the data alterations; based on the analysis results, it will be grant or refuse. Associations fabricate on open, translucent financial schemes base on blockchain skills when it institutes. Making financial transactions existing to everyone facilitates companies audit financial dealings in all good wishes. It is feasible to verify the occasion of any business transaction with high precision plus with no chance for any falsification. Other than all positive advantages, it faces one challenge, which is it makes audit operations complicated.

1.7   Security and Privacy Properties of Blockchain

Blockchain is famous for online financial transactions, so we start with security and privacy provisions for online and financial business transactions and their recognized vulnerabilities. Then, we discussed data privacy; furthermore, we mentioned famous techniques applied for security and privacy in the blockchain [4–8, 18–26, 29–40, 42–50].

1.7.1   Security and Privacy Necessities of Online Business Transaction

Before the invention of blockchain, long-established networks applied for online transactions, which are vulnerable to various active and passive attacks. Blockchain, with its high standard features or elements, overcomes the issues generated in long-established networks. However, some securities and privacy requirements must be applied on blockchain for proper online transactions, which are mentioned below.

    i. ***Reliability of the ledger across organizations:*** For online financial transaction, different companies have their structure and set of instructions, which make the issues or delays in the process of understanding, clearance, and insolvency between financial institutions or companies. This will also increase high transaction fees, prone to faults and variations among ledgers detained by dissimilar finance institutions. As a result, there is a need to design a consistent platform among institutions for effective transactions.

ii. *Unique intermediates supervise transactions' integrity:* Whenever an online transaction is placed for asset management or investment, the related items like notes, equity, income receipts, bonds, and other assets. This increases transaction costs, brings the threat of intentionally misrepresent or forge the certificate. Therefore, the structure must assure the reliability of transactions and averts transactions from being molested or tamper.

iii. *Accessibility of system and records:* The abusers, clients, or miners who take part in the online system ought to be talented to access the data of connections at any time from anyplace. At the structure point, the scheme must perform consistently even in the occurrence of any network related molest. At the business dealing stage, the information connections can be right to use through authoritative abusers, clients without being unfeasible, conflicting, or despoiled.

iv. *Prevention of double spending:* In the federal-based structure, an authorized, trusted central or federal moderator is accountable for confirming whether a digital coin two-fold compensated or not. Coming to decentralized-based blockchain technology, it is challenging to prevent double spending. By employing robust security mechanisms along with countermeasures, we can avoid double spending issues in decentralized online transactions.

v. *Confidentiality of Transactions:* Customers or clients who actively participate in financial-based transactions; mostly hide or not interest in expose their transaction and account-related credentials. Moreover, they believe that the system administrator will not disclose their personal information to other clients without their permission. Every client or abuser's data should be accumulated and continually access under security measurements, even under sudden malfunctions or malicious cyber-attacks. Such kinds of secrecy and privacy are wanted in numerous non-financial setups.

vi. *The anonymity of the abuser's personality:* In a decentralized financial transaction institute, it is challenging to authenticate dissimilar users efficiently and securely. Moreover, solitary or two parties to the contract might be hesitant to let the other party recognize respective authentic individuality in some special cases.

vii. **Unlikability of transactions:** Unlikability passes on to the incapability of shaping the correlation flanked by two interpretations or else two pragmatic individuals of the scheme by high self-assurance, secrecy, secrecy to the condition of being unrevealed plus undisclosed. Dissimilar entities that are not interested to announce their originality, abusers should involve that the connections connected to them cannot be allied. When the transaction is relevant to a client or abuser linked, it turns out that it is simple to assume additional information about the particular user like frequency transactions and remained balances. With the help of analysis of such statistical information regarding transactions plus accounts combined with little background facts about an abuser, interested or adversarial entities may estimate the accurate uniqueness of the abuser with soaring assurance. Naturally, the full secrecy of an abuser can only be confined by guarantee both pseudonymity and unlikability.

In some situations, along with the public blockchain's temperament, everyone tries to execute de-anonymization molests in secret exclusive of having the intention abuser even grasp entities' proper identity has tampered. As a result, the blockchain execution in Bitcoin only completes pseudonymity, although it is not unlikability and consequently not full secrecy challenged by pseudonymity by unlikability.

1.7.2   Secrecy of Connections and Data Privacy

Blockchain effectively provides confidentiality for all the sensitive data transformed and store in its database or distributed ledger. While the blockchain was formerly developed as a scattered large-scale record for the digital-cash organization Bitcoin, its probable capacity of appliances is heavier than virtual cash. Blockchain is proficiently applied in copyright proof, profit-making register, and smart contracts. Consider a situation, an abuser or client preferred for a smart contract to transmit a quantity of ETH to an additional abuser at a definite period. Suppose an opponent has backdrop details regarding one of the two entities; here, the opponent might reveal and link it. As a result, it is vital to propose and execute a more robust defense system for privacy-preserving well-groomed contracts.

Research on data privacy shows limitations on data privacy outflow from the past decade because of different known, and unknown molests. Such confidentiality outflow can escort to break the secrecy of transaction data. Hence, both secrecy and privacy cause a most important dispute for blockchain and its appliances that engage perceptive transactions and confidential data [46].

1.8 Privacy and Security Practices Employed in Blockchain

Researchers build various privacy and security techniques to enhance the popularity of blockchain in several domains. Here, we described some existing and future techniques [2–6, 14–18, 22–28, 39–46].

1.8.1   Mixing

It is a known fact that Bitcoin in the blockchain is not sure about user's anonymity since transactions utilize pseudonymous addresses which verify openly. People narrate user's transactions with his/her transaction history through a simple study of addresses employed in making Bitcoin. In an earlier section, we discussed that once the transaction's address is associated with real user individuality, which causes the leakage of all users' transaction records. Mixing is nothing but a random swap of user's coins with new users' coins.

    i. *Mixcoin:* Bitcoin is designed to avoid passive threats, which intend to produce anonymous payments in Bitcoin and its kind of currencies. Mixcoin offers anonymity similar to time-honored communication mixes; furthermore, it employs a responsibility system to notice stealing.

   ii. *CoinJoin:* The usage of coinjoin starts in 2013 as an optional practice for Bitcoin-based dealings. Coinjoin is mostly applied for joint payment, which means if one node wants to make a transaction, it searches or waits for another node interested in making payment. They jointly formulate payment in a single transaction. This will decrease the communication cost, and improperly implemented coin will reduce anonymity.

1.8.2   Anonymous Signatures

Digital signatures are digital credentials, and they implement with various modifications. Some specific digital signature models themselves can offer secrecy for the signer. These types of models are acknowledged as anonymous signatures.

> i. *Group Signature:* In this scheme, any component of a group could sign on the message on behalf of the whole group secretly through his/her private key; moreover, any component through the shared group's public key able to test then legalizes the engendered sign. Here, the sign authentication procedure exposes nothing but the signer's true uniqueness apart from the association of the group. Every group has its own elected administrator who controls the addition, deletion of members, quarrels, etc. This kind of operation is also needed in the blockchain scheme to build and cancel the group and dynamically attach fresh members or blocks to the group.
>
> ii. *Ring Signature:* As the name suggests, ring signature initiates from the signature derived technique which applies a ring-like structure and attains secrecy through signing by any group factor. Compared to the group signature, the ring signature is unique because, during the ring signature proposal, the signer's authentic personality could not be naked in the event of a quarrel, as no group manager. For suppose, n numbers of members employed in ring signature have a chance for 1/n probability of an adversary can effectively estimate an actual sender.

1.8.3   Homomorphic Encryption (HE)

HE is one of the hot researches, advanced, a powerful encryption technique, which executes various kinds of computations instantly on cipher-text and guarantees high privacy on data. On the other hand, decrypting on the outcome will engender matching results to those achieved by a similar plaintext process. Applying HE will effectively store data on a blockchain without any significant changes in blockchain properties. This will increase privacy concerns allied with public blockchain for auditing things.

1.8.4   Attribute-Based Encryption (ABE)

In ABE, attributes are the tricky and flexible features for cipher-text encryption with the secret key. Any individual can decrypt the encrypted information by the abuser's secret key if his/her attributes concur with the cipher-text aspects. This can guarantee if a molested abuser is associated with other valid abusers, he (molested abuser) cannot admit further data apart from the info that he (molested abuser) decipher with her/his private-key. However, till now, ABE is not installed in any outline on a blockchain for real-world action. Secure Access for Everyone (SAFE), Inter-Planetary File System (IPFS), and then Steemit are some of the well-known implementations of the ABE technique utilizing blockchain appliances continue to be an open dispute.

1.8.5   Secure Multi-Party Computation (MPC)

The MPC refers to a multi-user practice that allocates users to perform joint computation with their concealed facts inputs, not infringement respective input data confidentiality. Here, there is no chance for any opponent to learn the input of an authentic party. The accomplishment of applying MPC in distributed voting, personal request, and personal data recovery has made it a well-liked resolution to numerous real-world troubles. In the last few years, MPC has been broadly applied in blockchain schemes to guard the abuser's privacy. In [10], Andrychowicz *et al.* proposed a Bitcoin system with MPC protocol for secured multi-user lotteries without any trusted central authority. If an abuser infringes or hampers with the procedure, then he/she turns into a loser; moreover, her/his Bitcoins are transmitted to the sincere/truthful abusers.

1.8.6   Non-Interactive Zero-Knowledge (NIZK)

NIZK is an advanced version of zero-knowledge with powerful, influential privacy-preserving resources. Here, the fundamental design is that a recognized proof originated to prove that a program is finished with a few inputs in secret with no admission of any further info. In detail, a certifier confirms a verifier without giving any beneficial info to the verifier. When an abuser or client transmits money to an added abuser, he/she can confirm that she/he has a satisfactory balance by transferring zero-knowledge proofs, exclusive of enlightening the account balance. "Succinct Non-interactive Argument of Knowledge" is one of the extensions of zero-knowledge designed to support the Zcash procedure.

1.8.7 The Trusted Execution Environment (TEE)

TEE offers an entirely remote atmosphere for appliance executions, efficiently checking additional software appliances plus operating systems from being corrupt or tamper. The Intel Software Guard Extension (SGX) is a delegate skill to apply a TEE in various domains, especially in blockchain appliances. Multiple aspects are subjective for credit scoring: the quantity and nature of financial records, payment reports, and credit exploitation.

1.8.8 Game-Based Smart Contracts (GBSC)

GBSC designed based on a verification game that decides whether a computational assignment is properly executed or not. Moreover, in every stage of the "verification game", the verifier persistently tests less critical subsection of the calculation that permits TrueBit to diminish the commutating load on its nodes significantly.

1.9 Challenges of Blockchain

Blockchain is an incredible invention of this decade; at the same time, it has some significant challenges, which we discussed below. Even though considerable challenges, they can easily triumph over the ripeness and enrichment of the blockchain skill in the coming future.

1.9.1 Scalability

Due to the high volume of blockchain and its characteristics enhancement, the number of digital transactions also increased exponentially. Every transaction must store in a node block for authorization. The foundation of existing transactions desires to be legalized primary than the transaction deal to be authenticated. The adequate block size and then the intermission times play a huge role in introducing new blocks into the system. In some situations, the blocks' size may build unauthorized transaction delays in minute transactions since miners or clients mostly prefer to execute and prefer transactions for high transactional fees. By taking all these operations, scalability is a big issue in blockchain, and it classifies into storage optimization. Lightweight client or miner utilized to fix the scalability concern and redesigning of blockchains—where blockchain scattered into a critical block responsible for the leadership elections, a micro block accountable for business deal storing.

1.9.2   Privacy Outflow

When everyone on the network accesses the public keys, the blockchain defenseless against denial-of-service attacks leads to the outflow of transactional data. To overcome all these, various authors proposed dissimilar actions, those classified into mixing solution: Mixing suggests anonymity through transferring finances from manifold input address to manifold output addresses. Anonymous is another effective solution that unlinks the payment genesis for a transaction.

1.9.3   Selfish Mining

In selfish mining, some nasty or wicked miners or clients store the mined blocks in their database and tries to create a confidential branch that transmits only after reaching specific requirements. In such scenarios, truthful or sincere miners waste lots of time and resources since selfish miners or clients organize private chains.

1.9.4   Security

Security describes confidentiality, truthfulness, and availability, which are challenging tasks in public blockchains where keys are visible to all nodes. Confidentiality level is low in scattered systems, and truthfulness is the profession of blockchains; even though it faces different issues, accessibility in blockchains is high in terms of legibility compared to writing accessibility.

1.10   Conclusion

Blockchain is a broadly renowned technology, which got massive interest from various research communities around the world. It consists of different key techniques that support various requirements in different human life areas like healthcare, financial transactions, elections, and markets. However, it faces many challenges associated with security and privacy. So, in this chapter, we made a systematic study on blockchain safety measurements in recent years. We made an explicit discussion on blockchain development, working procedure, structure and key technologies, and IoT inclusion with blockchain. Moreover, we described various security and privacy properties and respective practices; finally, we discussed challenges in the blockchain.

References

1. Dorri, A., Steger, M., Kanhere, S.S., Jurdak, R., BlockChain: A Distributed Solution to Automotive Security and Privacy. *IEEE Commun. Mag.*, 55, 12, 119–125, 2017.
2. Xie, J., Tang, H., Huang, T., Yu, F.R., Xie, R., Liu, J., Liu, Y., A Survey of Blockchain Technology Applied to Smart Cities: Research Issues and Challenges. *IEEE Commun. Surv., Tutor.*, 21, 3, 2794–2830, 2019.
3. Archana Prashanth, J., Han, M., Wang, Y., A Survey on Security and Privacy Issues of Blockchain Technology. *Math. Found. Comput. Am. Inst. Math. Sci.*, 1, 2, 121–147, 2018.
4. Zhang, R., Xue, R., Liu, L., Security and Privacy on Blockchain. *ACM Comput. Surv.*, 52, 3, Article, 51, 2019.
5. Ferrag, M.A., Derdour, M., Mukherjee, M., Derhab, A., Maglaras, L., Janicke, H., Blockchain Technologies for the Internet of Things: Research Issues and Challenges. *IEEE Commun. Surv.*, 6, 2, 2327–4662, 2018.
6. Lao, L., Li, Z., Hou, S., Xiao, B., Guo, S., Yang, Y., A Survey of IoT Applications in Blockchain Systems: Architecture, Consensus, and Traff Modeling. *ACM Comput. Surv.*, 53, 1, Article 18, 2020.
7. Zheng, X., Zhu, Y., Si, X., A Survey on Challenges and Progresses in Blockchain Technologies: A Performance and Security Perspective. *Appl. Sci.*, 9, 2, 4731, 2019.
8. Restuccia, F., D'Oro, S., Kanhere, S.S., Melodia, T., Das, S.K., Blockchain for the Internet of Things: Present and Future. *IEEE Internet Things*, 1, 1, 1–8, 2018.
9. Bach, L.M., Mihaljevic, B., Zagar, M., Comparative Analysis of Consensus Algorithm, in: *MIPRO 2018*, Opatija Croatia, May 21-25, 2018, IEEE, pp. 218–225, 2018

10. Conti, M., Kumar, E.S., Lal, C., Ruj, S., A Survey on Security and Privacy Issues of Bitcoin. *IEEE Commun. Surv. Tutor.*, 20, 4, 3416–3452, 2018.
11. Melhem, A., AlZoubi, O., Mardini, W., Applications of Blockchain in Smart Cities., in: *DATA '19: Proceedings of the Second International Conference on Data Science, E-Learning and Information Systems*, December 2–5, 2019, Association for Computing Machinery, New York, NY, USA, Article 358, pp. 1–7, 2019.
12. Mohanta, B.K., Jena, D., Panda, S.S., Sobhanayak, S., Blockchain technology: A survey on applications and security privacy Challenges. *Internet Things*, 8, Article 100107, 2019.
13. Sapirshtein, Sompolinsky, Y., Zohar, A., Optimal selfish mining strategies in bitcoin, in: *Financial Cryptography and Data Security: 20th International Conference, FC 2016*, Christ Church, Barbados, 2017, Springer, Berlin Heidelberg, pp. 515–532, 2017.
14. Lei, A., Cruickshank, H., Cao, Y., Asuquo, P., Ogah, C.P.A., Sun, Z., Blockchain-based dynamic key management for heterogeneous intelligent transportation systems. *IEEE Internet Things J.*, 4, 6, 1832–1843, 2017.
15. Mettler, M., Blockchain technology in healthcare: The revolution starts here, in: *2016 IEEE 18th International Conference on e-Health Networking, Applications and Services*, pp. 1–3, Sept 2016.
16. Biswas, K. and Muthu kumarasamy, V., securing smart cities using blockchain technology, in: *2016 IEEE 18th International Conference on High Performance Computing and Communications*, pp. 1392–1393, 2016.
17. Dalipi, F. and Yayilgan, S.Y., Security and privacy considerations for iot application on smart grids: Survey and research challenges, in: *Future Internet of Things and Cloud Workshops (FiCloudW), IEEE International Conference on. IEEE*, 2016, pp. 63–68, 2016.
18. Laszka, A., Dubey, A., Walker, M., Schmidt, D., providing privacy, safety, and security in iot-based transactive energy systems using distributed ledgers, in: *Proceedings of the Seventh International Conference on the Internet of Things*, ACM, p. 13, 2017.
19. Lombardi, F., Aniello, L., De Angelis, S., Margheri, A., Sassone, V., A blockchain-based infrastructure for reliable and cost-effective iotaided smart grids, in: *Living in the Internet of Things: Cybersecurity of the IoT-2018*, pp. 1–6, 2018.
20. Mylrea, M. and Gourisetti, S.N.G., Blockchain for smart grid resilience: Exchanging distributed energy at speed, scale and security, in: *Resilience Week (RWS)*, 2017, IEEE, pp. 18–23, 2017.
21. Kalkan, K. and Zeadally, S., Securing internet of things (iot) with software defined networking (sdn). *IEEE Commun. Mag.*, 56, 9, 186–192, 2017.
22. Ziegeldorf, J.H., Matzutt, R., Henze, M., Grossmann, F., Wehrle, K., Secure and anonymous decentralized Bitcoin mixing. *Futur. Gener. Comput. Syst.*, 80, 448–466, Mar 2018.

23. Yang, C., Chen, X., Xiang, Y., Blockchain-based publicly verifiable data deletion scheme for cloud storage. *J. Netw. Comput. Appl.*, 103, 185–193, Feb 2018.
24. ElGamal, T., A Public Key Cryptosystem and a Signature Scheme Based on Discrete Logarithms, in: *Advances in Cryptology. CRYPTO 1984. Lecture Notes in Computer Science*, Blakley, G.R., Chaum, D. (Eds), Springer, Berlin, Heidelberg, vol. 196, pp. 10–18, 1985.
25. Gai, F., Wang, B., Deng, W., Peng, W., Proof of reputation: A reputation-based consensus protocol for peer-to-peer network, in: *Database Systems for Advanced Applications*, pp. 666 681, 2018.
26. Garay, J., Kiayias, A., Leonardos, N., The Bitcoin backbone protocol: Analysis and applications, in: *EUROCRYPT 2015*, pp. 281–310, 2015.
27. Garg, S., Gentry, C., Halevi, S., Sahai, A., Waters, B., Attribute-Based Encryption for Circuits from Multilinear Maps, in: *Advances in Cryptology. CRYPTO 2013. Lecture Notes in Computer Science*, Canetti R., Garay J.A. (Eds), Springer, Berlin, Heidelberg, vol. 8043, pp. 479–499.
28. Gentry, C., Fully homomorphic encryption using ideal lattices, in: *STOC*, pp. 169–178, 2009.
29. Xu, X., Weber, I., Staples, M., Zhu, L., Bosch, J., Bass, L., Pautasso, C., Rimba, P., A taxonomy of blockchain-based systems for architecture design, in Software Architecture (ICSA). *2017 IEEE International Conference on Communication Security*, IEEE, pp. 243–252, 2017.
30. Zhang, L., Cai, Z., Wang, X., Fakemask: a novel privacy preserving approach for smartphones. *IEEE Trans. Netw. Service Manag.*, 13, 335–348, 2016.
31. Zheng, X., Cai, Z., Li, J., Gao, H., Location-privacy-aware review publication mechanism for local business service systems, in: *INFOCOM 2017-IEEE Conference on Computer Communications*, IEEE, pp. 1–9, 2017.
32. Zheng, X., Cai, Z., Li, Y., Data linkage in smart iot systems: A consideration from privacy perspective. *IEEE Commun. Mag.*, 56, 55–61, 2018.
33. Zheng, X., Luo, G., Cai, Z., A fair mechanism for private data publication in online social networks. *IEEE Trans. Netw. Sci. Eng.*, 7, 880–891, 2020.
34. Zheng, Z., Xie, S., Dai, H.-N., Chen, X., Wang, H., Blockchain challenges and opportunities: A survey. *Int. J. Web Grid Serv.*, 14, 4, Article 352, 2018.
35. Zheng, Z., Xie, S., Dai, H., Chen, X., Wang, H., An overview of blockchain technology: Architecture, consensus, and future trends, in Big Data (Big Data Congress). *International Congress on IEEE Communications*, pp. 557–564, 2017.
36. Zyskind, Nathan, O., *et al.*, Decentralizing privacy: Using blockchain to protect personal data, in: *Security and Privacy Workshops (SPW)*, pp. 180–184, 2015.
37. Gilad, Y., Hemo, R., Micali, S., Vlachos, G., Zeldovich, N., Algorand: Scaling Byzantine Agreements for Cryptocurrencies. *Cryptology ePrint Archive*, 2017.
38. Miller, A., Xia, Y., Croman, K., Shi, E., Song, D., The honey badger of BFT protocols, in: *CCS*, pp. 31–42, 2016.
39. Restuccia, F. and Das, S.K., Optimizing the lifetime of sensor networks with uncontrollable mobile sinks and qos constraints. *ACM Trans. Sens. Netw. (TOSN)*, 12, 1, 2, 2016.

40. Jagannath, J., Polosky, N., Jagannath, A., Restuccia, F., Melodia, T., Machine learning for wireless communications in the internet of things: A comprehensive survey. *Ad Hoc Networks*, 93, Article 101913, 2019.

41. Restuccia, F., D'Oro, S., Melodia, T., Securing the internet of things in the age of machine learning and software-defined networking. *IEEE Internet Things J.*, 5, 6, 4829–4842, 2018.

42. Restuccia, F., Ghosh, N., Bhattacharjee, S., Das, S.K., Melodia, T., Quality of information in mobile crowd sensing: Survey and research challenges. *ACM Trans. Sens. Netw. (TOSN)*, 13, 4, 34, 2017.

43. Bekara, C., Security issues and challenges for the IoT-based smart grid. *Proc. Comput. Sci.*, 34, 532–537, 2014.

44. Frustaci, M., Pasquale, P., Gianluca, A., Fortino, G., Evaluating critical security issues of the IoT world: Present and future challenges. *IEEE Internet Things J.*, 5, 4, 2483–2495, 2017.

45. Alrawais, A., Alhothaily, A., Hu, C., Cheng, X., Fog computing for the internet of things: Security and privacy issues. *IEEE Internet Comput.*, 21, 2, 34–42, 2017.

46. Agrawal, R., Chatterjee, J.M., Kumar, A., Rathore, P.S. (Eds.), *Blockchain Technology and the Internet of Things: Challenges and Applications in Bitcoin and Security*, CRC Press, UK, 2020.

Toward Smart Cities Based on the Internet of Things

Djamel Saba*, Youcef Sahli and Abdelkader Hadidi

Unité de Recherche en Energies Renouvelables en Milieu Saharien, URER-MS, Centre de Développement des Energies Renouvelables, CDER, Adrar, Algeria

Abstract

A smart city is a modern technology that aims to improve the quality of daily life and reduce costs. However, organizational, technological, and societal changes in today's cities are driven by their desire to be a part of the response to climate change. Smart city seeks to reconcile the cultural, social, and environmental pillars through approaches that combine participatory governance and rational management of available resources. The smart cities appeared in recent years, benefiting from technological advances illustrated by ubiquitous computing and artificial intelligence, forming ambient intelligence. It includes connected objects that make the city itself connected, or communicating. Then, connected objects allowing the city to react automatically according to events and new technologies based on the Internet of Things (IoT) which is widely dispersed. This study is carried out to provide valuable information about technology environments and support researchers; it is necessary to understand the choices and the gaps available in this area.

Keywords: Internet of Things, decision-making, smart city, interoperability, ambient intelligence

Corresponding author: saba_djamel@yahoo.fr

Vishal Kumar, Vishal Jain, Bharti Sharma, Jyotir Moy Chatterjee and Rakesh Shrestha (eds.) Smart City Infrastructure: The Blockchain Perspective, (33–76) © 2022 Scrivener Publishing LLC

2.1 Introduction

The smart city concept has been implemented by digital companies wishing to provide technological solutions for the daily life of the individual and society. As the cities that adopted these solutions became pioneers in many areas and, in turn, suffered from some setbacks, such as the insufficiency of some services provided around the real needs of the regions, or even the loss of sovereignty associated with technological dependence as well. The increasing automation of management processes is often addressed in a sectoral fashion (water, electricity, transportation, etc.). In this sense, we can talk about a "digital city" or a "connected city" [1].

Then, a second movement emerged in recent years, aiming to return the goals of local public action and social innovation to the center of attention, rather than considering that technological progress alone can meet the challenges. Therefore, institutions are more and more concerned with citizens and socio-economic actors, by promoting citizen participation and opening regional governance. We then talk about a "collaborative city" or "agile" or even "open", given the technological innovation of digital.

Some define a smart city as a city that relies mainly on ICT to promote better interaction with its citizens and to ensure that its residents improve quality and the living environment, which affects three basic aspects: the economy, society, and the environment [2]. All three are working with the same objective of ensuring a favorable context for development. Then, the smart city is a platform that uses Internet of Things (IoT), computer technology, control technology, and communication technology to connect various objects via the network to provide more convenient control and management. It effectively serves residents by communicating with a variety of IoT-based digital objects. The main goal in the future is to achieve solid and transparent communication between all organisms [2]. Smart city technology based on the IoT has changed human life by achieving communication between everyone [3]. City automation systems have become more sophisticated. These systems provide the infrastructure and tools to exchange all types of information and services on the objects [4]. A smart city is a domain, which allows a network connecting between different elements like, sensors, actuators, and management programs. In addition, the smart city includes installed detection and control objects. These switches consist of sensors attached to a central axis, also called "gates". The latter is a control system that includes a user interface that interacts with other devices such as a tablet, mobile phone, or computer as the network connection of these systems is managed by the IoT [5].

In the field of energy and electricity consumption, buildings occupy the largest share of energy consumption and carbon dioxide emissions [6]. In parallel, the current civilization has become more and more digital, through the emergence of new technologies in the ways of consuming electricity through the dependence of smart city management in centralized systems and control devices to achieve an economy in electric energy [7].

In addition, the use of a smart city should achieve a comfortable standard of living [8] by using smart energy management interfaces [9, 10], which is known as the Home Energy Management System (HEMS) [11]. The device is seen as a tool to support managing and balancing individuals' electrical energy consumption without compromising their comfort. However, the smart city is an emerging field full of promise and aspirations, accompanied by much empirical research. Also, the availability of a variety of smart cities in the global market has encouraged researchers to explore the original concept of a smart city and develop their research in many problems, the most important of which is the relationship of the smart city with the green city and sustainable development. Finally, many advantages should be available in smart cities, including the following [2]:

- The smart city can achieve the interaction between the user and the electricity grid, such as obtaining data about electricity consumption, determining energy consumption plan [12], and optimum utilization of energy resources without neglecting the environmental aspect.
- A smart city can improve comfort, safety, and the interaction between people's lives and improve lifestyle.
- The ability to communicate with the city via mobile phone and remote network.
- Through the smart city, it is possible to read on the meters (water, electric power, gas, etc.), which provides more practical conditions for high-quality service.

The remainder of this paper can be organized as follows. Section 2.2 introduces the origin of smart city technology. Section 2.3 presents the smart and sustainable city. Section 2.4 explains the smart city areas and sub-areas. Section 2.5 details the IoT. Section 2.6 provides examples of smart cities. Section 2.7 explains the benefits of using smart city technology. Next, an analysis and discussion of the work done in Section 2.8. Finally, Section 2.9 concludes the research paper.

2.2   Smart City Emergence

The use of smart city technology dates back to the late 1980s and early 1990s. Often, three phenomena are identified to explain their origin.

2.2.1   A Term Popularized by Private Foundations

Although some associate the origin of the smart city with the concept of "smart growth" introduced by new urban planning in the 1980s, this term is primarily the fruit of a strategy developed by IBM [13]. Wanting to increase its profits during the recession, the company has identified cities as an important market by connecting them with information and communication technologies [14]. More specifically, IBM's idea is based on two assumptions. The first concerns three pillars in the heart of the city: 1) service planning and management; 2) infrastructure services; and 3) human services. The second assumes that each of these columns forms a single system [14]. Later, IBM spread this technology and "sold" it to cities [13]. In other words, the spread of the term "smart city" is the product of an advertising campaign in its pursuit of profit. The term's popularity goes hand in hand with a variety of somewhat similar expressions that are sometimes used to distinguish or to try to define a "smart city" (Figure 2.1) [15].

The term "smart city" is also an expression used to define the city of the future. For some, the term includes other terms and characteristics that are not very different from the term "smart city". Albino *et al.* assert that the

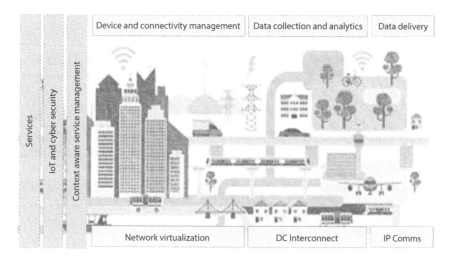

Figure 2.1 Smart city according to Nokia.

Table 2.1 Extract of concepts often associated with the "smart city".

Concept	Definition
Intelligent city	Smart cities use information technology to transform people's lives. This designation refers to the ability to support learning, technology development, and innovation in cities. Therefore, every digital city is not necessarily smart, but every smart city contains digital elements [16].
Ubiquitous city	It has a direct relationship to digital city technology in many aspects. One of its characteristics is that it makes computing everywhere available to people. It also contributes to creating an environment that helps any citizen in obtaining any service, anywhere and at any time through any device [17].
Virtual city	The city has a hybrid concept because it is made up of many things like its physical entities and its real residents [18].

decision to refer to the adjective "smart" is a marketing choice: "Indeed, in marketing parlance, the term "intelligence" is a more user-friendly term than "intelligent" (Table 2.1) [13].

2.2.2 Continuation of Ancient Reflections on the City of the Future

Many urban thinkers have been interested in the city of tomorrow, a city in which technology still plays a role. The concept of "smart city" is a kind of culmination of these different ideas. The success of this label also stems from its appearance in a particularly convenient context. Cities will already face four major phenomena that require the implementation of a series of actions: increasing urbanization [19], climate change and awareness of the scarcity of resources, reducing budgets, and competition between cities. Additionally, thanks to technology, a "smart city" appears as a potential response. Indeed, "the link to technology is clear even if it refers to a variety of uses and levels of assignment". According to studies and research, to have a smart city, it must be effective in six aspects [20]:

- **A smart economy:** It is the city's economic competitiveness. It is measured through factors such as innovation, entrepreneurship, productivity, flexibility in the labor market, or even engagements in local and global trade tasks.

- **Smart citizens:** It mainly concerns the human elements and the city social relations. It is a question of the level of qualification of the population, but also its multiplicity, openness, creativity, quality of social interactions, or participation in public life.
- **Smart governance:** In other words, a transparent, transversal—and shared—mode of a city administration that includes citizen participation.
- **Smart mobility:** Giffinger emphasizes local and international access to the city, the existence of connected infrastructures exploiting ICT, innovative, sustainable, and safe transport systems [21].
- **Smart environment:** It is about the environment and resource management. So that the smart city should support and encourage a sustainable environment and rational management of all resources.
- **A smart lifestyle:** It brings together factors linked to the quality of life: culture, health, security, housing, education, tourism, social cohesion, etc.

2.3   Smart and Sustainable City

There are many terms that are directly related to the concept of smart city such as digital city, connected city and sustainable city. The latter represents a challenge for all countries and peoples of the world in their direct relationship with preserving the environment (Figure 2.2). The concept of the smart city emerged more than a decade ago, and since then rapid urbanization and the urgent need to develop a long-term viable model to deal with the expected increase in urban population led to the International Telecommunication Union (ITU) creating the term "smart and sustainable cities", giving priority to available resources as well as integration between technological and environmental elements [22]. But what exactly is a smart and sustainable city? Based on about a hundred definitions, the ITU has formulated a standard definition for a smart and sustainable driver [23]. During the conference held in Italy in 2014, experts agreed to define a smart city as a system that uses advanced information and communication technologies to improve the quality of daily life, taking into consideration the current and future needs of society in all fields [24]. Although the role of ICTs has not yet been fully defined, the services that ICTs can support,

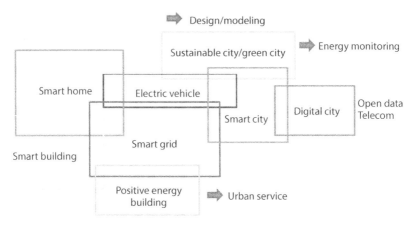

Figure 2.2 Elements of a smart city.

including water resource management, energy efficiency, and transportation infrastructure. The previous definition of the concept of the smart and sustainable city gives a starting point which makes it possible to understand the characteristics which these cities share and to develop key indicators, which will contribute to the development of an ICT infrastructure, methods of measurement, and policies related to this city type [2].

In addition, rapid urbanization poses many problems, such as defining methods of building infrastructure, providing services, citizen participation, and the links between different systems so that cities become more stable and sustainable places. Information and communication technology innovations are at the heart of this evolution [25]. Town planners are now moving toward this integrated approach; they no longer see cities as a set of distinct sectors but as a global network. The objective is to offer residents a better quality of life by combining technological and social innovations and by using ICTs to strengthen the efficiency of different sectors. According to Sekhar Kondepudi, "The essential characteristics of smart and sustainable cities are sustainability, quality of life and intelligence." Sustainability refers, among other things, to governance, pollution, and climate change [26]. Generally, the welfare of life has a basic relationship with the psychological state of the person as well as the available financial resources. As for the use of intelligence, it aims to improve the quality of life in all aspects [27]. Then, it is possible to assess smart and sustainable cities by four general criteria: those of society, the economy, the environment, and governance. The "society" criterion is used to determine whether the city serves the interests of its inhabitants. However, two concepts with similar meanings and goals are often confused, namely, the sustainable city and the smart city. Finally, organizational, technological, and societal changes in today's cities are driven by their desire to be a part of the response to climate change. According to Rudolf Giffinger, smart cities can be classified according to six main criteria, linked to regional and neoclassical theories of growth and urban development and based on theories of information and communication technologies [28].

2.4   Smart City Areas (Sub-Areas)

The intelligent transformation of cities under the impetus of new technologies has gradually integrated aspects of urban life in various fields. Then, faced with the growing variety of components of city intelligence, a classification of "smart" European medium-sized cities was proposed according to six dimensions: smart people, transportation, smart communications, smart commerce, etc. (Table 2.2) [21].

2.4.1   Technology and Data

The smart city is based on infrastructure communications that are very efficient (Table 2.3). In addition to a telecommunications network, the production of data requires the upstream implementation of technical devices, sensors, databases, and telecommunications networks. To do this, most cities have opened a data management center to create, collect, store, analyze, or disseminate information through an open data policy [29]. Then, a city's desire to open its data in an exploitable format aims at the development of internal and external services via the creation of platforms or applications disseminating these new services. The idea is that smart initiatives develop information and communication infrastructures so that, in turn, these infrastructures reinforce these initiatives by achieving environmental systems to provide services and collect data.

2.4.2   Economy

The data economy opens new markets and redistributes power relations across the digital and non-digital sectors (Table 2.4). The race for intelligence is first and foremost a race for the competitiveness of traditional and emerging companies to the point where the economic value of data is largely built by a host of actors from very different sectors [30]. New alliances are created between companies, innovation and research centers, governments, and citizens as a new map of many elements are formed (high-tech

Table 2.2 Smart city domains and sub-domains.

Domain	Sub-domains
Technology and data	• Telecommunications infrastructure • Data center • Digital platforms
Economy	• High-tech companies and digital transformation of companies • Innovation, entrepreneurship and creativity • Universities, research centers • Territorial marketing and international partnerships
Population	• Human and social capital • Attractiveness (brain drain) • Cohesion and social inclusion • Citizen proactivity
Transport and mobility	• Logistics • User information • Sustainable mobility and local accessibility
Quality of life and environment	• Public services • Smart grids • Renewable energy • Quality buildings and housing • Density and fight against urban sprawl
Touristic destination	• Tourist experience • Co-creation activities • Visibility
Governance	• e-government • e-Democracy • Interoperability and partnerships • Transparency • Citizen engagement and participation in • decision making • Protection

companies, corporate digital transformation, research centers, innovative and creative laboratories, entrepreneurship activities, and citizen projects). Strategic tools are often created to incorporate and strengthen the position of these actors in existing ecosystems (publications, events, participation in competitions, etc.).

Table 2.3 Summary of technology and data.

Sub-domains	Description
Telecommunications infrastructure	A city's communications system includes its telecommunications infrastructure, including means of communication such as phone, social media, the Internet, and others.
Data center	• A datacenter and digital device in the city that collects measure, store, analyze, and disseminates the information produced and co-produced with citizens. • Open data policy.
Digital platforms	• Services exploiting the data collected and the use of new technologies to improve them. • Survey on the diversity of distribution channels and the accessibility of these services via digital platforms (sites, applications, etc.).

Table 2.4 Economic overview.

Sub-domains	Description
High-tech companies and digital transformation enterprises	• Presence number of employees in "high-tech" companies. • Examination of the digital transformation of services and the functioning of other companies (small and medium in particular).
Innovation, entrepreneurship, and creativity	• Presence of alliances, partnerships, and multidisciplinary public-private research groups. • Presence of local incubators, business incubators, living labs or social innovation, or social purpose organization.
Universities and research centers	• Number of universities, research centers, training organizations.
Territorial marketing and international partnerships	• Creation of communication campaigns and publications on the procedures to be undertaken in the territory.

Table 2.5 Population domain summary.

Sub-domains	Description
Human capital	Set of skills, individual abilities, and the accumulated experience of individuals.
Attractiveness	The capacity of a city to welcome foreign students, tourists, and other non-residents by offering solutions adapted to their needs.
Social cohesion and inclusion	Measures to reduce the digital divide, i.e., to reduce the barriers to access to digital tools, to their learning, and participation in online activities (in particular about specific categories of citizens such as seniors and the disabled).

2.4.3   Population

The first smart city metrics focused on the spatial distribution of human capital to understand the increasing divergence between spaces with high concentrations of all levels of study (school, average, university, etc.) (Table 2.5). In the face of this observation, the attractiveness of talent is coupled with continuing education and strengthening of the human and social capital of the population. These results were largely inspired by studies of the creative classes that were converted to the new name "smart citizens" [31]. This is why some people incorporate creativity, openness, or ethnic diversity as a subfield.

2.5   IoT

The IoT is a technical realization of ubiquitous computing where technology is naturally integrated into everyday objects. We adopt this concept as the relationship between the physical world and the virtual world [32]. However, like other promising concepts, it faces many technical and non-technical issues that need to be addressed to enable the IoT to reach its full potential. In 1991, Mark Weiser [33] has presented de IoT concept as technology is slowly disappearing into the user environment, naturally integrated into the world. In addition, the technology is no longer represented by a single object, the personal computer, but on the contrary, presents itself in the form of specialized and devices capable of communicating with networks. In 1999, Kevin Ashton introduced the IoT as an aid to radio frequency identification [36]. However, the concept of the IoT could evolve and become more generalized toward connecting a large number of objects to the Internet, giving them their own identity and allowing them to provide services and collect information independently. The ambitious goal behind this interconnection is primarily to implement a large-scale machine-to-machine (M2M) communications infrastructure to allow these machines to better "perceive" the world that makes them surround them [34]. Second, there is a desire to provide the abstractions necessary for humans to interact with the physical and virtual world [35]. In other words, IoT users should be able to manipulate the physical environment in the same way they do today with higher-level abstractions, such as files, folders, web pages, hyperlinks, or personal files and relationships (for example, on social networks).

The term "cyber-physical systems" (CPS) is sometimes used to design concepts close to the IoT. Cyber physics systems share the same objective of linking the physical world and the virtual world (or cyber world). According to Cisco [43], the convergence of networks of people, processes, data, and objects, IoT goes to the IoE, or "Internet at all connects" (Figure 2.3). It is a multi-dimensional internet that combines many important elements such as big data and the IoT.

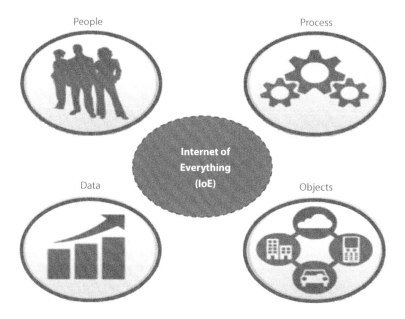

Figure 2.3 IoE.

- **People:** by connecting people in an effective way.
- **Process:** provides necessary information to a person (device) at the right time.
- **Data:** data is used to produce the most useful information for decision-making [44, 45].
- **Objects:** things are always connected to the Internet so you can make quick, accurate, and smart decisions [44].

The IoT is a global infrastructure that enables the following:

- The active objects of exchanging information or collecting information about passive objects, which is in line with the definitions of an M2M global network [35];
- To store and make accessible the identity of the objects, the information produced by them and all the knowledge necessary for the objects to gain autonomy, through representations, structures, and formats of data manipulable by machines [46];
- Human beings to access this information and interact naturally with the objects at the local and the global level, which includes data communication [47].

The IoT is influenced by the different usage scenarios that are considered today by the scientific and industrial worlds [35, 38, 48, 49] (Table 2.6), each of them has its tasks, limitations and goals. These scenarios can take place in private spaces, in which interactions with the outside are strictly controlled, or in public spaces open to all, with a host of differences. Indeed, a smart home that automatically regulates the brightness or temperature is a strictly private space while public parking that indicates to motorists which are the nearest free places is a strictly public space [50]. Various interactions will be able to exist between the different spaces through specialized interfaces. In the same way, some scenarios involve the direct participation of users; for example, a mobile application where users subjectively estimate the population density of a metro station or the cleanliness of a public place. Other cases of use are based on the sharing of certain objects belonging to the users, collaboratively. For example, as cars are increasingly equipped with GPS, it is possible to offer users the opportunity to contribute to the analysis of road traffic.

Table 2.6 Some definitions of the IoT.

Nature	Authors	Definition
Sociotechnical definition	Mohamed Younis [36]	It is an advanced communication and networking technology covers all aspects of our lives, and it is visible in the way people interact, shop, do business, etc.
Technico-economic definition	Asle Fagerstrøm *et al.* [37]	The IoT technology allows businesses to develop an infrastructure to create physical assets such as mobile phones, shopping carts, store shelves, digital displays, and even the product intelligent and enabling real-time interaction with customers either in the physical or the virtual store.
Technical definition	L. Atzori *et al.* [38]	The IoT sometimes considered synonymous with an Internet of Everything (IoE), represents "a variety of things or objects (...) that, thanks to the addressing system, they can interact with others to achieve common goals."
Socio-technical definition	Schatten M *et al.* [39]	With the rapid development of the IoT, so all devices should work as one institution to achieve the best services.
Technical definition	Behailu Negash *et al.* [40]	Interoperability remains one of the key challenges in realizing the IoT's vision.

(Continued)

2.5.1 A New Dimension for the Internet and Objects

With the advent of the IoT, the internet is acquiring a third dimension; in addition to the ability to connect anytime and anywhere, it is now possible to connect with any object. In addition, connected objects are uniquely identified and can collect environmental information (related to changes in environmental parameters, such as temperature) or behavioral

Table 2.6 Some definitions of the IoT. (*Continued*)

Nature	Authors	Definition
Technical definition	Das A *et al.* [41]	IoT is a network of things (a device, a person or a program) where they communicate with each other to achieve specific goals without human intervention (automatic) or human interaction with a computer (semi-automatic). In addition, the sensors are among the contributing elements in the work of the IoT and connect them to the Internet through protocols to achieve good communication and smart tracking, monitoring, and management.
Technical definition	Edewede Oriwoh *et al.* [42]	The IoT describes the interconnectedness of objects including identification, communication, and data collection. In this context, the objects range from traditional computing devices such as personal computers to standard household objects incorporating detection and/or communication capabilities through the use of multiple technologies.

information (resulting from state variations of the object itself or contextual objects), process them and communicate them on the Internet.

An object is an entity, this object has at least a unique identifier associated with an identity that expresses, on the one hand, its static properties (type, color, weight, etc.) and its state which is to say all its properties that could develop (position, battery level, etc.) [38]. However, many definitions agree that an object has computational, acquisition (sensor), and action (trigger) capabilities [35, 47, 51]. The IoT is also considered to consist of active organisms, able to perform mathematical operations, measure or influence the environment, and negative things, which do not have capabilities other than being tracked and discovered by active organisms. By extension, the passive object identity is not stored in it directly, except for the identifier, and it requires the use of a third-party infrastructure capable of storing this information. On the contrary, the active object can store all or part of its identity and exchange this information directly with other active objects. However, this ability to store one's identity is not mandatory for an active being and depends on (1) its physical resources, including memory, and (2) size (complexity) of the identity.

2.5.2   Issues Raised by the IoT

To enable the IoT to reach its fullest potential and concretize the scenarios that emerge, several aspects need to be studied. The promising concepts envisioned by the scientific researchers need to solve different problems: heterogeneous, the impact of the physical world (large continuous flows of data, the variability of the environment), the security of goods and people, etc.

2.5.2.1   IoT Scale

Of all the difficulties posed by the IoT, the global scale and very large number of objects involved are the most important, even if we exclude those that are only linked via proxy. The Internet can be seen as a promising candidate as it is widespread and thus represents a good basis for the IoT [52].

The various problems related to the size of the IoT are in the first place, as there are problems in processing and identifying things, which can be solved using current technologies (Table 2.7):

- IPv6 protocol for the addressing of objects.
- Electronic Product Codes (EPC), Internationalized Resource Identifiers (IRIs), or Universally Unique Identifiers (UUIDs) for the unique identification of objects.

2.5.2.2   IoT Heterogeneity

According to the uses for which they were designed, the properties and capabilities of objects vary significantly, contributing to making the IoT an ecosystem that is certainly rich, but also heterogeneous (Table 2.8). However, the characteristics of objects correspond to the constraints that

Table 2.7 Some scenarios for the IoT.

Scenario	Description
Optimize high racks of the warehouses	High bay warehouse operators can create a digital twin to optimize their collaboration with manufacturers and service partners. The digital pairing of the warehouse is mapped in the management software and displays the status and position of the assets it contains.
Enable standalone machines	Real-time interaction between machines and management systems enables efficient production at the command. Manufacturers can configure interfaces in their management software to allow communication between external systems and machines.
Streamline material flow in manufacturing	When we think of industry, we first think of sensors. Its uses include helping manufacturers track parts in real time and automated material flow from the warehouse. The parts are equipped with RFID tags that allow the sensors to transfer the position of each component to the corresponding management software in real time. This allows human operators to directly indicate where and when orders are ready to be processed, which increases the use of delays in the production process.
Monitoring and logistics	That makes it possible to track the time and location of an object, provided it is recognized (for example by an RFID tag). Today, this scenario is implemented by industrialists to track things in the production line (manufacturing, transportation, etc.).
Medical care and assistance to the person	By using the sensors to obtain real-time information about the patient's condition (heart rate, blood pressure, etc.), even when patients are outside the clinics, there are portable sensors, to respond quickly in the event of an imbalance in the patient's health.

(Continued)

Table 2.7 Some scenarios for the IoT. (*Continued*)

Scenario	Description
Smart environments	Adaptation of environmental standards in residences and offices (temperature, brightness, humidity, energy consumption, etc.). In the context of smart cities, analysis of various parameters (noise, pollution, and road traffic) can be done in real time and linking different elements of urban infrastructure to better manage all resources.
Social sensing shared sensing and participative sensing	Using sensors, the information can be collected and then combined with other groups. Also allowing users and organizations to share information from their systems on a large scale to collaboratively contribute to many analytical tasks such as road traffic, population flows, climatic conditions, etc.

Table 2.8 Summary of the impact of the scale on the IoT.

Scale impact	Description
Addressing and naming	Very large number of objects requires (1) important address space and (2) significantly increases the amount of information that name servers must store to fulfill their role of association between object names and their names addresses.
Discovery	Saving and searching for objects by name or by their characteristics is fundamental to the realization of scenarios where objects are not known in advance. In addition, storing and browsing all the objects in a centralized way is not possible on such a scale.
Access	Multitude of objects complicates data collection, while large volumes of data make their processing more complex (data mining and data aggregation).

condition how these objects are used and interact with their environment. For example, portable objects are more likely to experience choppy connectivity than static objects, and objects with low hardware resources are limited to uncomplicated tasks. Similarly, objects embed different sensors and actuators according to their functions, which has a direct impact on their ability to measure and influence their environment. Knowing that the IoT is a model in which various objects communicate and collaborate dynamically. In general, objects should be able to interact under all circumstances, regardless of the constraints imposed by their characteristics and their environment.

2.5.2.3   Physical World Influence on the IoT

The IoT is affected by features of the physical world (Table 2.9). This last is an environment that evolves naturally over time, on the one hand, because objects are added or withdrawn continuously and, secondly, because of the human beings and their objects mobility [53]. As many objects are brought up to dynamically discover their environment and communicate with other objects (i.e., initiate exchanges at time t with nearby objects that may not be available at present t + 1). Additionally, interactions, where specific objects move, can create a dynamic network structure. Therefore, organisms must be able to adapt dynamically to the changes that take place over time, both in terms of their states and their environment. Also, according to the needs expressed by the users, organisms must possess the means to interact according to situations that take place through cooperation with other organisms or the application of certain techniques.

Table 2.9 Summary of the impact of heterogeneity on the IoT.

Heterogeneity impact	Description
Functional heterogeneity	Objects have specific capabilities (static or mobile and hardware resources) and each of them corresponds to specific constraints (intermittent connectivity, lifetime, achievable tasks, etc.). Different methods and techniques must be considered to manage things according to the limitations and differences that exist between them.
Technical heterogeneity	It relates to the hardware (or software) technologies used to build objects and the independent collaboration between them. In addition, the development of applications is complicated, requiring developer's specific knowledge about the operation of each object.

Table 2.10 Summary of the impact of the physical world on the IoT.

Physical impact	Description
Data flow	The information produced by the sensors is naturally related to time and is in the form of measurements and data that are used for other tasks. This feature contrasts with the classic data set methods represented in the data model and the calculation model.
Sensors	One of the characteristics of sensors is that they regularly produce measurements that may be wrong, inaccurate or incomplete, without it being possible to predict the timing of the emergence. Specific techniques for detecting, correcting or mitigating errors must be implemented, especially in a multi-sensor environment such as the IoT.
Variability	Physical world is a changing environment, specifically in the context of mobile objects that have to deal with their energy limitations, intermittent connectivity, and the movements of their users. Also, objects must be able to adapt to changes that occur over time, according to the needs of users.

2.5.2.4   Security and Privacy

If the IoT presents many promising use cases, then it also poses many security and privacy issues (Table 2.10). Since things are physical entities that can influence their environment, the damage caused by a cyber-attack in such a context has a much greater impact. Such as those caused by snooping, taking off the site, stealing data, or denying service that we know at the moment. As an example, we can cite Stuxnet, which is a software solution that deals with Control Data Acquisition (SCADA) systems used in order to monitor industrial infrastructures [54].

2.5.3   Applications of the IoT That Revolutionize Society

Smart city is an economically sustainable urban development plan that offers a high standard of living to its residents. Technology has a key role to play in building smart cities. Smart urban infrastructure incorporates a variety of factors: ICT, IoT, public-private partnerships, social, and human capital.

2.5.3.1   IoT in the Field of Health

Sixty percent of global hospitals use the IoT to increase productivity and improve patient care. The most recent studies show that, by 2025, nearly 91% of health services will have integrated connected objects into their medical devices [55]. Connected objects are used daily to oversee and maintain medical institutions, surgeries, remote control, and geolocation services. Standardization of the IoT in the field of health inevitably leads to the creation of new business models that increase employee productivity and obtain reliable communication with patients.

Advances in medicine and technology have improved human life expectancy and have also led to the emergence of new types of diseases and health problems. Therefore, the IoT in the health sector can facilitate remote monitoring, thanks to smart sensors and activity trackers, and thus the operation of technologies. The IoT plays an important role in achieving e-health in a very effective way [56]. In addition, smart cities need smart health services that can track patients remotely, quickly provide emergency services, analyze patient data and use it for other activities and purposes. Besides medical applications, it creates sustainable development through better use of energy, hospital waste management, inventory management, etc. Finally, the future of smart cities will be incomplete without proper health and wellness centers for their residents.

2.5.3.2   Digital Revolution in Response to Energy Imperatives

AI is an important added value in energy management, which in the near future could represent a significant investment [57, 58]. The IoT addresses many important issues such as the depletion of natural resources, increasing global energy needs, instability of market prices, and human labor shortages. Also, the digital revolution has entered the debate on energy sectors through resource management: energy meters, the smart grid, and also the IoT in the smart home [59]. In addition, technology can make life easier, and it can harm our environment as well, such as using carbon natural resources. In this context, to ensure a prosperous future, countries of the world have made many investments in forms of renewable energy such as solar energy, wind energy, water, agriculture and oases [60]. For example, LED lights to reduce costs and improve longevity. In the renewable energy sector, European countries are at the forefront. Germany, the United Kingdom, France, and Italy made good progress in this segment. China, Australia, and Japan also use solar, wind, and hydroelectric power. The new form of energy consumption will be linked to IoT devices that will help individuals, regional institutions, and industries control energy fluids and metrics. In terms of the environment and sustainability, it is also about reducing water consumption and improving air quality, controlling wastewater disposal, and even recycling it. The IoT plays a major role in these areas in implementing smart sensor networks for environmental quality monitoring to obtain better information and make decisions [57, 61].

2.5.3.3   Home Automation (Connected Home)

The smart home is known for automating the things that are available inside the home such as smart TVs, connected speakers. Also, home automation allows for safety and electrical energy savings [62]. In addition to that, home automation includes many activities such as monitoring and programming various interventions inside the house, information sensors (alarm system, temperature changes, etc.) and triggers that allow programming and remote control of various electronic devices.

2.5.3.4   Connected Industry

In the industrialized world, the benefits of the IoT are endless. We cannot count it because it is everywhere. In all branches of the global industry, the IoT is used. This technology is deployed in-depth and today no industry operates without it. The technology depends on sensors installed in the systems to be monitored, and the data is returned to the computers that process and display it in a way that humans can understand [63].

Current components and sensors are performing higher than ever before. To use just a few numbers, the sensors that the IoT relies upon today consume 30 times less energy than older devices.

Industrial IoT improves production quality by providing comprehensive monitoring of the entire production chain. This 4.0 technology also helps prevent crashes by preventing potential system errors from occurring before they become final.

Previously, it was up to the technician to search for information by switching from one machine to another to check its condition, but now the model has been reversed. These are the connected devices that send important information directly to a connected interface managed by the technician. This is called predictive maintenance. In addition, maintenance is almost automatic thanks to the IoT, because many sensors present in all industrial processes allow information to be transmitted in seconds.

By connecting existing systems, faults can be predicted; stock depletion forecasts and loops within these systems can be accelerated.

The goal is to make an industrial enterprise safer, more reliable, interactive, productive, and more competitive. The integration of connected systems in the industry is also a priority if we wish to gain competitiveness. Finally, connected systems simplify industrial process data management.

2.5.3.5   IoT in Agriculture

The IoT is ubiquitous, in smartphones, homes, cars, businesses, and more. The rapid growth of world population, differences in eating habits, and climate disruption are three of the many factors that make modern agriculture change by the year 2050 which requires an increase in agricultural productivity of 70% to meet global demand [64]. This caused many governments to provide farmers with means that can be controlled remotely (smart) such as drones to collect the necessary information in real time on some environmental data. All these factors facilitate the ideal management of the farm, such as measuring the level of fertilizer and irrigation accurately on a particular plot and reducing financial and energy costs. Connected organisms are not only beneficial to farmers but also farmers who can closely monitor the health of their animals. Have you ever heard of connected cows? With a necklace with multiple sensors, there is the possibility to get real-time information about her health and behavior. In addition, any object can be part of the IoT once it is connected to the Internet by an electronic chip, sensor or network connection, which allows it to communicate with other objects, collect and exchange data. In the same network, the objects are interconnected which makes it possible to optimize their uses, while receiving multiple data and analyzes.

The M2M market in agriculture is expected to increase 17-fold between 2014 and 2024, reaching $225 million. By 2022, experts estimate that about 14 billion devices, including production machines, will be connected to the network and will greatly help improve production [65]. In 2024, the Asia-Pacific region will be the largest market for M2M agricultural applications with 54 million connected items. Europe will then be in second place with 51 million items. Thanks to these new technologies, Agriculture Operation Manager 4.0 can now control their devices remotely via a steering system, thus rationalizing their use. It can also monitor the position of the machine and detect the slightest anomaly. Implementing predictive maintenance also helps improve employee safety. In the latter it can be mentioned that the IoT has many other applications to cultivate tomorrow. Some examples:

- Manage the amount and composition of inputs according to the nature of the soil, climatic conditions and plant condition: Equipped farms achieve 15% to 20% savings on raw materials thanks to better utilization of big data.
- Automate time-consuming tasks thanks to robots (weeding, milking, etc.): Agriculture is already the second largest market for utility robots in France.
- Collecting and disseminating data that facilitate the operation of agriculture, such as geographic information through sensors and satellites, etc.

2.5.3.6   *Smart Retail or Trendy Supermarkets*

The supermarket or central market is a complex or multi-section building, and it may be multi-storey where foodstuffs and household items such as food, drinks, materials, and washing tools are bought and sold, and it also contains sections for sale of electronic devices, tools and electrical machines, which saves time and effort expended in frequency Different shopping areas and places. In general, if there is one technology that has the potential to transform the entire supermarket sector, then it is Artificial Intelligence and especially the IoT [66]. Some believe that the technology's applications are only limited to robots and voice assistants—but it is more than that. In New Zealand, for example, a food supermarket group is experimenting with an IoT solution by reading the contents of their shopping cart so that customers do not have to wait in long lines causing a waste of time and effort [67].

Commerce faces a strong challenge by automating this activity and leveraging the popularity of the IoT by combining e-commerce with traditional sales. So, commerce has taken the step of the digital revolution to enhance the sales experience and increase the rate of remittances [68]. One of the concepts of "smart retail" is RFID technology, which enhances the customer experience by providing a highly personalized customer experience. In addition to mobile applications, connected fund concepts are already designed to facilitate supermarket shopping, and merchants are also investing in mobile applications to build loyalty and attract customers to physical stores, for example, through promotional notifications.

Some studies indicate that future supermarket concepts such as "Amazon Go" may lose their luster over time as research studies indicate that consumer convenience is an important factor in placing marketing orders. The technological advancement of these types of stores can simplify the shopping experience in a way that makes customers happy to abandon the traditional supermarkets altogether. As the online shopping experience continues to improve and the digital world develops, it will be difficult for traditional stores to remain relevant in the future.

2.5.3.7   Smart and Connected Cities

Smart cities, or connected cities, have begun the digital transformation to meet the challenges of this modern society on the one hand, and on the other hand, urban planning, economics, and sustainable development are also important issues for the cities of tomorrow, which must meet the needs of an increasingly crowded population. In fact, pollution, along with overpopulation, is two major issues. In addition, the IoT is an important element in achieving smart city systems [61, 69]. Since per capita consumption is better managed, treatment is on a larger scale for city consumption (cost and pollution of public transport, urban transportation, waste treatment, electricity management, etc.). It also connects electronic devices (other than computers and smartphones) to the Internet in order to effectively monitor and manage daily activities. In urban development, ICT and the IoT are important building blocks for creating a smart infrastructure to manage, service, and support city dwellers. Additionally, IoT applications in the city allow optimization of building performance, energy consumption, and streets in particular as such.

Smart city infrastructure includes various factors: ICT, IoT, public-private partnerships, and social and human capital. The IoT connects devices (other than computers and smartphones) to the Internet for effective management of activities. In the field of urban development, ICT and the IoT are important building blocks for creating a smart infrastructure to manage, service, and support the ever-increasing urban population. A smart city needs technological efficiency in transportation and mobility, communications, services, security, civil relations, etc. However, IoT applications in the city make it possible in particular to improve: building performance, energy consumption, street furniture management, disposal of waste. Finally, the beneficiaries of these devices are consumers, citizens, regional institutions, and private companies.

2.5.3.8   IoT at the Service of Road Safety

The road and transportation sector is associated with high maintenance costs, car accidents, and the resulting heavy human and material losses.

Every year, road accidents kill hundreds of thousands of people around the world and cause similar injuries. Some are looking for solutions provided by both the IoT and machine learning, and day after day their prevalence grows and will one day become part of various aspects of daily life. Perhaps through the proper application of IoT technology, risks and damages can be reduced and costs saved. The use of connected smart sensors and machine learning-based analysis tools ensure that information is collected, predictions and decisions made that make roads safer. However, the human factor is still the main factor behind road accident deaths and other losses. Reckless driving, excessive speeding, driving under the influence of alcohol and drugs, driver distraction, and other bad habits increase the chances of road accidents [70]. Various countries apply regulations that impose and define safe driving, but these restrictions remain only reactions to the methods of drivers seeking to push them to safe driving in order to avoid penalties only. The IoT can provide advance assistance for drivers to follow proper driving habits. Geotab is using the IoT to help companies responsible for managing vehicle fleets reduce accidents [71]. "For fully self-driving cars to be launched, we must employ technology to help manage the human factor in driving cars," said the company's chief executive, Neil Kausey. Kawse has explained that data collection is the first step, as remote information technology enables an infinite number of things to know, for example, data about the car and the driver's behavior, in order to avoid the risks of traffic accidents and ensure safety of passengers and vehicles. Onboard diagnostics helps fleet management companies and insurance companies collect a wealth of information about cars and drivers' behavior, including measurable aspects such as speed, seat belt use, sharp cornering, and over-acceleration, which allows them to promote and encourage safe driving through procedures like scorecards and scores that rate drivers based on data about their driving. The second step, Kaosi said, is driver training; that is, using data to help drivers learn a safer driving style. Geotap uses collision avoidance systems, mobile cameras; video and audio alerts to identify dangers and receive direct warnings. Not only does this bring safety to people, but it also benefits companies looking to manage risk and control accident-related expenses. Moreover, the IoT and Telematics reduces the hassle of complying with regulations such as business hours rules that require drivers to record details such as when to start and stop driving and other important journey details. "This safety measure addresses drivers' accidents caused by lack of sleep hours," Kaosi said. Also, analyzing the data collected during accidents contributes to reducing future risks, such as being used to identify the most dangerous intersections of roads. This allows municipalities and transportation departments to direct their budgets to the areas and areas that are most needed and where they will have the greatest impact. He added that Geotap collects more than 900 million data points every day, pointing to the unlimited ways to invest this data.

In fact, providing timely maintenance for bridge networks, internal roads and highways, especially in large countries, is a very difficult and important task at the same time, and the mismanagement of transportation infrastructure leads to losses, including the collapse of bridges, poor road conditions, and traffic congestion. IoT can contribute to such situations, for example, sensors and smart concrete with sensors monitor the condition of road and bridge structures and alert them to defects before they escalate into disasters.

Controlling traffic and ensuring clear road visibility help reduce accidents that often occur due to poor road conditions and unfavorable weather conditions. Safe driving depends primarily on drivers' ability to clearly monitor the road and identify dangers. The sensors can provide the necessary data in real time.

Finally, more potential of the IoT will be revealed in ensuring safe driving while using fully self-driving cars and their ability to interact and make appropriate decisions. This may allow new capabilities such as preventing drivers from entering dangerous areas, helping to avoid collisions, and choosing bypass roads. Moving away from traffic bottlenecks and other perceptions in which the power of the IoT and machine learning combine to present new opportunities [72].

2.5.3.9   Security Systems

The safety and security of individuals is a strategic task for all countries. Without technology, it is hard to track down the negative elements in crowded cities. Where there is a need for high-quality monitoring software to eliminate the threats [73]. For example, IoT sound sensors can help security personnel with smart video surveillance, smart street lights, and the latest drone technology to quickly discover dangerous and suspected locations. In addition, IoT security systems can also help in effectively monitoring public places such as markets, malls, airports, hotels, metro stations, banks, and hospitals.

2.5.3.10 Waste Management

It is an important element in urban areas, where, for example, IoT-based waste monitoring devices contributes to keeping the environment meticulously clean [74]. In this context, some organizations are using smart solutions that rely on the IoT to measure the level of filling trash cans and thus improve the collection process. These solutions also contribute to determining the quality of the litter according to its characteristics: biodegradable, electronic waste, non-degradable, recyclable, etc. All of these solutions very effectively help in improving and preserving the environment. The novelty is the installation of sensors placed inside the containers that measure their filling level in real time [75]. Telemetry sensors collect this data, and its analysis can be used in different ways: in the form of a simple alert, released once the filling level is reached for rapid intervention or in a "smart" way by re-integrating the trash can. Complete for another collection tour already scheduled. The goal is to ensure that waste is collected and emptied at the right time and place. These areas of improvement are now possible at a lower cost, thanks to the democratization of connected objects and their networks.

2.6 Examples of Smart Cities

If there is no completely smart city today, then many are taking the path with more or less large-scale initiatives, among them, Barcelona and Vienna.

2.6.1 Barcelona, a Model Smart City

The Catalan capital acts as a benchmark in the world of smart cities by integrating intelligent sensors in many areas such as parking, waste collection, public lighting, irrigation of green spaces, and air quality [76].

For parking, sensors allow motorists to know, in real time, the availability of spaces to avoid going around unnecessarily, which helps alleviate traffic jams and thus gain time and comfort for people. There are also sensors to measure rainwater flows, humidity (air and soil), wind, sunshine, and atmospheric pressure to adjust the watering of public gardens, not only to assess the filling of garbage bins for more efficient collection but also to assess noise, air pollution, temperature, brightness, etc. [76].

2.6.2   Vienna, the Smartest City in the World

Conscious of the environmental impact of cities and their role to play for a sustainable future, Vienna has adopted a strategic plan, Smart City Wien, with objectives until 2050 to continue ensuring one of the best qualities of life to its inhabitants while preserving resources [77].

This ambition affects all areas: work, leisure, education, health, mobility, infrastructure, energy, and all aspects of urban development. To achieve this, it relies on a holistic vision integrating people and technology to innovate [78].

For example, to reach its target of 40% renewable energy by 2030, the city allows its citizens to become co-owners of solar panels operated by Wien Energy [79]. Each year, they receive a small nest egg depending on the amount invested and can, at any time, resell their shares at the price purchased. Since 2012, more than 6,000 Viennese have joined this program. In terms of mobility, the people of Vienna can count on the Grätzlards to replace the car when they need to combine volume and transport. These cargo bikes belonging to restaurants, shops, or companies that use them to deliver or transport large loads, are loaned free of charge to the population according to their need. All you need is an ID and a deposit. Some are even equipped to transport children. Nearly a hundred projects are currently underway to serve this smart city goal.

Among the cities that stand out for their intelligent development are also Stockholm, Copenhagen, and Lyon.

2.7   Smart City Benefits

According to recent statistics, in 2050, the proportion of the population in cities will reach 66%. It is, therefore, more urgent than ever to innovate and improve the efficiency of cities to cope with overcrowding and optimize the allocation of resources. Then, if cities and so-called "smart" technologies also have many practical and economic advantages, we will focus on the four main areas in which they have convinced the most in recent years.

2.7.1   Security

The priority of all cities is to ensure the safety of their residents. With the rapid technological development and availability of means, the use of

Table 2.11 Security and privacy issues in the IoT.

Security and privacy issues	Description
Vulnerability	The inability to use security techniques such as cryptography renders objects vulnerable to cyber-attacks that pose a threat to people and property.
Mass surveillance	Through integration with the environment, organisms can perform various measurements without the user being able to know where, when and who is collecting this data. Indeed, even in the absence of malicious intent on the part of the objects' owners, the extensive use of wireless networks facilitates eavesdropping. Finally, the unique identification of objects makes it possible to draw very detailed profiles of their owners and follow them on a large scale.

surveillance cameras has become widespread [80]. If video surveillance is nothing new, then the integration of new facial recognition technologies into these cameras, for the identification of a suspect or dangerous individuals before or after the facts, gives them a new youth. In addition to facial recognition, state-of-the-art CCTV cameras are also equipped with motion and smoke detectors and fire alarms. They can assess air quality, lock and unlock doors based on their situational analysis, and much more. In terms of security, cities could also put in place emergency hotlines and alarm buttons to reduce response times for police. Installing fixed alarm buttons across the city would allow law enforcement to pinpoint their location and manipulate traffic using smart technology to get to your destination faster. Ultimately, reducing response times could minimize or even eliminate the usually dramatic consequences of certain events (Tables 2.11 and 2.12).

2.7.2   Optimized Management of Drinking and Wastewater

"Smart water" is a recurring theme in smart cities. This concept refers to "a drinking water and wastewater management infrastructure that guarantees efficient management of the water" [84].

Among the many current problems related to water management are water losses due to unknown leaks or obstructions, overconsumption

Table 2.12 Some regions already equipped with intelligent security.

City (Country)	Description
Nairobi, Kenya	Creation of a video surveillance communication network for 195 police stations, and this network consists of 1,800 cameras [81].
Nanjing, China	Before hosting the 2013 Asian Games, Nanjing Municipality established an extensive video surveillance system that has since expanded to cover of the city [81].
Shanghai, China	Since the city implemented a video surveillance system similar to that of Nairobi and Nanjing, it has observed a drop of almost 30% in its crime rate. Another improvement: the average response time of the police force of 3 minutes per incident [81].
Washington, United States	The city has started using ShotSpotter "gunshot sensors" which immediately notify authorities when gunfire is detected [82].
Saudi Arabia	The country has adopted a national SMS alert system that uses the GPS function of mobile phones to warn people who are in or near a dangerous area [83].

compared to the volume of water required to complete a given task, unsatisfactory water quality for unidentified reasons, or the energy consumption required to transport drinking and used water.

Intelligent water management systems integrate into particular intelligent distribution networks, which ensure the availability and drinkability of water. These networks allow industry professionals to monitor more precisely the amount of water transported to allocate the right volumes for each use. They also allow them to test the quality of the water to ensure that it will still be potable once it reaches its destination.

Another solution "smart water" depends on smart meters, as unlike manual meters, they are more able to detect errors in many points, including the speed of water flow.

Finally, intelligent pumps and valves can adapt their activity rate to ambient conditions and the information provided by their sensors. Variable speed pumps are capable of analyzing sensor data to be able to slow or speed up their operation under these conditions. Likewise, smart valves adjust flow rates or block the water in pipes as needed (Table 2.13).

Table 2.13 Concrete use cases of "smart water" technologies.

City (Country)	Description
Baltimore, United States	Installing and automating more than 408,000 smart water meters to track high consumption and leakage. In addition, these solutions allow users to track their water consumption.
Netherlands	The country has equipped its dikes with sensors and installed pumping stations. It combines the data thus obtained with meteorological models to predict and combat the effects of floods and droughts in the region.
Castellón de la Plana, Spain	The city is currently installing 30,000 smart water meters, capable of communicating with each other and adjusting flow rates as needed to maintain network efficiency while consuming significantly less energy than traditional meters.

2.7.3   Better Visibility of Traffic/Infrastructure Issues

In smart cities, sensors installed on aircraft are used to monitor vehicle traffic [85]. The data collected can indicate places of traffic congestion or the presence of road faults in order to be avoided in advance by vehicle drivers, thus avoiding dangers and saving time. Intersections where many accidents are concentrated may be subject to increased surveillance and thus be redesigned to facilitate traffic flow. Drivers can, for example, suffer from poor visibility at a crossroads, leaving them little time to react and avoid a collision. In addition to improving traffic, smart solutions can detect damage to equipment such as traffic lights and pedestrian traffic lights. For example, in Las Vegas, in the United States, the city has installed sensors that measure carbon dioxide levels in the air and detect the nature of traffic. The objective: to determine whether the fact that light turns green faster helps to shorten vehicle stop time and the unnecessary emission of exhaust gases.

2.7.4   Transport

Transportation is one of the most important elements in cities, but the vehicle stops on the road too long, excessive dependence on personal cars, etc., which means inefficient transport means increased harmful emissions. The latter is one of the reasons that have forced cities to implement smart technologies in order to improve the quality of transportation services [86].

To achieve this, they rely in particular on mobile applications capable of estimating journey times by train, bus and other means of public transport. These applications must be able to estimate the transport times for each route and offer alternative routes through the city based on traffic at an instant T. This simple initiative can make all the difference in choosing to use public transport instead of the car.

Another big trend in smart cities is the switch to electric vehicles (EV). These vehicles eliminate the emissions usually generated by gasoline vehicles [87]. To encourage the use of this type of vehicle, many countries are creating "electric service stations". With EV charging stations in key areas of their cities. More and more cities are offering self-service bicycle rental (often via mobile apps) as an alternative to emissions-generating transport. Then, these solutions can reduce air pollution and thus protect the environment.

2.8   Analysis and Discussion

We all know that human beings are the ones who communicate with each other for various reasons, but can devices communicate with each other and talk to each other without referring to humans? The Internet is the technology that changed our entire world and allowed us to communicate with each other, so exchanging messages and getting news of the other side of the world became a normal thing and only needed several clicks from the fingertips on the smart device [88, 89].

After many years of human communication via the Internet, the field is now open to a new phase in which all the elements of the globe are connected, which is known as the integration between these elements to do larger and more distinguished work instead of connecting individual devices to the Internet and doing specific work only. We can imagine millions of applications that can be built on that in health, education, public services, and transportation. The IoT opens up a wide field to connect everything and anything, from humans and devices together, via the Internet. In a world that does not stop developing in a single moment, devices can communicate with each other to better provide their tasks, facilitate life and reduce a lot of wasted time, all through the IoT.

An advanced concept of using the Internet to connect things in general that can connect to the Internet to send, receive, and analyze data and organize the relationship between them in a way that allows the performance of required functions and control over them through the network.

Instead of having a limited number of powerful computing devices in our life (such as laptop computers, tablets, smartphones, and voice players) to carry out functions related to the Internet to complete them, it is possible on the contrary to make a large number of daily elements connect to the Internet to become active and perform the same tasks and more In order to create a better reality of life, and easier completion of tasks. For example, when you return from work in your car, only by connecting the car to a smart application is it possible to heat the food, and the refrigerator can also inform you of the food expiration date.

The IoT is an idea that stretches from ubiquitous computing, which conflicts with the way the world has become accustomed to that computing is as static in one place as it is in desktop computers.

There are basic ingredients to achieve the goal of the IoT, including:

- Mobility: Its goal is to provide the ability to access the Internet from any device, anywhere and anytime.
- Cloud computing: It means providing services and computer resources distributed over the network so that they can be accessed from anywhere at any time.
- Big Data: the amount of data increases with the increase in the number of devices connected to each other by means of networks and the Internet.
- The new generation of Internet addresses (IPV6): which will increase the number of addresses available to connect devices to the Internet from less than 4 billion addresses now to (X10 ^ 38 4) addresses, which means that connecting fifty billion devices to the Internet by the year 2020 will be something easy and possible.

The IoT can facilitate most operations on big data. Since IoT technologies will spread within most sectors, this will lead to the flow of very large volumes of data, and new methods of collecting and analyzing this data and benefiting from its information will emerge. The overlap between the IoT and big data will be within several areas, and there will be a great need for specialized skills if the institutions want to make the best use of this overlap. The request will be to analyze data, by coordinating the role of analytical tools that are subject to major developments and overseeing the data entry process. The IoT can achieve great results within a lot of sectors and can provide a wide range of technological jobs with great opportunities in the sectors of cloud computing, protection, growth, environment sectors, and various devices. The gains made by the IoT can be seen in the businesses of many of these sectors.

Since IoT is still in the development phase, it is necessary to create a stable, unified, secure and shared environment for IoT to overcome the identified drawbacks. The smart city is also a growing phenomenon that represents an investment for the future, synonymous with efficiency, sustainable development and quality of life, and without IoT systems, it is impossible to envision the future of our cities and capitals destined for significant growth.

2.9 Conclusion and Perspectives

A smart city is a city that relies on data collection and use to improve its organization and management. By using sensors, the city is aware of the behaviors and habits of its residents to provide them, in real time, with better information, better service delivery with better provision of resources. In addition, this "intelligence" affects many areas such as transportation (traffic, parking, etc.), electricity, water supply, and garbage collection.

In recent years, the smart city concept has evolved to be flexible and more adaptive to various risks, crises, and events to reduce their negative impact. It is also the idea of a smart city not only processing information but also integrating a societal dimension that places its residents at the heart of the project. Initially, this concept did not have the same challenges; nevertheless, they unite on their goal of creating a sustainable city.

IoT technology gives the ability to efficiently manage devices through communication with each other and cloud services, to exchange information so that each part can perform its task and the function it performs. So the really important part is not the machine that we will provide it with to be able to collect information from its surroundings, whether it is the periphery (sensors) or the thing, but rather the physical sensors, or the human body, as in smart lenses, for example.

Smart cities have several advantages including the following:

- Be able to implement infrastructure management including water, energy, information and communication, transportation, emergency services, public facilities, buildings, waste management and sorting, and others.
- Improving the quality of life for citizens.

- The existence of the wireless sensor network, which is a network of smart sensors to measure much information and transmit all data at the same time to the citizens or the concerned authorities.
- Creating an environment that attracts entrepreneurs and maintains economic growth.
- High levels of citizen participation in providing opinions and observations and communicating directly with the authorities.

Each city faces its challenges that differ from others, and these challenges increase with the delay of traditional solutions. Technical innovations provide support for city management to transform its human capital, natural resources, infrastructure, and intellectual assets. The smart city uses various communication and information technology solutions to integrate information within and between city systems and ranges and to engage citizens, companies, and society on a large scale in new ways. For the transformation to smart cities to truly take place, cities need to consider the following aspects of data: data sources and integration, analytics, and big data.

One of the characteristics of IoT applications is security challenges, such as ensuring security in IoT products and services have become a primary priority, and IoT devices and services can also be insecure and user data being stolen. Generally, the interconnected nature is considered a potential entry point for cyber-attacks on IoT devices. Accordingly, a collaborative approach toward more security will be needed to develop effective and appropriate solutions to the security challenges associated with IoT.

Finally, it is imperative to enrich this work with new information for IoT technology. It is also interesting to add examples of real applications of this technology.

References

1. Cocchia, A., Smart and Digital City: A Systematic Literature Review. In: Smart City, Springer, Cham. 2014, 10.1007/978-3-319-06160-3_2.
2. Saba, D., Sahli, Y., Berbaoui, B., Maouedj, R., Towards Smart Cities: Challenges, Components, and Architectures, in: *Studies in Computational Intelligence: Toward Social Internet of Things (SIoT): Enabling Technologies, Architectures and Applications*, A.E. Hassanien, R. Bhatnagar, N.E.M. Khalifa, M.H.N. Taha (Eds.), Springer, Cham, pp. 249–286, 2020.

3. Kim, T., Ramos, C., Mohammed, S., Smart City and IoT. *Future Gener. Comput. Syst.*, 76:159–162, 2017. https://doi.org/10.1016/j.future.2017.03.034

4. Zanella, A., Bui, N., Castellani, A., *et al.*, Internet of Things for Smart Cities. *IEEE Internet Things J.*, 1, 22–32, 2014. https://doi.org/10.1109/JIOT.2014.2306328

5. Risteska Stojkoska, B.L. and Trivodaliev, K.V., A review of Internet of Things for smart home: Challenges and solutions. *J. Clean. Prod.*, 140, 1454–1464, 2017.

6. larousse.fr, Encyclopédie Larousse en ligne - automatique, 2019, https://www.larousse.fr/encyclopedie/divers/automatique/187154. Accessed 1 Jan 2019.

7. Das, R., Dutta, S., Samanta, K. *et al.*, Security based Domotics. *Proc. Technol.*, 10, 942–948, 2013, https://doi.org/10.1016/J.PROTCY.2013.12.441.

8. Poland, M.P., Nugent, C.D., Wang, H., Chen, L., Smart Home Research. *Int. J. Ambient Comput. Intell.*, 1, 32–45, 2009, https://doi.org/10.4018/jaci.2009062203.

9. Liu, Y., Qiu, B., Fan, X. *et al.*, Review of Smart Home Energy Management Systems, in: *Energy Procedia*, 2016.

10. Saba, D., Degha, H.E., Berbaoui, B. *et al.*, Contribution to the modeling and simulation of multi- agent systems for energy saving in the habitat, in: *International Conference on Mathematics and Information Technology*, N. Djarfour (Ed.), IEEE, Adrar-Algeria, p. 1, 2017.

11. Saba, D., Sahli, Y., Maouedj, R., Hadidi, A., Energy Management Based on Internet of Things. *Stud. Syst. Decis. Control*, 335, 349–372, 2021.

12. Saba, D., Berbaoui, B., Degha, H.E., Laallam, F.Z., A generic optimization solution for hybrid energy systems based on agent coordination, Advances in Intelligent Systems and Computing, Springer, Cham, 639, 31 August. 527–536, 2018. 10.1007/978-3-319-64861-3_49.

13. Albino, V., Berardi, U., Dangelico, R.M., Smart cities: Definitions, dimensions, performance, and initiatives. *J. Urban Technol.*, 3–21, 2015, https://doi.org/10.1080/10630732.2014.942092.

14. Söderström, O., Paasche, T., Klauser, F., Smart cities as corporate storytelling. *City*, 18, 307–320, 2014, https://doi.org/10.1080/13604813.2014.906716.

15. Jadoul, M., Smart practices for building smart cities. *e i Elektrotech. Inf.*, 133, 341–344, 2016, https://doi.org/10.1007/s00502-016-0430-x.

16. Saharan, S., Bawa, S., Kumar, N., Dynamic pricing techniques for Intelligent Transportation System in smart cities: A systematic review. *Comput. Commun.*, 150, 603–625, 2020, https://doi.org/10.1016/j.comcom.2019.12.003.

17. Shin, D.H., A realization of pervasive computing: Ubiquitous city, in: *PICMET '10 - Portland International Center for Management of Engineering and Technology, Proceedings - Technology Management for Global Economic Growth*, 2010.

18. Yang, Y.-T.C., Building virtual cities, inspiring intelligent citizens: Digital games for developing students' problem solving and learning

motivation. *Comput. Educ.*, 59, 365–377, 2012, https://doi.org/10.1016/j. compedu.2012.01.012.

19. André, M., Mahy, G., Lejeune, P., Bogaert, J., Vers une synthèse de la conception et une définition des zones dans le gradient urbain-rural. *Biotechnol. Agron Soc. Environ.*, 18, 1, 61–74, 2014.

20. Pellicer, S., Santa, G., Bleda, A.L. *et al.*, A global perspective of smart cities: A survey, in: *Proceedings - 7th International Conference on Innovative Mobile and Internet Services in Ubiquitous Computing, IMIS 2013*, 2013.

21. Ismagilova, E., Hughes, L., Dwivedi, Y.K., Raman, K.R., Smart cities: Advances in research—An information systems perspective. *Int. J. Inf. Manage.*, 2019. https://doi.org/10.1016/j.ijinfomgt.2019.01.004.

22. Janssen, M., Bannister, F., Glassey, O. *et al.*, Electronic Government and Electronic Participation. *Joint Proceedings of Ongoing Research, Posters, Workshop and Projects of IFIP EGOV 2014 and ePart 2014*, 2014.

23. Ahvenniemi, H., Huovila, A., Pinto-Seppä, I., Airaksinen, M., What are the differences between sustainable and smart cities? *Cities*, 60, 234–245, 2017, https://doi.org/10.1016/j.cities.2016.09.009.

24. Nikki Han, M.J., Kim, M.J., A critical review of the smart city in relation to citizen adoption towards sustainable smart living. *Habitat Int.*, 108, 102312, 2021. https://doi.org/10.1016/j.habitatint.2021.102312

25. Albino, V., Berardi, U., Dangelico, R.M., Smart cities: Definitions, dimensions, performance, and initiatives. *J. Urban Technol.*, 2015. https://doi.org/1 0.1080/10630732.2014.942092

26. Macke, J., Rubim, Sarate J.A., de Atayde Moschen, S. Smart sustainable cities evaluation and sense of community. *J. Clean Prod.*, 239, 118103, 2009. https://doi.org/10.1016/j.jclepro.2019.118103

27. Balaji, K., An integrated ICT based framework for smart sustainable cities in a tropical environment Data. In: *Conference Proceedings of Sustainable Building*. 2013-2014. series. p 8.

28. Giffinger, R., European Smart Cities: the need for a place related Understanding Outlook: Smart metropolitan development, in: *Conference Creating Smart Cities*, 2011.

29. Camero, A. and Alba, E., Smart City and information technology: A review. *Cities*, 93, 84–94, 2019, https://doi.org/10.1016/j.cities.2019.04.014.

30. Vinod Kumar, T.M. and Dahiya, B., Smart Economy in Smart Cities, In: *Advances in 21st Century Human Settlements, 1st ed.* Springer, Singapore, pp. 3–76, 2017.

31. Silva, B.N., Khan, M., Han, K., Towards sustainable smart cities: A review of trends, architectures, components, and open challenges in smart cities. *Sustain. Cities Soc.*, 38, 697–713, 2018. https://doi.org/10.1016/J. SCS.2018.01.053.

32. Saba, D., Maouedj, R., Berbaoui, B., Contribution to the development of an energy management solution in a green smart home (EMSGSH), in: *Proceedings of the 7th International Conference on Software Engineering and*

New Technologies - ICSENT 2018, ACM Press, New York, NY, USA, pp. 1–7, 2018.

33. Weiser, M., The Computer for the 21st Century. *Sci. Am.*, 265, 94–104, 1991, https://doi.org/10.1038/scientificamerican0991-94.

34. Aggarwal, C.C., Ashish, N., Sheth, A., The Internet of Things: A Survey from the Data-Centric Perspective, in: *Managing and Mining Sensor Data*, pp. 383–428, Springer US, Boston, MA, 2013.

35. Miorandi, D., Sicari, S., De Pellegrini, F., Chlamtac, I., Internet of things: Vision, applications and research challenges. *Ad Hoc Netw.*, 10, 1497–1516, 2012, https://doi.org/10.1016/j.adhoc.2012.02.016.

36. Younis, M., Internet of everything and everybody: Architecture and service virtualization. *Comput. Commun.*, 131, 66–72, 2018, https://doi.org/10.1016/J.COMCOM.2018.07.008.

37. Fagerstrøm, A., Eriksson, N., Sigurðsson, V., What's the "Thing" in Internet of Things in Grocery Shopping? A Customer Approach. *Proc. Comput. Sci.*, 121, 384–388, 2017, https://doi.org/10.1016/J.PROCS.2017.11.052.

38. Atzori, L., Iera, A., Morabito, G., The Internet of Things: A survey. *Comput. Netw.*, 54, 2787–2805, 2010, https://doi.org/10.1016/j.comnet.2010.05.010.

39. Schatten, M., Ševa, J., Tomičić, I., A roadmap for scalable agent organizations in the Internet of Everything. *J. Syst. Softw.*, 115, 31–41, 2016, https://doi.org/10.1016/J.JSS.2016.01.022.

40. Negash, B., Westerlund, T., Tenhunen, H., Towards an interoperable Internet of Things through a web of virtual things at the Fog layer. *Future Gener. Comput. Syst.*, 91, 96–107, 2019, https://doi.org/10.1016/J.FUTURE.2018.07.053.

41. Das, A., Sharma, S.C.M., Ratha, B.K., The New Era of Smart Cities, From the Perspective of the Internet of Things, in: *Smart Cities Cybersecurity Priv.*, pp. 1–9, 2019, https://doi.org/10.1016/B978-0-12-815032-0.00001-9.

42. Oriwoh, E., Sant, P., Epiphaniou, G., Guidelines for Internet of Things Deployment Approaches – The Thing Commandments. *Procedia. Comput. Sci.*, 21, 122–131, 2013, https://doi.org/10.1016/J.PROCS.2013.09.018.

43. Iannacci, J., Internet of things (IoT); internet of everything (IoE); tactile internet; 5G – A (not so evanescent) unifying vision empowered by EH-MEMS (energy harvesting MEMS) and RF-MEMS (radio frequency MEMS). *Sensors Actuators A Phys.*, 272, 187–198, 2018. https://doi.org/10.1016/j.sna.2018.01.038

44. Saba, D., Sahli, Y., Hadidi, A., *The Role of Artificial Intelligence in Company's Decision Making*, Studies in Computational Intelligence. Springer, Cham. Hassanien AE, Taha MHN, Khalifa NEM. 911, 287–314, 2021. 10.1007/978-3-030-52067-0_13 pp. 287–314.

45. Hadidi, A., Saba, D., Sahli, Y., The Role of Artificial Neuron Networks in Intelligent Agriculture (Case Study: Greenhouse), In: *Artificial Intelligence for Sustainable Development: Theory, Practice and Future Applications. Studies in Computational Intelligence*, Hassanien A., Bhatnagar R., Darwish A. (eds) Springer, Cham, vol. 912, 2021. https://doi.org/10.1007/978-3-030-51920-9_4

46. Golpîra, H., Khan, S.A.R., Safaeipour, S., A review of logistics Internet-of-Things: Current trends and scope for future research. *J. Ind. Inf. Integr.*, 22, 100194, 2021. https://doi.org/10.1016/j.jii.2020.100194

47. Bendavid, Y., Fosso Wamba, S., Barjis, J., Special Issue on RFID - Towards Ubiquitous Computing and the Web of Things: Guest EditorsÂ´ Introduction. *J. Theor. Appl. Electron. Commer. Res.*, 8, 15–16, 2013, https://doi.org/10.4067/S0718-18762013000200008.

48. Singh, D., Tripathi, G., Jara, A.J., A survey of Internet-of-Things: Future vision, architecture, challenges and services, in: *2014 IEEE World Forum on Internet of Things (WF-IoT)*, IEEE, pp. 287–292, 2014.

49. Gubbi, J., Buyya, R., Marusic, S., Palaniswami, M., Internet of Things (IoT): A vision, architectural elements, and future directions. *Future Gener. Comput. Syst.*, 29, 1645–1660, 2013, https://doi.org/10.1016/j.future.2013.01.010.

50. Saba, D., Sahli, Y., Maouedj, R. *et al.*, Contribution to the Realization of a Smart and Sustainable Home, Artificial Intelligence for Sustainable Development: Theory, Practice and Future Applications. Studies in Computational Intelligence, Springer, Cham, vol. 912, 2021. https://doi.org/10.1007/978-3-030-51920-9_14

51. Teixeira, T., Hachem, S., Issarny, V., Georgantas, N., Service Oriented Middleware for the Internet of Things: A Perspective. *ServiceWave*, Springer-Verlag, 2011.

52. Adjih, C., Baccelli, E., Fleury, E. *et al.*, FIT IoT-LAB: A large scale open experimental IoT testbed, in: *IEEE World Forum on Internet of Things, WF-IoT 2015 - Proceedings*, 2015.

53. Ding, W. and Hu, H., On the safety of IoT device physical interaction control, in: *Proceedings of the ACM Conference on Computer and Communications Security*, 2018.

54. Karnouskos, S., Stuxnet Worm Impact on Industrial Cyber-Physical System Security. In: *IECON 2011 - 37th Annual Conference of the IEEE Industrial Electronics Society*. IEEE, Melbourne, VIC, Australia, 2011.

55. Farahani, B., Firouzi, F., Chang, V. *et al.*, Towards fog-driven IoT eHealth: Promises and challenges of IoT in medicine and healthcare. *Future Gener. Comput. Syst.*, 78, 659–676, 2018, https://doi.org/10.1016/j.future.2017.04.036.

56. Hassanalieragh, M., Page, A., Soyata, T. *et al.*, Health Monitoring and Management Using Internet-of-Things (IoT) Sensing with Cloud-Based Processing: Opportunities and Challenges, in: *Proceedings - 2015 IEEE International Conference on Services Computing, SCC 2015*, 2015.

57. Saba, D., Laallam, F.Z., Belmili, H., Hadidi, A., Contribution of renewable energy hybrid system control based of multi agent system coordination, in: *Symposium on Complex Systems and Intelligent Computing (CompSIC)*, Mohamed Cherif Messaadia University - Souk Ahras, Souk Ahras, Algeria, 2015.

58. Saba, D., Laallam, F.Z., Hadidi, A.E., Berbaoui, B., Optimization of a Multi-source System with Renewable Energy Based on Ontology. *Energy Procedia*, 74, 608–615, 2015, https://doi.org/10.1016/J.EGYPRO.2015.07.787.

59. Saba, D., Degha, H.E., Berbaoui, B., Maouedj, R., *Development of an Ontology Based Solution for Energy Saving Through a Smart Home in the City of Adrar in Algeria*, pp. 531–541, Springer, Cham, 2018.

60. Hadidi, A., Remini, B., Habi, M. *et al.*, The oasis of Tiout in the southwest of Algeria: Water resources and sustainable development, in: *AIP Conference Proceedings*, AIP Publishing LLC, p. 020007, 2016.

61. Saba, D., Sahli, Y., Abanda, F.H. *et al.*, Development of new ontological solution for an energy intelligent management in Adrar city. *Sustain. Comput. Inform. Syst.*, 21, 189–203, 2019, https://doi.org/10.1016/J.SUSCOM.2019.01.009.

62. Toschi, G.M., Campos, L.B., Cugnasca, C.E., Home automation networks: A survey. *Comput. Stand. Interfaces*, 50, 42–54, 2017, https://doi.org/10.1016/J.CSI.2016.08.008.

63. Fraga-Lamas, P., Fernández-Caramés, T.M., Castedo, L., Towards the internet of smart trains: A review on industrial IoT-connected railways. *Sensors (Switzerland)*, 17, 1457, 2017, https://doi.org/10.3390/s17061457.

64. Pachayappan, M., Ganeshkumar, C., Sugundan, N., Technological implication and its impact in agricultural sector: An IoT Based Collaboration framework. *Proc. Comput. Sci.*, 171, 1166–1173, 2020, https://doi.org/10.1016/J.PROCS.2020.04.125.

65. Elijah, O., Rahman, T.A., Orikumhi, I. *et al.*, An Overview of Internet of Things (IoT) and Data Analytics in Agriculture: Benefits and Challenges. *IEEE Internet Things J.*, 5, 3758–3773, 2018, https://doi.org/10.1109/JIOT.2018.2844296.

66. Saba, D., Sahli, Y., Maouedj, R. *et al.*, Towards Artificial Intelligence: Concepts, Applications, and Innovations, In: *Enabling AI Applications in Data Science. Studies in Computational Intelligence*, Hassanien AE., Taha M.H.N., Khalifa N.E.M. (eds), Springer, Cham, vol. 911, 2021. https://doi.org/10.1007/978-3-030-52067-0_6

67. Hamilton, S., Mhurchu, C.N., Priest, P., Food and nutrient availability in New Zealand: An analysis of supermarket sales data. *Public Health Nutr.*, 10, 1448–1455, 2007. https://doi.org/10.1017/S1368980007000134

68. Karjol, S., Holla, A.K., Abhilash, C.B., An IOT based smart shopping cart for smart shopping, in: *Communications in Computer and Information Science*, 2018.

69. Saba, D., Laallam, F.Z., Degha, H.E. *et al.*, Design and Development of an Intelligent Ontology-Based Solution for Energy Management in the Home, in: *Studies in Computational Intelligence*, 801st ed, A.E. Hassanien (Ed.), pp. 135–167, Springer, Cham, Switzerland, 2019.

70. Suthanthira Vanitha, N., Karthikeyan, J., Kavitha, G., Radhika, K., Modelling of Intelligent Transportation System for Human Safety using IoT. *Mater. Today Proc.*, 33, 4026–4029, 2020, https://doi.org/10.1016/J.MATPR.2020.06.421.

71. Ingemarsdotter, E., Jamsin, E., Balkenende, R., Opportunities and challenges in IoT-enabled circular business model implementation – A case study. *Resour Conserv. Recycl.*, 162, 105047, 2020. https://doi.org/10.1016/j.resconrec.2020.105047

72. Shafiq, M., Tian, Z., Bashir, A.K. *et al.*, Data mining and machine learning methods for sustainable smart cities traffic classification: A survey. *Sustain. Cities Soc.*, 60, 102177, 2020, https://doi.org/10.1016/j.scs.2020.102177.

73. Khan, M.A. and Salah, K., IoT security: Review, blockchain solutions, and open challenges. *Future Gener. Comput. Syst.*, 82, 395–411, 2018, https://doi.org/10.1016/j.future.2017.11.022.

74. Saha, H.N., Auddy, S., Pal, S. *et al.*, Waste management using Internet of Things (IoT), in: *2017 8th Industrial Automation and Electromechanical Engineering Conference, IEMECON*, 2017, 2017.

75. Adam, M., Okasha, M.E., Tawfeeq, OM, *et al.*, Waste Management System Using IoT, in: *2018 International Conference on Computer, Control, Electrical, and Electronics Engineering, ICCCEEE*, 2018, 2018.

76. Bakici, T., Almirall, E., Wareham, J., A Smart City Initiative: The Case of Barcelona. *J. Knowl. Econ.*, 4, 135–148, 2013, https://doi.org/10.1007/s13132-012-0084-9.

77. Vidiasova, L., Kachurina, P., Cronemberger, F., Smart Cities Prospects from the Results of the World Practice Expert Benchmarking. *Procedia Comput. Sci.*, 119, 269–277, 2017. https://doi.org/10.1016/j.procs.2017.11.185

78. Fernandez-Anez, V., Fernández-Güell, J.M., Giffinger, R., Smart City implementation and discourses: An integrated conceptual model. The case of Vienna. *Cities*, 78, 4–16, 2018. https://doi.org/10.1016/j.cities.2017.12.004

79. Saba, D., Laallam, F.Z., Berbaoui, B., Fonbeyin, H.A., An energy management approach in hybrid energy system based on agent's coordination, in: *The 2nd International Conference on Advanced Intelligent Systems and Informatics (AISI'16). Advances in Intelligent Systems and Computing*, Cairo, Egypt, 2016.

80. Lacinák, M., Ristvej, J., Smart City, Safety and Security, in: *Procedia Engineering*, 2017.

81. Feldstein, S., *The Global Expansion of AI Surveillance*, Washington, 2019.

82. Busljeta, A., How an Acoustic Sensor Can Catch a Gunman, *John Marshall J. Inf. Technol. Priv. Law*, 32, 211–234, 32, 2016.

83. Hussein, D., Alharbi, A., Alotaibi, M.F., Ibrahim, D.M., Comparative Study between Emergency Response Mobile Applications. *Artic Int. J. Comput. Sci. Inf. Secur.*, 17, 2, 5, 2019.

84. Larsen, T.A., Hoffmann, S., Lüthi, C. *et al.*, Emerging solutions to the water challenges of an urbanizing world. *Science*, (80-.) 352, 6288, 928–933, 2016. https://doi.org/10.1126/science.aad8641.

85. Debnath, A.K., Chin, H.C., Haque, M.M., Yuen, B., A methodological framework for benchmarking smart transport cities. *Cities*, 37, 47–56, 2014, https://doi.org/10.1016/j.cities.2013.11.004.

86. Šemanjski, I., Mandžuka, S., Gautama, S., Smart mobility, in: *Proceedings Elmar - International Symposium Electronics in Marine*, 2018.
87. Baucells Aletà, N., Smart mobility in smart cities, In: *Libro de Actas CIT2016. XII Congreso de Ingeniería del Transporte. Universitat Politècnica València, Valencia.* ISBN 978-84-608-9960-0. pp. 1209-1219. https://doi.org/10.4995/CIT2016.2016.3485. 2016.
88. Kumar, A., Payal, M., Dixit, P., Chatterjee, J.M., Framework for Realization of Green Smart Cities Through the Internet of Things (IoT), in: *Trends in Cloud-based IoT*, pp. 85–111.89, 2020.
89. Jha, S., Kumar, R., Chatterjee, J.M., Khari, M., Collaborative handshaking approaches between internet of computing and internet of things towards a smart world: a review from 2009–2017. *Telecommun. Syst.*, 70, 4, 617–634, 2019.

Integration of Blockchain and Artificial Intelligence in Smart City Perspectives

R. Krishnamoorthy[1], K. Kamala[2], I. D. Soubache[3], Mamidala Vijay Karthik[4]
and M. Amina Begum[5]*

[1]*Prathyusha Engineering College, Chennai, India*
[2]*SRM Valliammai Engineering College, Kanchipuram, India*
[3]*Rajiv Gandhi College of Engineering and Technology, Puducherry, India*
[4]*CMR Engineering College, Hyderabad, India*
[5]*Sree Sastha Institute of Engineering and Technology, Chennai, India*

Abstract

Improvement of life in urban areas requires continuous development where integrated policies are implemented by interoperable, safe, and secure technological innovations. Potential of Artificial Intelligence (AI) and blockchain is recognized by public administration to solve local community problems. Innovative perspective is offered by blockchain for smart cities organization which was perceived initially with Bitcoin—the crypto currency. It also offers an economic model which is more transparent for resource management. This chapter focuses on involvement of AI and blockchain for the contribution of smart cities development to form smart city ecosystem. This model of smart city ecosystem is based on authentication of Self-Sovereign Identity (SSI) model involving smart contracts between citizens, administrators, and entities. It also discusses various domains where AI and blockchain are applicable. This chapter focuses on exploring the contribution and potential of blockchain in the perception of smart cities by in depth review of various scientific researches on basics of blockchain and real-time applications of it especially in smart cities. It also summarizes applications of blockchain which have won the gift of success along with exploration of opportunities and challenges of blockchain technology in smart cities.

Corresponding author: amina.gtec@gmail.com
R. Krishnamoorthy: ORCID: https://orcid.org/0000-0002-2750-3578
K. Kamala: ORCID: https://orcid.org/0000-0003-4266-0886
I. D. Soubache: ORCID: https://orcid.org/0000-0001-6889-2779
Mamidala Vijay Karthik: ORCID: https://orcid.org/0000-0001-7149-7868
M. Amina Begum: ORCID: https://orcid.org/0000-0003-3775-8758

Vishal Kumar, Vishal Jain, Bharti Sharma, Jyotir Moy Chatterjee and Rakesh Shrestha (eds.) Smart City Infrastructure: The Blockchain Perspective, (77–112) © 2022 Scrivener Publishing LLC

Keywords: Robotics, industrial automation, Internet of Robotic Things, SCADA, Artificial Intelligence, smart environment, Industrial Internet of Things

3.1   Introduction

Incorporation of new technologies for developing smart cities is necessary to provide innovative smart services necessary for the future of smart communities. Main goal of smart cities is enhancing the quality of life for its inhabitants and businesses by involving smart technologies that reduces source deterioration, thereby reducing overall maintenance cost. From this perspective, much attention is received by blockchain technology in recent years as it is offering innovative alternatives in the context of smart cities for both individuals and organizations. This chapter provides a good knowledge of the new technology, Blockchain, especially in the point of view of smart cities [1]. When powered by Artificial Intelligence (AI), blockchain technology becomes the most advance development of information and technology (IT) taking place in the market of cryptocurrency and blockchain. Several features are provided by AI for managing the monetary decentralized systems. Application that integrate AI and blockchain helps the customer to compare information with ease allowing the investors to get broad knowledge for making decisions and investing in business involved in smart cities. Usage of AI is efficient due to its smart networks implemented in various smart sectors of smart cities. More efficiency is achieved by involving AI which is effective in delivering various services, obtaining consensus mechanisms for implementing blockchain in different scenarios of different operations in smart cities. Primarily blockchain was mainly linked with Bitcoin but developments have explored its usage in logistics, financial transactions and securing contracts [2]. Blockchain has potential to be implemented with trust in digital community as well as in local community. This innovative technology has the ability in enhancing transparency between regional and local organizations while making communication of sensitive data easier without any compromise of privacy and security. Smart cities provide smart solutions to its citizens to enjoy a decent life quality in a sustainable clean environment as shown in Figure 3.1.

Blockchain technology manages and integrates the infrastructure for providing better services with ensured efficiency and utilization of resources available in an optimal way. New technologies are incorporated for developing smart cities providing innovative ways for various services. Various applications by integrating blockchain and AI together that can be implemented in smart cities are discussed such as securing

Figure 3.1 Smart city—Conceptual framework.

data communication, smart contracts, citizen participation, economy and employment, health, education, property registration, auction, renewable energy, waste management, safety, and smart assets. Hence, to implement all these applications in smart cities, incorporation of sensors and actuators is promoted operated through the technology of AI. New possibilities are put front by this technology which greatly contributes to the sustainability of urban area. A new framework is proposed for binding the AI technology along with blockchain technology for integrating key dimensions such as governance, metabolism and culture of smart cities [3]. Rapid growth is obtained in urbanization due to the advancements in smart cities implemented by blockchain technology and AI. Management of smart cities is done in better way by providing solutions for waste management, water management, energy management, and various other services of e-governance.

Smart cities focus on using modern technologies as follows:

1. Blockchain
2. Internet of Things,
3. Artificial Intelligence
4. Machine learning
5. Big data

All these technologies aim to create urban environment which utilizes resources optimally thereby reducing the cost. This chapter focuses on adopting solutions based on blockchain technology and AI with its applications in the development of smart cities, as these technologies are secure, immutable, and more transparent. A security framework based on blockchain enables secured communication of data in a smart city where unique features are provided by blockchain technology such as scalability, faster operation, capability of fault tolerance, improved reliability, and faster response [4]. Digital transaction between the parties is performed without any involvement of third party is termed as smart contract which is trackable and cannot be reversed with transaction performance verification that can be negotiated if required. All sorts of situations can be handled by smart contracts including legal and financial processes, agreements and insurances. Urban development is promoted by smart cities by various technologies as shown in Figure 3.2.

Decentralized voting platforms based on blockchain is more secure providing unique system for voting which removes complexities or any other inefficiencies in voting process. Citizens will be able to provide feedback and raise grievances for improving the facilities of smart cities. This technology of blockchain is useful in registration of local business beginning from inception till dissolution. It increases the ease of operation while reducing the cost of business implementation. An efficient solution in the field of logistic management is provided by blockchain technology which removes unwanted verification layers acting as barrier in creation of chain of sustainable value. Employment register based on blockchain can be implemented for employees, which is transparent and secure in maintaining their history of employment [5, 6]. This indicates the quality of their service making assignment of job easier as this system based on blockchain is a trusted system and nothing is hidden. In this chapter, several other applications of blockchain are explained where smart thinking of the devices in these smart cities is through the technology of AI. In the medical field, single health record can be maintained by the technology of blockchain which is secure and flexible both for the patients and medical practitioners. Patients can avoid carrying any health records as their consultant

Figure 3.2 Trend in development of smart cities.

will be able to view medical history of the patient with utmost reliability. Medical services are better controlled as they are transparent with pharmaceutical supplies using blockchain technology. In the field of education, blockchain technology is used for maintaining the records of credentials of student in a secure way that cannot be explored by unauthorized individuals and shared with stakeholders by proper mechanism of consent. Overall, this chapter discusses the impact of technology of blockchain and AI for various solutions involved in smart cities.

Aim of this chapter is to provide holistic vision of AI and blockchain for developing smart cities in urban areas. A better understanding is provided on blockchain for identifying open issues that can be investigated by the research community. A comprehensive view is provided on the selected field for introducing the basic ideas to the reader behind AI and Blockchain applicable for smart cities.

The chapter is organized as follows. Section 3.2 focuses on providing an overview of concept of smart cities, Blockchain technology, and AI in the perspective of development of smart cities by integrated with the technologies. It discusses the basic terms involved in blockchain technology along with its features and its basic working strategy. It also includes the basic definitions and categorization of AI. Section 3.3 describes the model of smart city based on blockchain technology along with integration of blockchain technology for implementing its various applications in smart cities. Section 3.4 provides the integration of AI in the development of smart cities which includes importance of AI and provides various application domains of AI in the perspective of smart city. Finally, the chapter concludes with Section 3.5 presenting the conclusion and future work.

3.2 Concept of Smart Cities, Blockchain Technology, and Artificial Intelligence

3.2.1 Concept and Definition of Smart Cities

This section provides a conceptual view of smart cities which includes origin of smart cities, novel definitions applicable for it, fundamental characteristics of smart cities along with its significant components.

Concept of smart city is expressed in different ways in the literature.

- ➢ Smart cities is defined by Komninos as regions with higher capacity for innovation and learning with its population incorporating creativity with digital infrastructure institutions for operating digital space of smart cities. Uncertainty of this concept is causing problem in understanding how the smart cities develop is influenced by adopting information technology.
- ➢ Smart city is also defined as collection of paradigms found across various domains, namely, environment, economy, government, life, people, and mobility addressing several cases such as monitoring of environment, analysis of traffic, smart public transport, monitoring of utility, reporting of real-time incidents, smart medical services, e-commerce, and electronic voting system. Infrastructure of city administration can be improved by analyzing data collection obtained from various domains for optimizing services.
- ➢ A smart city can also be defined as an environment with communication technologies for creating interactive spaces with integrated information to bring efficient capability of computation to the physical world [7].
- ➢ Smart city includes significant components which allow centralization of data, components able to take several forms,

compatible to specialized hardware which includes simple website to highly complex applications.

➢ Data accessibility is provided to all citizens so that they can access freely and are able to propose any changes in an interactive way to make corrections. Urbanization benefits can be ensured by providing full exploitation with accessing to electronic infrastructure by management policies of urban growth in order to provide innovative services to all the residents.

➢ Sensitive data acquisition is the major objective of smart cities through Internet of Things (IoT) ensuring data security with primary importance. Due to this reason, most of the administrators invest huge amount on developing smart cities thereby providing various facilities to its inhabitants.

➢ Smart city is a huge network of technical innovations with interconnected technologies, which was predicted by Cisco [8] as by 2030, it is expected that 500 billion devices connected to Internet.

➢ Gartner [9] predicts that, by 2022, smart cities will be using 10 billion smart objects that are interconnected.

3.2.1.1 Integration of Smart Cities with New Technologies

New technologies can be integrated to construct smart cities, where its overall framework is as shown in Figure 3.3.

- Perception layer in the framework involves in handling tasks based on technology of IoT, hence related to collection of information and perception of data.
- Platform layer involves in analyzing and processing of information obtained from various platforms and components of the host network.
- In the smart city technology, entire network is terminated with application layer which deals with applications related to personal applications, business applications, and that relate to public service.
- A system of network security is necessary for smart city with five in one capability, namely, defense, monitor, combating, governing, and evaluating in order to build a system meeting its needs of standardization.

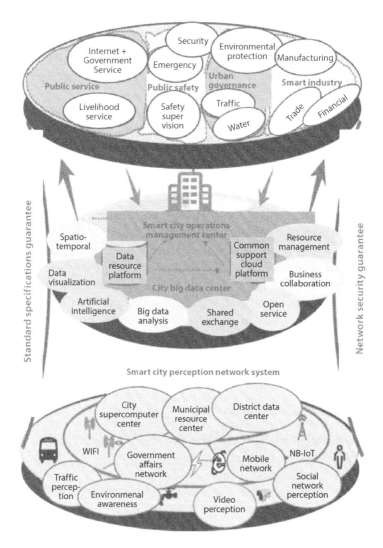

Figure 3.3 Integration of technologies in smart cities.

Development of smart cities has the following overall trend where indispensable role is played by information in the development of smart city.

1. Internet from mobile acts a good channel for the people in collecting, exchanging, transmitting and sharing information thereby makes this technology as a significant part in human life.

2. As mobile internet is already integrated in the lives of people, consumers have changes their habits in society by maintaining relationships through networks hence creates mobile type of lifestyle in their lives interfering in every aspect of life of a person.

3. Thirdly, mainstream involves intelligence, as digitization has started penetrating in all walks of our life and has become gradually center of cultural forms, currently hence ushers a new round of ecology in the cultural field.

4. In the current era, changes are leaded by information technology occupying the fourth part. It involves technologies such as cloud computing, big data, IoT, AI, and blockchain for developing the quality of solutions of smart cities. Urban activities are transformed continuously to obtain optimization with continuous progress attained by these technologies.

5. Fifth, Internet Thinking integration is focused for innovative thinking on big data, users involved, platforms used and cross border link which encourages reevaluation of chain of traditional value realizing innovations oriented both to integration and applications in all walks of real life.

6. Sixth, urban development is promoted by smart cities by combining multiple technologies to implement multiple applications operated by one center having unified chains with four platforms.

7. Here, one center indicates big data which caters to the demands of the smart city and four platforms indicates service platforms with integrated information necessary to provide smart management of city, smart livelihood of people, smart management of government affairs, and managing economy in a smart way.

8. Multiple technologies indicate various technologies such as IoT, mobile internet, cloud computing, and AI. Multiple applications indicate list of smart applications necessary in a smart city and unified chains indicate trusted information ecology in smart city by utilizing blockchains.

3.2.1.2   *Development of Smart Cities by Integrated Technologies*

Integrated innovative wisdom model can be formed by integrating technologies such as IoT, mobile internet, cloud computing, AI, blockchains, and big data, where data is core of these technologies and hence involves collection of data, analysis of data, services related to decision making, and data mining. This model is based on strategies, namely, integrated collaboration, intelligent system, interconnected empowerment, and continuous evolution, assuring management of smart cities in an accurate and effective way along with monitoring and law enforcement in order to take decisions. A comprehensive support is provided by the integration of these innovative information technologies in constructing smart cities. For example, in real-time data of the city is collected by IoT, information integration and business flow is realized by mobile internet, collected data is shared, verified, and traced using blockchains creating a mechanism for data sharing for the platforms of AI and big data while Service mechanisms and urban operation driven by data for its development and formation is promoted by deep level mining. Additionally, urban management with its decision-making has mining and analysis of big data as its base with data center construction based on cloud computing which enhances the supporting capacity of massive data center where allocation of resources on demand is realized by cloud computing with billing based on volume promoting extension based on resource scale, labor of specialized division having network services of innovation.

3.2.2 Concept of Blockchain Technology

The term blockchain technology appeared coined by Haber and Stornetta in their publication in 1991 [10]. Basic concepts necessary to understand blockchain technology are discussed as follows:

- **Nodes:** Nodes are the significant rudimentary elements of blockchain technology, which is a network made of nodes. Computers are the nodes in real time.
- **Transactions:** Transaction is represented by each share involved in Blockchain. Creation of new transaction occurs whenever a value on Blockchain changes, where transaction involves sending of virtual currency from one account to other account. Any transaction will be accepted only if at least 50% of the nodes existing approve it.
- **Block:** Holding of data by blockchain is represented by block which contains information from various transactions. A cryptographic hash is used to link each of the blocks with the previous block with all the blocks being stored in each of the node.
- **Account:** Each account in blockchain consists of two variables, namely, private key and public key. Private key holder

is the owner of the account. If this private key is lost by its owner, then there is no possibility of claiming the account back in blockchain like "Forgot Password" other centralized technologies where there is chance of claiming the lost account.

3.2.2.1   Features of Blockchain Technology

Features of blockchain technology are discussed as follows:

- **Decentralized:** Blockchain is a huge network and hence consists of several nodes, and data is available in several places and hence is not centralized.
- **Scalability:** Blockchain allows the feature of scalability, which means nodes in the network can be scalable as required ideally infinite.
- **Security:** Breaking blockchain is impossible theoretically, with the available current technology [11–13]. As we know already that any transaction must be accepted by more than half of the nodes to get approved in the network. If the hacker is able to hack a blockchain by altering one particular data, then he may create a new block which has to be verified by all nodes in the network of blockchain. In this operation, if any one node responds differently, then checking of cryptographic hash of that particular node is done; thereby, the network ignores that particular node automatically until it is able to return to a version of real data. Hence, hacking is possible only if the hacker is able to modify half plus nodes at the same time for breaking blockchain leading to fraudulent transaction which is not at all possible with the available technology.
- **Smart:** Blockchain technology is able to write separate custom code for each of the application such that possibility of various rules can be added specific for an application along with cases.
- **Auditable:** In blockchain technology, a hash links each block with the previous block hence navigation is possible in blockchain along all the blocks by which we can reach the starting origin block of the blockchain termed as Genesis block; hence, it is possible to track all changes chronologically.

3.2.2.2   Framework and Working of Blockchain Technology

Blockchain is defined as a technology with distributed ledger peer-to-peer recording the transactions, contracts, agreements, and sales validating transactions, thereby creating verified ledger of information which cannot be altered. Blockchain technology has various features listed as follows:

- Transparency
- Openness
- Sharing
- Storage
- Peer-to-peer communication

These characteristics are necessary to get it operated through Internet. We know that blockchain has two types of keys, namely, public key and private key. Main difference between both keys is that public key operates in an open decentralized environment without any restrictions on number of people who can join the network, whereas private key operates only within a confined number of people along with a controlling entity [14–16].

Working of the blockchain is described by the following steps as shown in Figure 3.4.

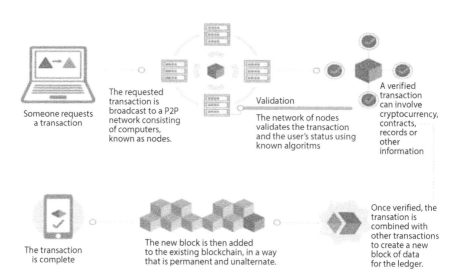

Figure 3.4 Basic working of blockchain technology.

- If someone requests a transaction, then the requested transaction is broadcasted to a P2P network consisting of nodes which are the computers involved in the network.
- Then, the transaction along with status of the user is validated by the nodes involved in the network utilizing known algorithms of validation. A verified transaction is then combined with other transactions in creating new blocks of data for the ledger.
- This newly created block is then added to group of existing block in the blockchain with a permanent status that cannot be altered, completing the transaction.
- Enormous potential is possessed by Blockchain technology in shaping the smart communities in an enhanced way for providing better quality of living in the future.
- Blockchain technology is able to provide solution for a large variety of problems occurring generally in smart cities. But, in practice, implementing this technology depends on community preferences and administration.

3.2.3   Concept and Definition of Artificial Intelligence

This section provides a conceptual overview of AI in specific Machine Learning (ML) applicable for applications of smart cities. The term AI indicates that the entity is able to capture data, process it and respond to inputs from various sources. This definition of AI can be extended as "artificial entity such as software or computer system is able to achieve planned goals in an environment of variable conditions. But intelligent term indicates that the system is able to provide response to previous environmental unknown condition through adapting and learning continuously.

In broader sense, ability of entity or computer system to estimate the intellectuality of real human beings is termed as AI. In order to mimic the behavior of human AI is divided into six divisions, namely, ML, computer vision, knowledge representation, robotics, natural language processing and automated reasoning. In smart devices, the system is able to adapt itself to new circumstances with the help of ML which involves data processing, data analysis, pattern extrapolation and finally prediction. Learning ability of AI is represented by ML essentially which converts experience of the system into knowledge of the system. Algorithms of ML possess two diverse advantages in comparison with the convention algorithms. These are as follows:

1. ML algorithms can operate on unknown data without previous experience over it for which the system is not trained for.
2. ML algorithms are able to adapt it to data changes.

3.2.3.1 Classification of Artificial Intelligence–Machine Learning

ML algorithms must learn from previous experiences adding knowledge to the system. Based on the learning type, ML algorithms are classified into three types as shown in Figure 3.5, also represented as follows:

- Supervised Learning
- Unsupervised Learning
- Reinforcement Learning

Supervised Learning: In this type of ML algorithm, training data is the labeled pair of input and output and learning of the system is based on given instances. Learning problem typically in supervised learning are, namely, classification and regression. In the case of classification, sorting of data is done based on predefined categories whereas in regression, calculation of output is done corresponding to each input data.

Unsupervised Learning: In the case of unsupervised learning, training data is unlabeled in contrast to supervised learning. In this case, grouping of data is done based on commonalities.

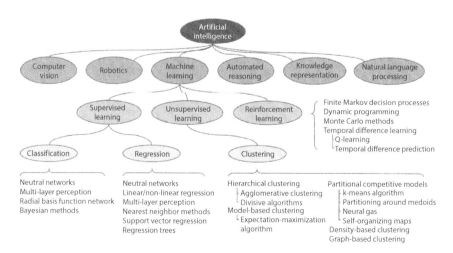

Figure 3.5 Categorization of artificial intelligence.

Reinforcement Learning: In this case, there is no availability of training data but a strategy of maximizing predefined reward cumulatively is developed by the system.

3.3   Smart Cities Integrated with Blockchain Technology

Primarily, blockchain technology was apparent with Bitcoin only, but recently, it has found place in several other applications such as logistics, system management, and smart contracts. Researchers have harnessed the potential of this technology which has increased the trust of users in digitial communities [17, 18]. Decentralized nature along with its openness to users, blockchain technology is used as single point of starting for novel initiatives. Blockchain technology has the ability of increasing the transparency of regional and local institutions along with sensitive data communication in a secured way facilitating confidentiality. Hence, this blockchain technology is able to act as an interoperable platform for developing smart cities where the citizens are able to participate actively in the process of decision-making thereby affecting the communities to which they belong to. Blockchain also serves as an tool in managing the company's reputation in context to the environmental activity.

- Smart city administration generates huge amount of sensitive data and hence demands huge volume of storage where the generated data can be saved in a secured way with predetermined policies for data accessing.
- Based on recent cases of threat, online transactions still have the security issue of cyber-attacks in real time, which can be mitigated specifically the phenomenal effects, distribution model is utilized by blockchain technology for increasing the degree of entropy with implicit reduction of system vulnerability which it supports.
- As this technology is based on the architecture of cryptography, transactions are unlikely to get altered or reversed. Every time broadcasting of a new transaction occurs in the network, each nodes has to validate it and thereby has to include in the distributed ledger, if in case the transaction has got invalidated, then it has to be ignored by the nodes.

- A consensus is achieved by the nodes if most of the nodes decide for single state to make up network along with which, each of the participants possess a signature or key used for creation of transaction.
- Association is allowed by this key between the creator of a particular transaction, i.e., one of the user and the recipient indicating the other user.
- As the ledger has to be validated by the total network and also as it is distributed every transaction can be associated only with one user and there is no possibility of registering of a single transaction several times on a particular blockchain.
- Different technologies are integrated in the development of infrastructure of smart cities for ensuring the residents of the urban area with better life quality, a better environment for development of business with resource optimization and public administration in a transparent way.
- Attaining of these goals is by utilizing blockchain technology acting as a tool for ecosystem with distributed and decentralized nature. Empowerment of smart cities is through features of blockchain such as information sharing, validation of information, transparency, and database updating with security [19].
- This technology allows the local government and citizens to interact with each other without any central authority needed in between in a distributed manner. Smart communities are able to function in an optimized way by implementing smart contracts which can execute transactions in a smart way automatically without the necessity of any operator as a intermediate person. Model of smart city based on blockchain utilizing Self-Sovereign Identity (SSI) is as shown in Figure 3.6.

Infrastructure based on blockchain is able to connect local community of smart city to interact with public administration. Specialty of this technology is that each of the member of the community is allowed to access the ledger where a copy of the ledger is available with every member. In transactions, authentication of a person is done by utilizing the Digital Sovereign Identity. Instead of having central authorities, an interconnected network is utilized as a community of peers with each peer possessing its

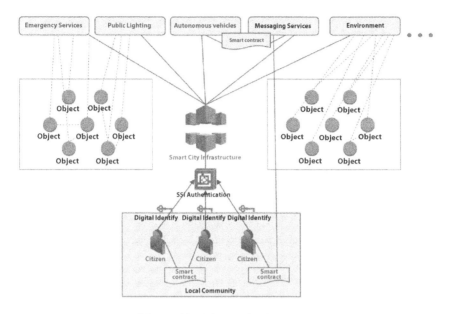

Figure 3.6 Smart city model using blockchain technology.

own identity. In the ecosystem, IoT devices are involved that are placed at various locations for recording and transmitting real-time data concerning the environment of the smart city [20]. Smart contracts is also possible between the public authorities as well the citizens; it can also be defined even in between the citizens where these smart contracts are safely stored where there is reduced attempts of frauds in the blockchain.

3.3.1 Applications of Blockchain Technology in Smart City Development

In the development of smart cities, several applications can be implemented using the technology of blockchain in various fields such as secured communication of data, smart contracts, smart energy management, smart waste management, and smart assets, as shown in Figure 3.7 which are discussed as follows.

3.3.1.1 *Secured Data Transmission*

In smart city, huge amount of data is generated which has to be transmitted to remote places in a secured way, such that no hacking is allowed. A unique feature of blockchain technology is to provide secured data

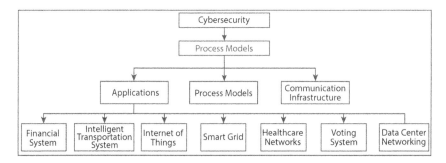

Figure 3.7 Applications in smart city using blockchain technology.

communication with improved reliability, faster transmission with reduced delay, scalability, and capable to tolerate faults with operation performed in an efficient way by avoiding many threats [21].

3.3.1.2   Digital Transaction—Smart Contracts

Transactions can be performed between two parties digitally in the form of smart contracts without the involvement of third party. These digital transactions can be negotiated and its performance can be verified if necessary; hence, these transactions have irreversibility property as well as can be tracked. These smart contracts are applicable for all situations which include process related to finance such as agreements related to crowd funding, financial services, insurance premiums also related to legal documents such as property law. Stronger contracts can be developed by blockchain technology which can be accessed only by the parties of the contract directly involved in it, while third party are allowed to access the authenticity of the contract by utilizing the measures of general security and hashed crypto keys. Generally, Ethereum and solidity are used for the development of smart contracts. Generally extra cost is incurred for the practice of contracting overheading the real cost, but these smart contracts based on blockchain technology enables reduction of cost incurred by notaries-a branch of legal profession. These smart contracts not only provide security and acts as replacement for notaries but also provide convenient, speedy, and reliable process of certification.

3.3.1.3   Smart Energy Management

Energy management is the prime sector in which blockchain technology is used for accelerating the enforcement of various energy usage pricing models in real time. These models are able to promote renewable energy sources, such that energy demands are met by local power generation within the smart city. It helps in power supply management thereby balancing the load. Recording of consumption of energy is done based on which electricity bill is generated in an automatic way. Citizens are enabled to invest in farms of micro renewable energy such that they are able to produce energy for their requirement and excess production of energy is sold to the grids [22].

3.3.1.4   Modeling of Smart Assets

Initially, blockchain was involved in tracking of cloud-based smart assets later the idea of modeling of smart asset was evolved where monitoring of products and components was done permanently in the supply chain with update set of predefined characteristics. This provides data to the distributed systems in real time about the availability of products [23]. Optimal transportation of products along with increased availability whenever demanded indicates better information.

Model of the smart asset is designed such that storage of merchandise along with distribution is well adapted to the situation with increased storage generally outside the smart cities. Turning of products into itemized smart assets increases efficiency of distribution by effectively using the space available in the city as shown in Figure 3.8. As the requirement of storage space is less, indicates management of inventory is done by

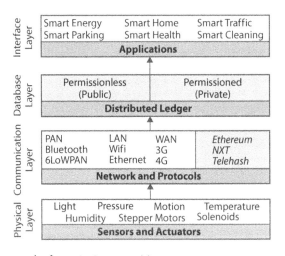

Figure 3.8 Framework of security in smart cities.

implementing Just in Time and Just in Case conditions. This results in distribution of products in optimized way; hence, smart cities provide several benefits such as more green space and diverse availability of products with more innovative products and functions with less storage space.

3.3.1.5   Smart Health System

Citizens residing at smart cities can be beneficial as blockchain technology is able to create single e-record of their health such that it is more secure, flexible, and trustworthy for the health providers as well as the patients to maintain such decentralized records, and there is no need for the patients to carry or maintain bundle of hardcopy of the health records every time they visit the consultant [24]. They are able to access the health record any time from any place along with which they are able to register any appointment with care providers or practitioners online without any problem. Any possibility of exchange of medical records is avoided with better control over the medical services as the history of the patient is transparent for the medical practitioners using the technology of blockchain. Approval of insurance claim becomes easier by the usage of smart contract providing faster settlement.

3.3.1.6   Smart Citizen

Development and planning of smart city requires contribution of citizen as a significant part. A platform is developed using blockchain termed as loyalty and rewards platform based on blockchain where right contributors are rewarded for their involvement in the development of smart city. Citizens can use voting platforms based on blockchain which provides more security as it is decentralized acting as a unique voting system as it removes inefficiencies and complexities involved in other ways of voting [25]. These platforms are used where feedback can be provided by the citizens raising their grievances which are resolved at an earlier rate such that facilities in the smart city are improved.

3.3.1.7   Improved Safety

Improved security can be provided by the blockchain technology, where originality of the documents cannot be altered. This technology is also able to verity the originality of documents, for instance, evidence submitted to the court can undergo alteration to hide the truth which delays the process at courts wasting the time of law enforcing agencies adding burden to their work. Such proofs can be cryptographically verified in an unambiguous way by identifying whether the proofs are altered or not. This allows faster proceedings of cases minimizing evidence tampering. Digitized system using blockchain technology can be used for registration of birth and death ensuring accurate records where the data is encrypted using public keys and private keys for securing the information.

3.4   Smart Cities Integrated with Artificial Intelligence

In the current era, developments in AI specifically ML is utilized in advanced applications of smart cities. Essential component of smart city is termed as smart infrastructure which comprises of wireless sensor networks that collects structured data, analyzes it, and communicates this data autonomously which is referred as smart monitoring [26–28].

Algorithms of AI have ability to process huge amount of data with pattern and feature detection that are not possible to detect using conventional approaches. In spite of having such capabilities, mistrust is seen among engineers as these AI algorithms involve opaque inner processes hence called as black box. In order to increase the trust on AI algorithms for smart monitoring, this black-box nature has to be explained prior to engineers leading to Explainable AI (XAI). Proper categorization of AI algorithms is required for improved explanation about the AI algorithms via XAI. In the previous section, we have seen wide categorization of AI algorithms, in precise ML algorithms applicable for smart monitoring.

Advanced urban regions with its organizations and people are ultra-connected in terms of technology is termed as smart cities. It is a system with interconnected intelligent subsystems. These subsystems consist

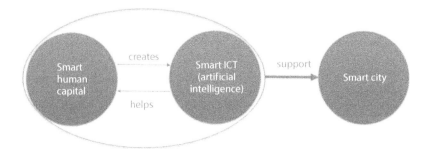

Figure 3.9 Role of AI in developing smart city.

of components, which work together integrated with each other thereby providing quality products and services with real-time access with sustainable development characteristics in a socio-economic environment. Information and communication technologies (ICTs) are utilized by these systems for stimulating the economic growth to provide improved quality of life, integrating hardware technologies with software technologies finally to provide smart urban management. The term smart city is facilitated mainly by ICTs evolution, in specific AI which has the possibility of replacing human being in harmful complex activities. However, smart cities involve smart human race able to create smart ICTs prepared with AI as shown in Figure 3.9. Smart people with their integrated creativity utilize smart technologies and, with total cooperation, can solve problems related to pollution, urban agglomerations, natural resources depletion, etc.

3.4.1   Importance of AI for Developing Smart Cities

In this section, main focus is on importance of AI for developing various aspects of smart cities. In a smart city, AI can be utilized in several areas such as stock market, smart transportation, security applications, and rescue management [29]. In the development of smart cities, several complex factors arises such as restructuring of economic status, protection of environment, issues related to government laws and mobility constraints. For example, intelligent buildings can achieve sustainable development by using AI which used systems driven by software, electronic devices and other technologies which are able to perceive the environment of the building based on which action is taken to optimize performance of the system [30–32]. AI provides convenient solution in designing, construction of system, maintenance of smart transportation, and scheduling of time of the transport system. It not only involves in developing intelligent efficient transport system to be operated in smart cities but also utilized for resolving problems of complex system of transport at a faster rate by processing large amount of data.

In smart transport system, AI is integrated; hence, real-time report about current traffic conditions and occurrence of accidents is generated solving essential problems of smart cities such as overcrowding, degradation of environment, and congestion due to traffic. This issue of traffic flow is found increased in cities, and hence to overcome this problem, physical infrastructure is required for managing with advanced technologies and new ways of thinking. A four-layer pyramidal infrastructure for designing smart cities is as shown in Figure 3.10.

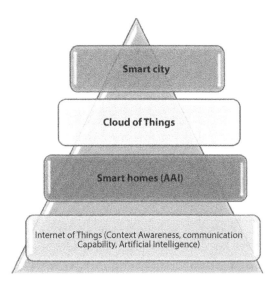

Figure 3.10 Infrastructure of four-layer smart city.

A collection of IoT devices are involved at the bottom layer which are able to interact with the users directly. Learning and prediction of individual's behavior with their preferences is obtained by gathering of contextual information by smart home systems available in layer 2. System findings contextually in combination with AI is utilized for providing services of new category such as smart lighting, smart heating, smart supervision system for providing security, smart assistances generating alarms during problems, smart monitoring of elders or children, environmental monitoring which are tailored based on the requirement of the user. Combining all these four layers provides all advantages and facilities required by a smart city. Management of energy, environment, and water, meeting requirements of issues related to administration, public safety and government, and health care with social programs are given preference in infrastructure of smart cities [33].

3.4.2 Applications of Artificial Intelligence in Smart City Development

In this section, various applications of AI are discussed in the development of smart cities. Applications related to AI in specific ML particularly Deep Reinforcement Learning (DRL) is focused. Based on the reports from international organization, 50% of the population lives in urban area and by 2050 two third of the population will start living in cities thereby providing huge opportunities to technical companies involved in development of smart cities [34–37]. Based on the report of International Data Corporation, more than 130 billion dollars is spent on developing smart cities to make it more livable with system for social management with facilities of advanced infrastructure. A big role is played by AI in smart cities to make urban areas smarter to attain sustainable growth for equipping cities with advanced features with utmost safety and convenience. Let us analyze each of the applications in brief.

3.4.2.1   Smart Transportation System

Smart transportation system is an integrated application comprising of advanced sensors, actuators, and intelligent control systems along with ICT which generates big data impacting effectively future of smart transportation system and smart cities [38–40]. A vital role is played by AI in specific ML specifically DRL to monitor precisely the flow of traffic data estimating it in real time in urban environment acting as a key element in this application. In this section, developments of smart transportation are discussed, playing a significant role in realization of smart cities. Several issues such as traffic flow accessing, management of fleet, MEC channel estimation, estimation of possibilities of accidents, and passengers hunt are focused in smart transportation system to be utilized in smart cities as shown in Figure 3.11.

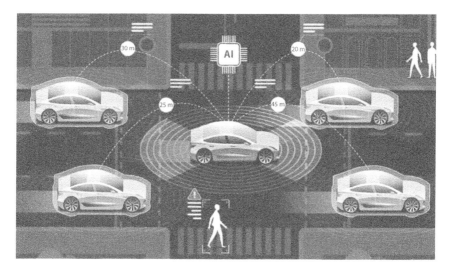

Figure 3.11 Operation of autonomous vehicles using AI and LiDAR technology.

- Driving with enhanced behavior based on DRL with decision-making is done in environment of heterogeneous traffic. Smart driving involves data preprocessor which converts data collected into a matrix of hyper grid, from which essential latent features are extracted using a two-stream deep neural network (DNN) with optimal policy attained by DRL.
- Validation of the proposed method is done by simulating the resulting for various scenarios of traffic with connected vehicles. Securing issues arising in mobile edge computing is focused for handling security threats successfully based on the approach of DRL in order to learn possible attacks via unsupervised learning.
- Smart parking in real time by creating traffic maps is possible by utilizing road surface sensors incorporated along with CCTV camera in the parking spots of smart cities provides updated information of empty parking space to the drivers saving their time avoiding delays to move smoothly without creation of traffic.
- Traffic sensor supported by AI utilizes 3D cameras for collecting real-time data of vehicle density on road which is thereby sent to the patrol control center where data obtained from various points are collaborated. Based on the results obtained from this collaboration of data, signal timings are adjusted at various points ensuring smooth vehicle flow [41].
- Public transport can also be converted into smart transportation by integrating with AI with lots of opportunities to improve public transit. Even commercial cab services like Ola and Uber have started using AI for providing better service to the customers with better riding experience. Hence, in smart cities, AI is implemented in traffic management and smart vehicle parking as most of inhabitants of smart cities possess their own car along with commercial vehicles involved in transportation of goods for these inhabitants.

AI also includes autonomous vehicles which are able to self-drive by themselves based on sensor-based technology which makes AI successful in reaching various fields. In autonomous vehicles, LiDAR is the promising technology, by which the vehicle is able to get awareness about its surroundings. This awareness of this sensor-based technology helps the vehicle to drive safely without any risk of collision with neighboring vehicles [42–45].

LiDAR is one of the sensors used by automated AI vehicle where it has 3D sense which have paved way for this indispensable technology evolutes from driver assistance vehicle to autonomous vehicles. LiDAR is able to collect critical data about the surrounding of the environment that helps autonomous vehicle to provide safety reliably.

3.4.2.2   Smart Surveillance and Monitoring System

Enhanced security can be provided in smart cities by utilizing cameras and sensors enabled by AI which always keeps an eye on the environment as well as in the neighborhood of the smart cities. Unusual activities of people in the areas are tracked by such cameras to recognize their face as found in restricted areas [46–48]. Movement of vehicles registered in the database of the smart city is tracked using camera system of AI security system enabled with high resolution which can monitor density of the crowd and environmental cleanliness of public places such as smart parks, smart swimming pool and smart refreshment centers all throughout day and night.

- AI also uses the data collected by different departments such as police department, in order to predict type of crime along with its intensity based on activities already occurred in that area. A big role is played by security camera enabled by AI, providing more security and trouble free life to the people.
- Training data is needed for creating such high-tech video device which can operate integrated with surveillance system. Development of security camera system is done using large amount of data sets obtained from videos and from image obtained from other cameras similar to this prototype.
- In the technology of face recognition, AI is able to detect different people based on their faces and their personal identities. Security cameras integrated with AI along with drones are able to recognize faces of human and matches with that of databases in order to trace the identity of the person and finally authenticate persons living in the smart city, restricted areas and smart societies.
- AI-based face detection model utilizes the land marking annotation technique for training the system such any new faces entering the smart city will be checked whether matching with database of crime list such persons are tracked

Figure 3.12 Smart surveillance by night vision thermal camera system.

continuously and information is provided to crime department as shown in Figure 3.12.

- Humans are tracked using autonomous flying drones which also monitors movement of the traffic thereby providing imagery 2D aerial view mapping for city urbanization in a better way. It is utilized by crime squad and security departments for providing advanced surveillance and security [49].

3.4.2.3 Smart Energy Management System

Urban area development mainly depends on sustainability of energy which play key role in providing power to all smart devices. AI is acting as a catalyst in parallel in urbanization which aims at optimization of smart services from design level even in the field of energy management acting as a paramount in energy domain along with its consumption. Critical support is provided by AI into pilot energy systems in order to attain energy

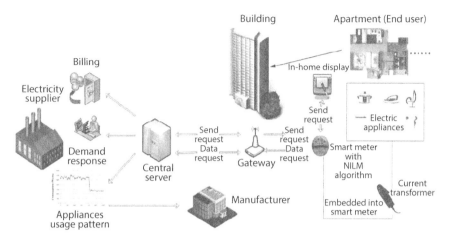

Figure 3.13 Smart energy management system with NILM algorithm.

sustainability in the case of smart cities as shown in Figure 3.13. To attain this smart metering along with non-intrusive load monitoring (NILM) for adding value to electric appliances by consuming less amount of electricity [50–52].

- Optimization problem of multi-objective of NILM is solved by implementing hybrid genetic algorithm with approach of multiple kernel learning with support vector machine.
- This algorithm is applicable for 25 types of appliances as it provides the design for optimal kernel function based on the properties of various kernel, with the indicators of performance are specificity, sensitivity, and classifier's overall accuracy.
- Utilization of energy and its sustainability in urban areas is achieved by integrating AI along with big data and IoT. These technologies together provide energy sustainability for optimal smart cities.
- Major consumers of energy are smart cities as they collaborates various smart devices operating together; hence, there is always correlation between consumption of energy and footprint of environment in terms global warming where sustainability of energy is emerging as the key question beholding the stakeholders which includes decision makers, industries and society.

- Old infrastructure of electric system is replaced by smart grid acting as effective addressing way for the challenges of energy system raised globally. In the context of developing smart grids, important role is played by applications of microgrid such as framework of transactive energy, advanced market of retail electricity along with energy management.
- Generally, renewable resources such as solar energy, wind power, or generators support microgrids typically in order to backup power requirement of smart cities acting as supplement to the main grid of power whenever there is power cut or high demand of power.
- Redundancy is provided by strategy of microgrid which integrates power from solar energy and wind energy essentially such that localized disaster affects operation of main grid to a little extent.
- Smart grid functions based on the conditioning of its key feature, namely, smart metering. Currently, 800 million smart meters are in usage worldwide with rate of penetration of just 50%. Greater efficiency can be attained by increasing the usage of more smart meters in a smart grid in order to optimize it.
- This is possible by implementation of AI integrated with the context of smart metering along with optimization of smart grid for yielding positive results with reduced consumption of energy and higher sustainability of energy. Integration of AI in energy management for smart cities involves following steps:
  - Method for load monitoring is considered which highlights the monitoring of non-intrusive load.
  - Empirical testing is done for the algorithm of AI implemented for energy management.
  - Finally, analysis is performed for evaluating the performance of the energy management system.
- Advanced computational techniques are introduced for electricity forecasting and recognition of pattern. Great impact is viewed in the techniques of smart metering and smart data in terms of efficiency providing solution in the field of smart energy management.

- Energy consumption is optimized by the integrating the techniques of AI along with the approaches of smart grid as they can set up services that are sophisticated.
- New predicting capabilities are offered by ML algorithms which are of more demand nowadays. Further, problem complexity increases with the context of Big data hence requires techniques of novel mining which are meant for behavioral analytics based on time series of energy.
- Hence, there is direct linkage between user behavior and data analysis leading to the integrating of modeling of smart energy, behavioral analytics, metering along with its solutions [53].
- Recently, NILM technique is focused for its advantages in the field of energy management.
- Monitoring of load is able to reduce 20% consumption of energy. This technique of NILM is sensing of single point which used only one smart meter per apartment. But theoretically, higher efficiency is yielded by having more number of smart meters but practically more the number of smart meters, more the cost, with complex configuration of the network with increased complexity of management of the appliances.
- Smart energy management system with load monitoring benefits users, manufacturers and suppliers as prediction of demand is known prior, thereby meeting the gap between total supply of electricity and demand reducing the waste of energy [54].
- Energy management in smart cities is done in a smart way which formulates reduction in electricity bill in specific in the case of appliances of power hunger. Every appliance is monitored about how much energy is consumed and if any failure is intimated to the server for immediate recovery.

3.4.2.4   Smart Disposal and Waste Management System

In smart cities, management of waste has to done in a smart way and has to disposed based on the category of the waste [55–58]. Human intervention is reduced as sensors are fixed in the waste bins for smart waste management.

- Large amount of waste is generated by the people living in smart cities which act as a challenging task for the urban municipality corporation.
- In smart cities, cleanliness is the main goal hence garbage has to be maintained in a smart way to maintain the level of hygiene in the environment.
- Smart cameras enabled by AI are able to detect trash on the street sides and generates notification to the authorities indicating the presence of waste.
- This smart technique is also able to categorize the type of waste collected which is useful in disposing the waste based on its category [59, 60].
- Collection of waste is efficient, when sensors are installed on waste bins in turn enabled by AI.
- Notifications are received by authorities whenever the waste bins are almost filled.
- Timely dispose will reduce the cost of operation of waste management avoiding any unnecessary pickups.
- Dynamic collection is done from the waste bins based on the optimized schedule proposed in a smart way.

3.5   Conclusion and Future Work

Involvement of the technologies of blockchain and AI in the development of smart cities has resulted in rapid growth of urban areas with new infrastructure both for the citizens and the public administration. As development increases, governance of cities also becomes complex which is overcome by these technologies. Smart cities are able to adapt itself to address the problems related to socio economic issues even when challenges occur both in the environment and transformations in technologies. These smart cities developed by digital technologies are able to improve the quality of life as well the performance level of the residents in real time. Direct contact between the citizens and public administration provides excellent management of the society as third party is totally restricted to interfere. Blockchain technology would really benefit both local administration and city officials based on novel way of connecting the public with the facilities available. Smart cities possess specialized infrastructure of hardware consisting of components which collects and stores data in a secured way. Integration of new applications is allowed and the applications are able to interoperate between themselves with the possibility of reusing the existing infrastructure. Smart contracts make the legal process more transparent avoiding any fraudulent in real time.

Smart cities possess the smart infrastructure as the key component which is able to monitor its components and applications in a smart way leading to more reliable, cost effective, and durable infrastructure than the existing conventional models. AI have several algorithms which able to impart intelligence to machines to analyze automatically the data collected by the sensors where the nature of black box is used in smart monitoring specifically in ML algorithms. But it causes mistrust and intransparency, and hence, full potential of ML algorithms is hindered. However, transparency is enhanced by XAI technique increasing the confidence of engineers on ML algorithms which is drawing the applications of ML toward it specifically smart monitoring and its deployment. In future, these technologies can be explored still to introduce several other innovation applications in smart cities.

References

1. United Nations Organization (ONU), Revision of world urbanization prospects, United Nations, New York, 2018, https://www.un.org/development/desa/en/news/population/2018-revision-ofworld urbanization-prospects.html.
2. Liu, Y., Wei, J. and Rodriguez, A.F.C. Development of a strategic value assessment model for smart city. *Int. J. Mob. Commun.*,12, 4, 346–359, 2014.
3. Komninos, N., *Intelligent Cities:Innovation, knowledge systems and digital spaces*, p. 320, Spon Press, London and New York, 2002.
4. Nasulea, C. and Mic, S.-M., Using Blockchain as a Platform for Smart Cities. *J. Eng. Technol.*, 9, 2, 37–43, 2018, 10.6025/jet/2018/9/2/37-43.
5. Gori, P., Parcu, P.L., Stasi, M.L., SmartCities and Sharing Economy, vol. 96, 2018. Robert Schuman Centre for Advanced Studies Research Paper No. RSCAS.
6. Albino, V., Berardi, U., Dangelico, R.M., Smart cities: Definitions, dimensions, performance, and initiatives. *J. Urban Technol.*, 22, 1, 3–21, 2015.
7. Steventon, A. and Wright, S. (Eds.), *Intelligent spaces: The application of pervasive ICT*, Springer-Verlag, London, 2006.
8. Cisco, Internet of things at-a-glance, Cisco, Canada, https://www.cisco.com/c/dam/en/us/products/collateral/se/internet-of-things/at-aglance-c45-731471.pdf, 2.16.
9. Gartner, *Smart Cities Will Include 10 Billion Things by 2020*, 2015, https://www.gartner.com/en/documents/3004417.

10. Haber, S. and Stornetta, W.S., How to time-stamp a digital document, in: *Conference on the Theory and Application of Cryptography*, Springer, Berlin, Heidelberg, *Lecture Notes in Computer Science, 537*, pp. 437–455, 1990.

11. 6 Key Features of Blockchain: This is what makes Blockchain so exciting!, New York, Online: https://thefintechway.com/6-keyfeatures-of-blockchain/. Accessed: October 2019.

12. Pal, O., Alam, B., Thakur, V., Singh, S., Key management for blockchain technology. *ICT Express*, 2019.

13. Viriyasitavat, W. and Hoonsopon, D., Blockchain characteristics and consensus in modern business processes. *J. Ind. Inf. Integr.*, 13, 32–39, 2019.

14. Lee, J.Y., A decentralized token economy: How blockchain and cryptocurrency can revolutionize business. *Bus. Horiz.*, 62, 6, 773–784, 2019.

15. Hebert, C. and Di Cerbo, F., Secure blockchain in the enterprise: A methodology. *Pervasive Mob. Comput.*, 101038, 59–68, 2019.

16. Szabo, N., Smart Contracts: Building Blocks for Digital Markets. *EXTROPY: J. Transhumanist Thought*, 16, 16–32, 1996.

17. Boncea, R., Petre, I., Vevera, V., Building trust among things in omniscient Internet using Blockchain Technology. *Romanian Cyber Secur. J.*, Spring, 1, 1, 2019.

18. Tapscott, D. and Alex, *Blockchain Revolution: How the Technology Behind Bitcoin Is Changing Money, Business and the World*, Penguin, Toronto, 2016.

19. Aggarwal, S., Chaudhary, R., Aujla, G.S., Kumar, N., Choo, K.K.R., Zomaya, A.Y., Blockchain for smart communities: Applications, challenges and opportunities. *J. Netw. Comput. Appl.*, 13–48, 2019.

20. Beck, R. and Müller-Bloch, C., *Blockchain as Radical Innovation: A Framework for Engaging with Distributed Ledgers as Incumbent Organization*, 2017, 10.24251/HICSS.2017.653.

21. Swan, M., *Blockchain: Blueprint for a new economy*, 1st edition, O'Reilly Media Inc, Sebastopol, CA, 2015.

22. ISO 24760-1, A framework for identity management - Part 1: Terminology and concepts, ISO & IEC, Switzerland, 2019, https://www.iso.org/standard/77582.html.

23. Smolensky, N., Identity and Digital Self-Sovereignty, America, 2016, https://medium.com/learning-machineblog/identity-and-digital-selfsovereignty1f-3faab7d9e3-. 3jcgvnbok.

24. Payam Almasi, P., The Identity Revolution - Self Sovereign Powered by Blockchain, California, 2019, https://blog.goodaudience.com/howblockchain-could-become-the-onramptowards-self-sovereign-identitydd234a0ea2a3.

25. Vranken, J., *Social Challenges of Cities of Tomorrow*, Centre OASeS, 2011, https://ec.europa.eu/regional_policy/sources/docgener/studies/pdf/citiesof-tomorrow/citiesoftomorrow_social.pdf.

26. Acatech – National Academy of Science and Engineering, *Industry 4.0, Urban development and German international development cooperation (Acatech position paper)*, Herbert Utz Verlag, Munich, Germany, 2015.

27. Adadi, A. and Berrada, M., Peeking inside the black-box: A survey on explainable artificial intelligence (XAI). *IEEE Access*, 6, 2018, 52138–52160, 2018.

28. Abdeljaber, O., Avci, O., Kiranyaz, S., Boashash, B., Sodano, H., Inman, D., 1-DCNNs for structural damage detection: verification on a structural health monitoring benchmark data. *Neurocomputing*, 275, 2018, 1308–1317, 2018.

29. Bach, S., Binder, A., Montavon, G., Klauschen, F., Müller, K.R., Samek, W., Onpixel-wise explanations for non-linear classifier decisions by layer-wise relevance propagation. *PloS One*, 10, 7, e0130140, 2015.

30. Bao, Y., Chen, Z., Wei, S., Xu, Y., Tang, Z., Li, H., The state of the art of data-science and engineering in structural health monitoring. *Engineering*, 5, 2, 234–242, 2019.

31. Barredo Arrieta, A., Diaz Rodriguez, N., Del Ser, J., Bennetot, A., Tabik, S. *et al.*, Explainable artificial intelligence (XAI): Concepts, taxonomies, opportunities and challenges toward responsible AI. *Inf. Fusion*, 58, 2020, 82–115, 2019.

32. Kabalci, E. and Kabalci, Y., *From smart grid to Internet of Energy*, 1st edition, Academic Press, London, UK, 2019.

33. Kelley, T., Symbolic and sub-symbolic representations in computational models of human cognition: What can be learned from biology? *Theory Psychol.*, 13, 6, 847–860, 2003.

34. Langley, P., The changing science of machine learning. *Mach. Learn.*, 82, 3, 275–279, 2011.

35. Legg, S. and Hutter, M., Universal intelligence: A definition of machine intelligence. *Minds Mach.*, 17, 4, 391–444, 2007.

36. Li, R., Gu, H., Hu, B., She, Z., Multi-feature fusion and damage identification of large generator stator insulation based on Lamb wave detection and SVM method. *Sensors*, 19, 7, 3733, 2019.

37. Martins, J., Towards smart city innovation under the perspective of software-defined networking, artificial intelligence and big data. *RTIC – Rev. tecnologia dainformação e comunicação*, 8, 2, 1–7, 2018.

38. Bilek, J., Mittrup, I., Smarsly, K., Hartmann, D., Agent-based concepts for the holistic modeling of concurrent processes in structural engineering, in: *Proceedings of the10th ISPE International Conference on Concurrent Engineering: Research and Applications*, Madeira, Portugal, July 26, 2003.

39. Bisby, L.A. and Briglio, M.B., *ISIS Educational Module 5: An introduction to structural health monitoring. SAMCO Final Report 2006*, ISIS Canada, Winnipeg, Manitoba, Canada, 2005.

40. Burkov, A., *The hundred-page machine learning book*, 2019.

41. Nomura, Y. and Shigemura, K., Development of real-time screening system for structural surface damage using object detection and generative model based on deep learning. *J. Soc. Mater. Sci.*, 68, 3, 250–257, 2019.

42. Nosratabadi, S., Mosavi, A., Keivani, R., Ardabili, S., Aram, F., State of the art survey of deep learning and machine learning models for smart cities

and urban sustainability, in: *Proceedings of the 18th International Conference on Global Research and Education Inter-Academia*, Budapest, Hungary, September 4, 2019.

43. Ogie, R.I., Perez, P., Dignum, V., Smart infrastructure: An emerging frontier for multidisciplinary research. *Proceedings of the Institution of Civil Engineers–Smart Infrastructure and Construction*, 170, 8–16, 2017.

44. Organisation for Economic Co-operation and Development (OECD), *Enhancing the contribution of digitalisation to the smart cities of the future*, Online: https://one.oecd.org/document/CFE/RDPC/URB(2019)1/REV1/en/pdf, last accessed: January 20, 2020.

45. Pan, H., Azimi, M., Lin, Z., Yan, F., Time-frequency based data-driven structural diagnosis and damage detection for cable-stayed bridges. *J. Bridge Eng.*, 23, 6, 04018033, 2018.

46. PricewaterhouseCoopers, *Creating the smart cities of the future*, Online:https://www.pwc.com/gx/en/sustainability/assets/creating-the-smart-cities-of-the-future.pdf, last accessed: January 21, 2020.

47. Ribeiro, M.T., Singh, S., Guestrin, C., Why should I trust you?: Explaining the predictions of any classifier, in: *Proceedings of the 22nd ACM International Conference on Knowledge Discovery and Data Mining*, San Francisco, CA, USA, August 13, 2016.

48. Russel, S.J. and Norvig, P., *Artificial intelligence: A modern approach*, 3rd edition, Pearson Education Ltd, Harlow, Essex, UK, 2014.

49. Salehi, H. and Burgueno, R., Emerging artificial intelligence methods in structural engineering. *Eng. Struct.*, 171, 170–189, 20182018.

50. Santos, A., Figueiredo, E., Silva, M., Santos, R., Sales, C., Costa, J., Geneticbased EM algorithm to improve the robustness of Gaussian mixture models for damage detection in bridges. *Struct. Control Health Monit.*, 24, 3, e1886, 2016.

51. Senniappan, V., Subramanian, J., Papageorgiou, E., Mohan, S., Application of fuzzy cognitive maps for crack categorization in columns of reinforced concrete structures. *Neural Comput. Appl.*, 28, 1, 107–117, 2016.

52. Shalev-Shwartz, S. and Ben-David, S., *Understanding machine learning From theory to algorithms*, Cambridge University Press, New York, NY, USA, 2014.

53. Sierra-Perez, J., Torres Arredondo, M.A., Alvarez-Montoya, J., Damage detection methodology under variable load conditions based on strain field pattern recognition using FBGs, nonlinear principal component analysis, and clustering techniques. *Smart Mater. Struct.*, 27, 1, 015002, 2017.

54. Smarsly, K., Lehner, K., Hartmann, D., Structural health monitoring based on artificial intelligence techniques, in: *Proceedings of the International Workshop on Computing in Civil Engineering*, Pittsburgh, PA, USA, July 24, 2007.

55. Soomro, K., Bhutta, M., Khan, Z., Tahir, M., Smart city big data analytics: An advanced review. *Wiley Interdiscip. Rev.: Data Min. Knowl. Discovery*, 9, 5, e1319, 2019.

56. Anbuchezhian, N., Velmurugan, T., Suganya Priyadharshini, T., Krishnamoorthy, R., Novel Design of Hybrid Steam Turbine Reflector Based Controller for Solar Power Plant, 14, 9, 572–578, 2020, https://doi.org/10.15866/ireme.v14i9.19510.

57. Krishnamoorthy, R., S. Priya, L., Aswini, S., Guna, C., Design and Implementation of IoT based Energy Management System with Data Acquisition. *2020 7th International Conference on Smart Structures and Systems (ICSSS)*, Chennai, India, pp. 1–5, 2020.

58. Steiner, M., Legatiuk, D., Smarsly, K., A support vector regression-based approach towards decentralized fault diagnosis in wireless structural health monitoring systems, in: *Proceedings of the 12th International Workshop on Structural Health Monitoring*, Stanford, CA, USA, September 10. 2019.

59. Kumar, A., Payal, M., Dixit, P., Chatterjee, J.M., Framework for Realization of Green Smart Cities Through the Internet of Things (IoT), in: *Trends in Cloud-based IoT*, pp. 85–111, 2020.

60. Jha, S., Kumar, R., Chatterjee, J.M., Khari, M., Collaborative handshaking approaches between internet of computing and internet of things towards a smart world: a review from 2009–2017. *Telecommun. Syst.*, 70, 4, 617–634, 2019.

4

Smart City a Change to a New Future World

Sonia Singla[1]* and Aman Choudhary[2]

[1]Bangalore University, Bangalore, Karnataka, India
[2]Lingayas University, Faridabad, Haryana, India

Abstract

During ancient times, we used to see in Mahabharata great epic that Sanjay was telling about the battle fought between Kauravas and Pandavas in Kurukshetra; it was just the technology that we have known as television and similarly flying aircraft, etc. Now in this time, the world is heading toward the need for a smart city to solve all the problems associated with it like air pollution, water crisis, and safety.

AI along with IoT is the best solution to solve this problem, but as India is a vast country with 60 different languages spoken, so making every person educated with new technology and removing the bridge gap of the language barrier is a big challenge.

In this paper, we have tried to focus on how AI will be able to solve the problems of a smart city.

Blockchain innovation is not just the premise of the cryptocurrency Bitcoin. This framework also has an activity to facilitate, coordinate, and control distinctive city administrations with straightforwardness, proficiency, and protection.

Keywords: Artificial Intelligence, information and communication technology, smart city, agriculture, education

4.1 Introduction

A smart city, as the name suggests, deals with city life to make it better, cleaner, and inexpensive. It uses information and communication

---

**Corresponding author*: ssoniyaster@gmail.com

Vishal Kumar, Vishal Jain, Bharti Sharma, Jyotir Moy Chatterjee and Rakesh Shrestha (eds.) Smart City Infrastructure: The Blockchain Perspective, (113–126) © 2022 Scrivener Publishing LLC

technologies (ICT), and the data is collected to analyze traffic, crimes, healthcare, transportation, and other services. The population of few larger Cities of India as shown in Figure 4.1. It is a wave of the future and is expected to have 60% of the population living in the city by 2050 [2–5].

The principle of utilizing blockchain is that it gives various unique features, for example, improved unwavering quality, quicker and productive activity, and scalability. The future works will intend to plan a system-level model to explore the interoperability and scalability of various stages utilized in a keen city [5]. The principle of utilizing blockchain is that it gives various unique features, for example, improved unwavering quality, quicker and productive activity, and scalability. Hence, mix of blockchain development with contraptions in a brilliant city will make an average stage where all gadgets would have the choice to pass on securely in an appropriated climate. The future works will intend to plan a system level model to explore the interoperability and scalability of various stages utilized in a keen city [5].

ICT as shown in Figure 4.2 includes all communication technologies like internet, mobile, laptop, software, and social networking, etc. It, in fact, is the expanded term for information technology (IT). In other words, ICT provides all its information via telecommunication [5].

Four main applications of ICT include the following:

1. Internet access
2. Marketing
3. Management
4. Processing

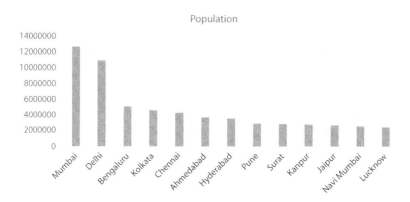

Figure 4.1 Population in few larger cities of India [6].

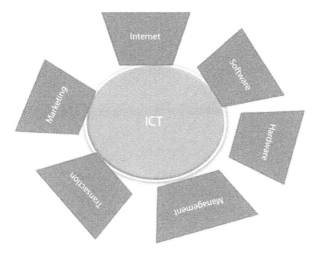

Figure 4.2 Information and communication technology (ICT) [15].

4.2   Role in Education

Teachers referred to as Guru are the building blocks of society; they give rise to scientists, politicians, doctors, Engineers, etc. To make the teaching skills creative, attractive, and adapt to future technologies, schools and colleges are making efforts to enable students to learn new techniques and adapt to it. It is highly beneficial during lockdown where online teaching was being given to students. However, to adapt to new technologies, internet access should be available in school and colleges and most important teachers must be highly educated to know the new technologies to enable them to teach the students and to give their best [6].

In the computerized period, the smart city can turn into an insightful society by using progress in developing advancements. In particular, the quick appropriation of blockchain innovation has driven a change in perspective to another advanced brilliant city biological system. Besides, the combination of Artificial Intelligence (AI) and blockchain innovation is reforming the savvy city network design to assemble manageable biological systems. In any case, these headways in advance bring the two chances and difficulties with regard to accomplishing the objectives of making an economical keen urban area [18].

These days, with regard to security, we cannot be excessively cautious. Savvy cities have been setting IoT gadgets around to help convey more elevated levels of security just as proceed with the progress of a carefully improved future [26, 27]. With higher quantities of IoT gadgets, come higher expected possibilities for programmers to assault feeble zones. By utilizing blockchain, we must carry availability to a huge scope without bargaining security all the while. IoT gadgets cannot have a blockchain; however, the framework combined with cryptographic keys can be utilized to build up a personality for gadgets. Explicit gadgets can introduce their security-secured accreditations to take an interest in the IoT conditions it is permitted and approved [19, 20].

Cash on movement and logistics organization are the fundamental challenges took a gander at by online business associations, especially in horticultural countries [20, 24]. Furthermore, online business retailers moreover need to manage time-mentioning little demands with various things, which cause high working costs for online business associations [21–23, 30].

4.3   Impact of AI on Smart Cities

First question that arise in making city smart city is how we can make it cleaner?

In the world, in top 16 polluted countries, India's five states are mentioned: Faridabad, Gurgaon, Ghaziabad, Noida, and Delhi as shown in Figure 4.3 [7].

About approx. 4.2 million deaths occur due to bad air quality in the whole world.

Data from different sources and AI advancement could allow us to enter down on incredibly close by issues [8].

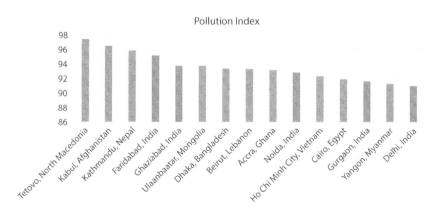

Figure 4.3 Air pollution in world [7].

Second question arise is how we can make the city safer? One rape occurs in every 15 minutes in India. About 87 rape cases daily were reported in 2019, 7% rise from previous year [8].

4.3.1   Botler AI

Established by Ritika Dutt, the Botler AI uses regular language handling to decide if an episode groups as inappropriate behavior or other wrongdoing. It is made by utilizing 300,000 client record cases in Canada and the USA. In addition, its conversational AI centers around giving the rape and assault survivor an understanding, regardless of whether their experience falls under the Violation of US criminal code or Canadian Law. This innovation is yet under the beginning stage, however, essentially centers to draw rape matches from the declarations of the people in question.

4.3.2   Spot

Spot is another chatbot, used by associations to alleviate the occurrence of rapes. Frequently, the protests of rape are either gotten by some unacceptable individual or are inappropriately archived. By coordinating AI into the framework, the chatbot archives more data forthright, lessens examination time, and catches 29% more insights concerning the occurrence in introductory reports.

4.3.3   Nimb

Nimb is another innovation that helps in forestalling rape cases. Planned as a ring, Bluetooth is incorporated at the focal point of the ring. In a crisis circumstance, by squeezing the ring, the Bluetooth sends cautions to pre-recorded contacts in the telephone. The reaction time is 30 seconds.

4.3.4   Sawdhaan Application

Established in 2018, this innovation is supposed to be the principal AI-based application to forestall rapes and assaults in India. This application is accessible in the play store and can be enacted by utilizing the versatile application. Once the application becomes initiated it sends trouble message and call to the essential contact like clockwork in a crisis circumstance. With the assistance of the AI innovation, a united report is made about the individual's area, and the encompassing voices, which will be shipped off the gatekeepers by means of SMS. This is explicitly valuable to

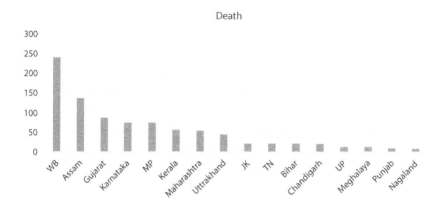

Figure 4.4 Death caused by flood [10].

subdue down occurrences of gangrape like Hathras, Hyderabad, and New Delhi [9].

Third question which comes up in mind is how we make our cities powerful? About approx. one fifth of death in India is because of flood as shown in Figure 4.4 [10].

Another question which comes in mind is how can we make our city efficient? Delhi, Kolkata, and Mumbai recorded the highest traffic in world top twenty countries [11].

The traffic AI utilizes AI and machine learning to improve the traffic [12].

4.3.5 Basic Use Cases of Traffic AI

The three different ways to improve traffic the executives and advantage drivers.

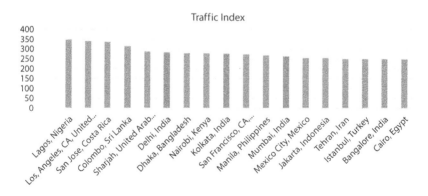

Figure 4.5 World road traffic [11].

1. Traffic Signals

    Traffic AI frameworks can enhance traffic signals and decrease holding up time at crossing points. The AI recognizes vehicles in pictures from traffic cameras. The data is shipped off a control place, where calculations examine traffic thickness. In the event that the framework distinguishes blockage, it can guide traffic signals to re-course traffic, in light of continuous information, example, the world road traffic as shown in Figure 4.5.

2. Traffic Patterns

    Using perceptive assessment, traffic AI structures can perceive traffic plans and hinder or alleviate road obstruct before it occurs. Sharp metropolitan regions can facilitate a traffic AI structure with their Intelligent Transport System (ITS) or join the AI with their Advanced Traffic Management System (ATMS).

3. Safety

    Traffic AI structures can make emergency organizations and public transportation safer and more capable. Traffic AI isolates between kinds of road customers and can put together traffic stream moreover. At the point when the AI perceives an emergency vehicle, it can re-course traffic to help emergency work power show up at their goal speedier. If a vehicle is caught in busy time gridlock, then the AI can help it with making a stop on time [12].

How AI and IoT can be used to reduce dry waste and e-waste?

Significant organizations can utilize AI and IoT for ecological supportability alongside eco-accommodating equipment to lessen the harmful effects. With appropriate methods set up, the disposed of gadgets can be revamped and reused, sparing great many dollars for the endeavour in the assembling of new items.

4.4   AI and IoT Support in Agriculture

Soil contamination is a significant issue confronted today because of populace development, serious cultivating, and different exercises. 50,000 deaths happen each year everywhere on the world because of pesticide harming. Food creation is the way to food of human life on earth. Use of AI and IoT for ecological maintainability incorporates strategies to screen yields and soil and augment crop creation with a low effect on the climate. IoT and AI innovations can possibly change customary rural practices [22]. The rural population in India has risen as shown in Figure 4.6. They make ready

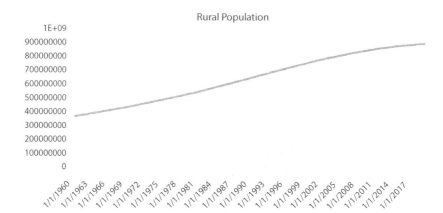

Figure 4.6 Rural population in India [6].

for more secure farming techniques and eventually advantage individuals' wellbeing. Shrewd observing gadgets and sensors can be connected to yields to screen their development continually. Oddities can be identified and settled right away. Boundaries, for example, hydration, plant nourishment, and illnesses can be observed continuously. The information would then be able to be used to decide water system designs and suggest the best watering cycles. A superior assortment of harvests having high wholesome substance can be cultivated utilizing AI, which can likewise bring down our utilization of destructive pesticides [13].

Last but not the least, how AI can save the city from terrorist?

Numerous fear terrorist attacks are cultivated by bringing dangerous gadgets covered up with common looking items to public spots. In such case, it is practically difficult to separate a fear-based oppressor from common individuals just from the secluded appearance. Nonetheless, important signs may be found through investigating a progression of activities of a similar individual. Anomalous practices of article getting, store, or trade openly places may demonstrate possible assaults [14].

4.5   Smart Meter Reading

Automated meter reading (AMR) and generating bill by pressing the button just like an old Polaroid camera printing picture itself.

Automated meter reading and detection of water leakage and meter errors and if meter is being operated by itself and bill generate itself can be used same like car alarm theft or protecting your home sitting far from it due to the sensors installed. Example of smart meter is shown in Figure 4.7.

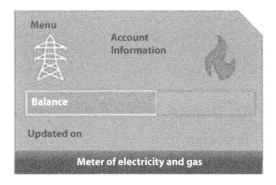

Figure 4.7 Illustration image of smart meter reading [2].

Main advantages

1. Bill will be not misplaced.
2. Water leakage will be prevented but in fact it will give warning message if any leakage is there.

Interfacing a water sensor to an Arduino is an incredible method to distinguish a hole, spill, flood, downpour, and so on. It tends to be utilized to distinguish the presence, the level, the volume, as well as the shortfall of water.

AI in Healthcare

AI-controlled retinal imaging structures, perceptive showing programs, glucose sensors, insulin siphons, wireless applications are available in today world.

It can change diabetes care to achieve better blood glucose control, decrease hypoglycemics scenes, and decline diabetes comorbidities and disarrays [1].

Electronic health record (EHR) has helped clinicians distinguish and define persistently sick patients. EHR can improve quality consideration by utilizing the information and examination to forestall hospitalizations among high-hazard patients.

M-health, in other word, is monitoring of public health by mobile, cellphone, and smart watches. It is further branch of e-health for monitoring health.

There are different difficulties looked by the healthcare areas, for example, putting away the clinical record of the patient, keeping up hospital information system, upkeep of clinical hardware, medicine blunder and parcel more. Presently, the hospitals rely upon ICT to patch up the entire cycle of the medical services area. Through ICT the metropolitan—rustic variations have been broken and abbreviated. In the event that a specialist has the correct correspondence channel, it is anything but difficult to convey treatment and care for the patient who is found anyplace around the globe. The framework causes the doctor to consistently screen the patient's set of experiences and indicative report and to track the current medical issue. The doctor can likewise interface with understanding, prescribe to take clinical assessment, and endorse medication.

The town population needs legitimate medical services mindfulness because of the nonattendance of precise data. The transportation troubles in country territories are additionally a detriment taking the patient to the medical clinic on schedule.

This is a significant purpose behind the expanded number of irresistible sicknesses and demise rates in towns. This can be tended to by introducing appropriate correspondence channel so the doctors in the towns can speak with the close by towns and along these lines the life of numerous individuals can be spared [15, 16].

What can we expect in smart city?

1. Clean air
2. Clean water
3. Recycle of waste
4. Eco-friendly
5. Green energy
6. Safe transport
7. Less traffic
8. Safe home, school
9. Inexpensive treatment

How AI is shaping the food industries?

The food business is not known for its initial reception of innovation. However, prodded by imaginative new businesses, computerized reasoning (AI) may demonstrate the special case. Here are six instances of how the food business is as of now utilizing AI or could be utilizing it in the exceptionally not so distant future.

Growing new items

AI indicates to help food organizations do that precisely. Their innovation utilizes AI and prescient calculations to demonstrate purchaser flavor inclinations and foresee how well they will react to new tastes. The information can be fragmented into segment gatherings to assist organizations with growing new items that coordinate the inclinations of their intended interest group [17].

The framework, which they call Self-Optimizing-Clean-In-Place, or SOCIP, utilizes ultrasonic detecting and optical fluorescence imaging to gauge food buildup and microbial trash in a bit of gear and afterward advance the cleaning cycle.

4.6   Conclusion

AI and blockchain are the backbones for smart cities; however, it is quite challenging with language barrier for farming in rural area. Blockchain, AI, and IoT promise a bright future with clean air, safe transport, clean water, etc. Further research is required in this area so that combination of blockchain and AI benefits can be utilized.

References

1. Singla, S., AI and IoT in Healthcare, in: *Internet of Things Use Cases for the Healthcare Industry*, P. Raj, J. Chatterjee, A. Kumar, B. Balamurugan (Eds.), Springer, Cham, 2020, https://doi.org/10.1007/978-3-030-37526-3_1.
2. Smart cities: A cheat sheet - TechRepublic, https://www.techrepublic.com/article/smart-cities-the-smart-persons-guide/. Accessed 21 Oct 2020.
3. Smart city - Wikipedia, https://en.wikipedia.org/wiki/Smart_city. Accessed 21 Oct 2020.
4. Cook, D.J., Duncan, G., Sprint, G., Fritz, R., Using smart city technology to make healthcare smarter. *Proc. IEEE Inst. Electr. Electron. Eng.*, 106, 708–722, 2018.
5. Biswas, K. and Muthukkumarasamy, V., Securing smart cities using blockchain technology. *2016 IEEE 18th International Conference on High Performance Computing and Communications; IEEE 14th International Conference on Smart City; IEEE 2nd International Conference on Data Science and Systems (HPCC/SmartCity/DSS)*, IEEE, pp. 1392–1393, 2016.
6. Population of Cities in India, 2020, https://worldpopulationreview.com/countries/cities/india. Accessed 21 Oct 2020.
7. Pollution Index by City 2020 Mid-Year, https://www.numbeo.com/pollution/rankings.jsp. Accessed 21 Oct 2020.
8. #BeatAirPollution-HowAIandIoTcouldhelppeoplecombatairpollutionissues, https://www.capgemini.com/gb-en/2019/06/beatairpollution-how-ai-and-iot-could-help-people-combat-air-pollution-issues. Accessed 21 Oct 2020.
9. Top 10 AI Technologies to Mitigate Rape and Sexual Assault, https://www.analyticsinsight.net/top-10-ai-technologies-mitigate-rape-sexual-assault. Accessed 21 Oct 2020.

10. India - number of deaths due to floods and landslides by state 2020 | Statista, https://www.statista.com/statistics/1147398/india-flood-landslides-death by-state/. Accessed 21 Oct 2020.

11. Traffic Index by City 2020 Mid-Year, https://www.numbeo.com/traffic/rank ings.jsp. Accessed 21 Oct 2020.

12. Traffic AI: Why, How, and a Real-Life Use Case, https://mobility.here.com/learn/smart-transportation/traffic-ai-real-life-use-case. Accessed 21 Oct 2020.

13. How IoT And AI Can Enable Environmental Sustainability, https://www.forbes.com/sites/cognitiveworld/2019/09/04/how-iot-and-ai-can-enable environmental-sustainability/36d6b26568df. Accessed 21 Oct 2020.

14. Geng, X., Li, G., Ye, Y. *et al.*, Abnormal behavior detection for early warning of terrorist attack, in: *AI 2006: advances in artificial intelligence*, A. Sattar and B. Kang (Eds.), pp. 1002–1009, Springer Berlin Heidelberg, Berlin, Heidelberg, 2006.

15. Information Communication Technology in HealthCare | Uses of ICT, https://www.frontenders.in/blog/information-communication-technology healthcare.html. Accessed 21 Oct 2020.

16. Artificial Intelligence in Healthcare: Examples, Pros/Cons & Future - Business Insider, https://www.businessinsider.com/artificial-intelligence healthcare?r=US&IR=T. Accessed 21 Oct 2020.

17. Examples of Artificial Intelligence in the Food Industry - Food Industry Executive, https://foodindustryexecutive.com/2018/04/6-examples-of artificial-intelligence-in-the-food-industry/. Accessed 21 Oct 2020.

18. Singh, S., Sharma, P.K., Yoon, B., Shojafar, M., Cho, G.H., Ra, I.-H., Convergence of blockchain and artificial intelligence in IoT network for the sustainable smart city. *Sustain. Cities Soc.*, 63, 102364, Dec. 2020.

19. Blockchain Technology and Smart Cities, [Online]. Available: https://dynamicconsultantsgroup.com/blogs/blockchain-technology-and-smart cities/. [Accessed: 22-Oct-2020].

20. Babich, V. and Hilary, G., What operations management researchers should know about blockchain technology. *SSRN J.*, 22, 1, 2018.

21. Karame, G., On the security and scalability of bitcoin's blockchain, in: *Proceedings of the 2016 ACM SIGSAC Conference on Computer and Communications Security*, Association for Computing Machinery, New York, NY, pp. 1861–1862, 2016.

22. Crop Yields - Our World in Data, [Online]. Available: https://ourworldin data.org/crop-yields#oilcrops. [Accessed: 22-Oct-2020].

23. Xu, X., Pautasso, C., Zhu, L., Gramoli, V., Ponomarev, A., Tran, A.B. *et al.*, The blockchain as a software connector, in: *Proceedings of the 2016 13th Working IEEE/IFIP Conference on Software Architecture (WICSA)*, Institute of Electrical and Electronics Engineers, Piscataway, NJ, pp. 182–191, 2016.

24. Chod, J., Trichakis, N., Tsoukalas, G., Aspegren, H., Weber, M., Blockchain and the value of operational transparency for supply chain finance. *SSRN J.*, 1, 1, 2017.

25. Reddy, N.A. and Divekar, BR., A Study of Challenges Faced By E-commerce Companies in India and Methods Employed to Overcome Them. *Proc. Econ. Financ.*, 11, 553–560, 2014.

26. Jha, S., Kumar, R., Chatterjee, J.M., Khari, M., Collaborative handshaking approaches between internet of computing and internet of things towards a smart world: a review from 2009–2017. *Telecommun. Syst.*, 70, 4, 617–634, 2019.

27. Kumar, A., Payal, M., Dixit, P., Chatterjee, J.M., Framework for Realization of Green Smart Cities Through the Internet of Things (IoT), in: *Trends in Cloud-based IoT*, pp. 85–111, 2020.

5

Registration of Vehicles With Validation and Obvious Manner Through Blockchain: Smart City Approach in Industry 5.0

Rohit Rastogi[1]*, Bhuvneshwar Prasad Sharma[2] and Muskan Gupta[3]

[1]Dept. of CSE, ABES Engineering College, Ghaziabad, India
[2]Dept. of IT, ABES Engineering College, Ghaziabad, India
[3]B.Tech. CSE Final Year, ABES Engineering College, Ghaziabad, India

Abstract

Blockchain technology replaces centralized applications to distributed computing. Modern economy is estimated by the place of motor transport in the infrastructure of the national economy. An automobile registration system is a unified information system. This information system takes care of every information of an automobile registration. It is administered by a national registry entity and has access by other government and non-government of services that handles automobile information. Cyber-physical system (CPS) is defined as the combination of computation and physical process. It is mainly used in ICT section. It is also focused on resolving the problems related to authors of the data regarding transparency, media, and storage problems by technical handling.

The presented manuscript uses all above concepts at one place and integrate them to build a useful application. The presented frame allows car manufacturers, owner, repairing companies, and insurance agencies to register and add new entries for cars in a simple method. Four different smart contracts control block share updated in DriveLoop. In addition, database technology has been leveraged to cache intermediate data. It efficiently uses the Industrial IoT and 5G technologies.

Many researchers have been called for rules and applications to draw old maps into the Blockchain based on distributed applications. New protocols are available in this work for the International Automated Vehicle Management System, called DriveLoop, was proposed and developed.

---

*Corresponding author: rohit.rastogi@abes.ac.in; ORCID: https://orcid.org/0000-0002-6402-7638

Vishal Kumar, Vishal Jain, Bharti Sharma, Jyotir Moy Chatterjee and Rakesh Shrestha (eds.) Smart City Infrastructure: The Blockchain Perspective, (127–162) © 2022 Scrivener Publishing LLC

Keywords: DriveLoop, Blockchain, peer-to-peer (P2P), hashing algorithms, car registration, overlay network

5.1   Introduction

An individual, whenever bought one's own vehicle or have sold it, or have been a part of an automobile manufacturing or dealing at any stage of the cycle, one would be familiar with the complication that is process of vehicle registration. Given the fact that all these vehicles in the market have been sold and resold as they are passed through multiple hands, it becomes a cumbersome task to maintain a legitimate record of the history of each vehicle and make it available when needed.

But before one goes on to talk about the problems of the process of vehicle registration, one first needs to understand why vehicle registration is such an important aspect of automobile dealing. Car ownership may get changed as many times as you can imagine.

Whether you look at it in the terms of dealing in spare parts or in assembled vehicles, dealings by the middlemen or by the retailer who makes the final sale to a consumer, or in terms of the resale of a second-hand vehicle, there are a number of stakeholders who would very much want to know about all the history of the vehicle they are buying. Not to mention the insurance agencies, the police and other authorities, and, well, the government too need to keep tabs on the automobiles for various reasons.

The fact of the matter is that all these stakeholders need information about the vehicles, starting from its manufacturing story, covering its first sale, the accidents, if any, that it has been in, and any all repairs and maintenances. This is crucial not for just to maintain a track record of the vehicle in question to determine its market value but also for legal and insurance purposes.

Vehicle registration is a way to facilitate this record keeping by maintaining a link between the vehicle and its owner. It might be or not be compulsory, depending on the law of the land. This helps the authorities with regard to taxation, insurance, or crime detection purposes. Also, it is a way for the automobile dealer to keep a track of their vehicles [1, 6, 15].

5.1.1   Concept of Smart Cities

The urban development has resulted in a change of archetype in 21st century. Research activities for smarter cities have become priority task. The life had been improved in the last century in terms of technologies and services. Smart city is the demanding solution of sustainability and urbanization.

Smart cities may lead to a dystopian world that is regulated by technocratic governments which propel citizens to subaltern roles. However, the massive industrialization and the increasing population in the big cities has been a big challenging for urban planner, architects, and administrators [28, 29].

The service platforms of smart cities are Internet of Things (IoT), big data systems, and mobility. Connected automobile with its advanced technology reduces the chances of accident and help drivers to save time and gasoline in their limits. Increase in population in urban areas often leads to the problem of parking spaces. Smart parking is one the most important parts of smart city. Sensors are placed in smart cities with good internet connectivity. More urban our planet becomes, smarter the cities have to be. The cities of tomorrow will be more prone to transformation embellishment than the cities of yesterday [12].

5.1.2   Problem of Car Registration and Motivation

The process of registering a car has always been difficult. This is a lengthy process involving several parties, and there is also the risk of manipulating information, replicating data and various errors. In this case, critical information can be very vulnerable to fraud or data falsification, or even available for tracking.

By bringing the power of Distributed Ledger Technology called Blockchain into the picture and moving the entire process of registering a car on to Blockchain, a lot of these vulnerabilities can easily be resolved [16].

5.1.2.1   Research Objectives

Blockchain comes to the rescue by reducing the average response time. The Blockchain will allow parties to send data in the form of an intellectual contract or chain code, which will eventually become the single source of unchanged data for all parties. In addition, the Blockchain in the vehicle registration ecosystem will help reduce the risk of fraud and aggression, since only authorized personnel can use the data when updating the private key in province.

In fact, any attempt to track fake data can be easily done on the Blockchain. The best part is that Blockchain provides one single idea of the lifecycle of the car in one book, which is not currently available [2].

5.1.2.2   Scope of the Research Work

This research experiment is a generalized project implemented using open source technologies developed by Linux Foundation called Hyperledger

Fabric in a permission model. Anyone can use this project by taking the authorization and adding their stakeholders into the system.

5.1.3   5G Technology and Its Implications

With an advanced access technology and with an increase in the demand of the users, 4G will now be easily replaced with 5G. There are several reasons to switch to 5G: have higher capacity, increase data rate, lower end-to-end interruption, massive device connectivity, reduced cost, and consistent quality of experience [18].

5G consists microcells, small cells, and relays and hence heterogeneous. Device-to-device communicative (D2D) and IoT are major concerns. 5G provide a good policy for future 5G standardization network MBB mobile broadband. 5G will allow wireless networks to matter data rates and use case that are currently handled by fiber access. One of the widely used technologies in today's era is IoT. IoT further consists two technologies. These technologies used to describe a key focus area for the ICT sector [4, 5].

a)   Cyber-physical system (CPS): This system is used to describe a key focus area for the ICT section. It is basically defined as the unification of computation and physical processes.

b)   Machine to machine (M2M): It represents the way in which machine can communicate between themselves.

5G validate IoT for new use cases and economic sectors. Objective of 5G is to meet projected mobile traffic demand and to heuristically address the communications needs most sectors of the economy. Also, the aim of group is to promote the development of 5G technologies in China. South Korea's 5G forum is also a public private partnership program that is formed in May 2013.

5.1.4   IoT and Its Applications in Transportation

Application in Automobile

If you have ever bought your own vehicle or have sold one or have been a part of an automobile manufacturing or dealing at any stage of the cycle, then you would be familiar with the complication that is vehicle registration.

Given the fact that all vehicles in the market have been sold and resold as they are passed through multiple hands, it becomes a cumbersome task to maintain a legitimate record of the history of each vehicle and make it available when needed. By applying Blockchain and IoT technologies and the whole process of registering of vehicles in Blockchain, many of these problems can be easily solved.

5.1.5   Usage of AI and ML in IoT and Blockchain

A good working model could be IoT generating data from a multitude of sensors and analytics, Blockchain storing data and, AI/ML drawing intelligence from the same data. An example of the above is in a supply chain, where IoT can measure a lot of different metrics from environment to trip record to motion sensing, use Blockchain to store that data and then use AI on that data to make human-like decisions. The purpose of Blockchain in this solution is to provide transparency across organization and immutability of data as well as executing smart contracts.

This is not just true for supply chain but is possible in many sectors such as healthcare manufacturing, identity, and security applications and even finance industries. For example, a bank offering line of credit to SMEs may depend on these technologies to make faster, accurate, and error-free assessment by using IoT to measure goods, raw materials, finished products, assets, etc., of an SME, store these in Blockchain for audit and other decision-making purposes and employ AI to make recommendations [4, 6, 7].

Each technology in itself is capable of transformation. They do not need one another to be useful. But together, they are even more powerful catalysts to solve problems that are difficult to handle otherwise. Take an example of healthcare. Healthcare issues such as surgical infections, hygiene, and negligence can have a bad impact on the patient as well as the hospital in itself. The combination of IoT, Blockchain and AI can be used effectively to bring accountability, efficiency, and better and faster patient recovery [19].

5.2   Related Work

Blockchain is not a new technology. It is a set of existing methods, which are organized in a new specific order to solve problems related to different strengths, security and sharing. Many applications are suggested to move from a normal or normal operation to a Blockchain. In addition, many surveys were written to obtain information about applications. The following are some of the previous works related to DriveLoop. Two important Blockchain systems for this application are CarChain and Fabcar IBM Blockchain [20].

5.2.1   Carchain

The Carchain is a distributed and decentralized system that connects the car owner and tenant and securely leases and secures financial exchange based on the time spent. The system operates in the open network Blockchain - Ethereum and can be moved to a private Blockchain - Hyperledger.

It consists of an intellectual agreement that integrates systems and applications into the system (for web application owners, for the user's mobile phone), to manage the system, to send information to the Blockchain, and to make changes to the system. It uses an electronic signature method that allows you to unlock the car on arrival.

5.2.2   Fabcar IBM Blockchain

This code demonstrates network configuration on the standard IBM Blockchain platform and the implementation of the Fabcar smart contract on the network. We then configure our application to interact with the network, including identity, to send transactions in a smart contract. The application is configured with Node.js using the Fabric Node SDK to handle network requests and the Angular client to open the web interface [21].

Nowadays, career opportunities are rising rapidly. To achieve success, every field needs lots of dedication and hard work. Automobile engineering career is one of the best careers that is very creative and fast paced. It mainly deals with construction, manufacturing, and design of automobile. Due to rapid growth of auto component in automobile sector because of an advanced technology, the jobs in automobile engineering is increasing every day and the reason behind it are automobile engineers.

5.2.3   Blockchain and Future of Automobiles

The author Pham and team explained the future scope and limitations as follows:

As future perspective, it can be said that, nowadays, career opportunities are rising rapidly. Any field requires lots of dedication and hard work to learn any profession and achieve the success.

Basically, in this research, authors have presented a write-up for an automobile registration or automobile parking using Blockchain. Here, scientists are using an automobile which is designed for passenger and is run by an internal combustion engine with the help of volatile fuel. In today's world, people prefer vehicle to go anywhere whether it is miles away or it is near to the location. It is the daily need of the person as they have to go for their work or to fulfil their needs. The smoothing lubrication of an automobile helps to move vehicles fast and easy which make our life so simple.

As it is known, nowadays, people move to the big cities for better jobs, excellent education and of their bright future. This migration often leads to the increase in population which further leads to the problem of parking spaces. Mostly, many people cannot find safe parking spaces in a crowded area. So, this is insecure solution of centralised based car parking system. An automobile registration system is a unified information system. These information system controls of every information related to an automobile registration. Blockchain is being used nowadays as one of the most emerging domains [14, 17].

The authors' team have applied the methodology for the help of assigned unique ids and without disclosing their personal information, vehicles can communicate with deployed parking lots. Then, register vehicle book parking by requesting the controller. Then, the controller check for parking space around their establishment when receive a request from the ordinary. Then, the complete information is sent to the ordinary node and then the ordinary node reserves the parking and pays for it.

In limitations, one can see that the study was a good learning process and was a very satisfying experience. Yet there are several factors that limited this researches plan to study as every researcher desired limitations are as follows.

a) **Access to Documentation and Information**
   - Required data was not readily available. The process of documentation during design and development is not a regular practise. Due to confidentiality of the companies, an R&D and Design activity, the information shared was limited about the processes that are followed for a particular product category.

b) **Automobile Industry**
   - The R&D and Design executives in the automotive industry are tied up because of many rules and policies.

- Data sharing is very limited. It is not the general practise in the corporation culture to openly and willingly share the information.

In concluding remarks, they explained that they implemented the Blockchain technology to maintain trust, security, and clarity in the system. We use many technologies and one of the technologies is IoT, Ethereum.

They tested proposed idea on the basis of latency of Blockchain, the throughput of Blockchain, the accuracy of transactions, latency upon TAIVs, and throughput upon TAIVs [13].

5.2.4 Significance of 5G Technology

One of the widely used technologies in today's era is IoT. IoT further consists two technologies. These technologies used to describe a key focus area for the ICT sector. b) M2M: It defines the way of communication of machine between them.

The purpose of 5G is as follows:

a) To meet projected mobile traffic demand [24, 25].
b) To address the communications that is mostly needed by the economy sectors.

5.3 Presented Methodology

With Blockchain, stakeholders, such as automotive vehicle manufacturers, agents, customers, and agencies, can easily participate in accessing and updating vehicle data based on their access to security. The solution also ensures that the most secure and complete information is stored and shared securely and economically [8].

To further explain it, let us first look at the roles of the various stakeholders involved in the vehicle registration process. We also looked at some basic workflows and understood how they were simplified with Blockchain.

a) **Manufacturer:** Push the vehicle toward Blockchain by adding details including make, model, version, chassis number, engine number, and the selling date of vehicles.
b) **Dealer:** Car sales are applied to end customers.

c) **Insurance Agency:** Checks customer and car information and provides insurance.
d) **Registration Authority:** The RTO will be responsible for approving registries and providing registration numbers, sending vehicle transfers and resetting vehicles.
e) **Police:** It issues vehicle licenses and transfer certificates, as well as traffic invoices.
f) **Service Center:** Parts of the service are included as work cards and replacement parts.
g) **Customer/Car owners:** Allow the exchange of confidential information as PII [27].

5.4   Software Requirement Specification

The following software requirements have to be fulfilled.

5.4.1   Product Perspective

This idea is not totally implemented anywhere in this world. There exists an app named "Carchain" which provides a way to connect the car owner and tenant securely leases and secures financial exchange based on the time spent.

5.4.1.1   Similarities Between Carchain and Our Application

a. Both Carchain and this application are service-based applications.
b. In both the applications, there are customers who want to avail the services and the professionals who want to provide those services.
c. One can join as a service provider in both applications.
d. Feedback can be provided for both the applications.

5.4.1.2   Differences Between Carchain and Our Application

a. Our application provides an automated way of purchasing a car right from the first step to the last step. Carchain does not involve selling cars.

b. Carchain uses the Ethereum network to implement the Blockchain but our application uses hyperledger fabric—a private network.

5.4.2   System Interfaces

a. HTML5, JavaScript, CSS3, and Bootstrap are used for the front end portion of the application.
b. Node JS is used to write the chain codes for the backend.
c. Docker is used as a service product that uses OS-level virtualization to deliver software in packages called containers. The containers are isolated and group their own software, libraries and configuration files; they can communicate through clearly defined channels.
d. Hyperledger Fabric is used as a platform to operate the application.
e. Two databases are used—LevelDB for storing the transaction data and CouchDB for storing the asset data.
f. Visual studio code is used as a source code editor.
g. Postman is used to create, share, test, and document APIs.

5.4.3   Interfaces (Hardware and Software and Communication)

We use many interfaces like

a) **Login/Signup:** This interface lets a customer enter the application and avail services and if someone is not a customer to this application, it also helps them to become a registered customer.
b) **Main Page:** This interface consists of all the services available also it is a connecting medium to all interfaces.
c) **Contact us:** This interface lets any customer with any issue to contact us.
d) **Manufacturer:** This interface lets the manufacturer push the vehicle toward Blockchain by adding details including make, model, version, chassis number, engine number, etc., and whenever one sells vehicles.
e) **Dealer:** Car sales are applied to end customers.

f) **Registration Authority:** The RTO will be responsible for approving registries and providing registration numbers, sending vehicle transfers, and resetting vehicles.

g) **Police:** It issues the vehicle license and transfer certificate.

h) **Customer:** Allows the exchange of confidential information as PII.

5.4.3.1 Hardware Interfaces

a) Processor: Intel i5-6200U/Intel Core or better.

b) GPU: 2.30 GHz.

c) Ram: 8 GB or more.

d) Hard Disk: 20GB or more.

e) Operating System: Linux/Mac.

f) Input Device: Standard Keyboard, Mouse and USB.

g) A browser which supports HTML and Java script.

h) Internet Connection.

5.4.3.2 Software Interfaces

a) **Ubuntu 20.04:** Team has chosen Linux operating system for its best support and user friendliness for this project.

b) **Hyperledger Fabric v0.20:** It is used as a modular Blockchain structure, which serves as the basis for the development of Blockchain-based products, solutions, and applications using plug-and-play components intended for use in private companies.

c) **NodeJsv12.16.0-x64:** It is been used to write down the back end logic, i.e., Chain code for the automation of the transactions.

d) **Docker 19.03.8:** It is used as a service product that uses OS-level virtualization to deliver software in packages called containers.

e) **Postman 7.24.0:** It is used to create, share, test and document APIs. This is achieved because users can create and save simple and complex HTTP/s requests and their responses. This results in more effective and less tiring work.

5.4.3.3   Communications Interfaces

This project supports all types of web browsers. The team is using simple forms for the registration forms, feedback, availing the services, etc.

Memory Constraints

Primary Memory: 8 GB or above.
Secondary Memory: 20 GB or above.

5.4.4   Operations (Product Functions, User Characteristics)

Following operations will be performed by our software.

5.4.4.1   Product Functions

a)   It allows people to register onto the application who want to use its services.

b)   The manufacturer can add a new car into the Blockchain for the sale purpose.

c)   The dealer can sell a car and can change the ownership of the car after some validations.

d)   The registration authority can validate a car for changing its ownership from one person to another.

e)   The customer can check all the steps involved in a registration process directly from a single dashboard.

f)   Any change done anywhere is reflected everywhere in the network.

5.4.4.2   User Characteristics

a)   Only 18+ adults can register or can provide service to other needed people.

b)   Basic technical knowledge of using the computer system is required.

c)   Two-week hands-on training is enough for using the software.

5.4.5   Use Case, Sequence Diagram

5.4.5.1   Use Case

The following are the various use case diagrams of the various actors involved in the project.

Manufacturer: Figure 5.1 depicts the relationship of manufacturer and the various use cases.

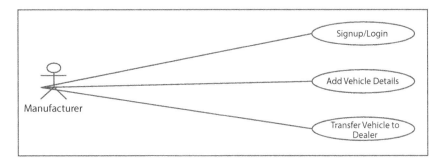

Figure 5.1 Use case of manufacturer.

Dealer: Figure 5.2 depicts the relationship of dealer and the various use cases.

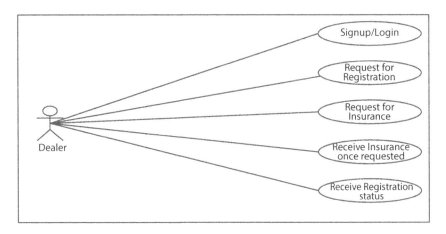

Figure 5.2 Use case of dealer.

Registration Authority: Figure 5.3 depicts the relationship of the Registration Authority and the various use cases.

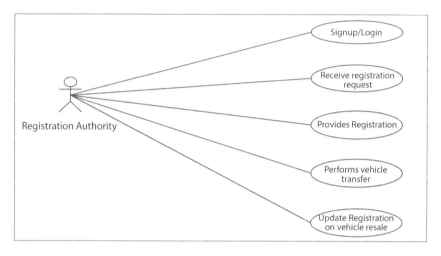

Figure 5.3 Use case of registration authority.

Police: Figure 5.4 depicts the relationship of police and the various use cases.

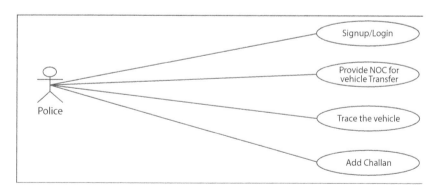

Figure 5.4 Use case of police.

Customer: Figure 5.5 depicts the relationship of customer and the various use cases.

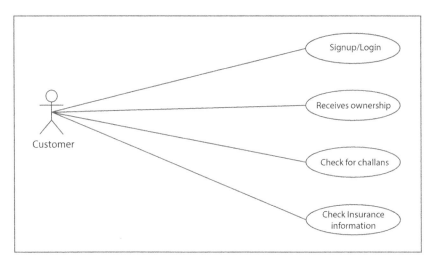

Figure 5.5 Use case of customer.

5.4.5.2   Sequence Diagrams

A sequence diagram shown in Figure 5.6 basically depicts collaboration between articles in a sequential order. This diagram shows how the client

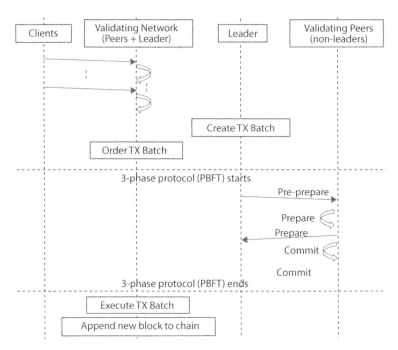

Figure 5.6 Sequence diagram.

enters into the network and a new block of transactions is created and finally added into the Blockchain network.

5.4.5.3   System Design

System design is the way toward defining the engineering, modules, interfaces, and information for a system to fulfill indicated prerequisites.

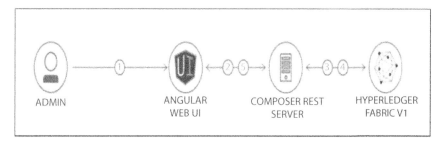

Figure 5.7 High level view of architecture.

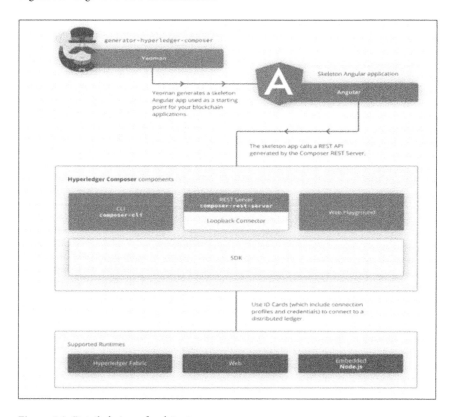

Figure 5.8 Detailed view of architecture.

Architecture diagrams, data flow diagrams, activity diagram, ER diagram, and database schema diagrams are shown in Figures 5.7 to Figure 5.13.

5.4.5.4 Architecture Diagrams

The following is the system architecture design for the project.

5.4.5.4.1 Data Flow Diagram

Level 0: The following is the level 0 data flow diagram of the project.

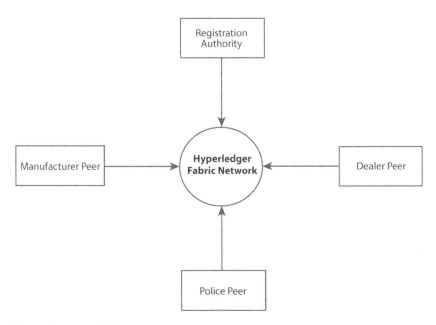

Figure 5.9 Level 0 DFD.

Level 1: The following is the level 1 data flow diagram of the project.

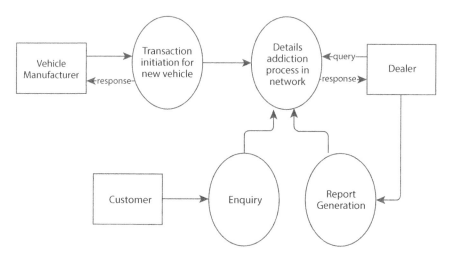

Figure 5.10 Level 1 DFD.

Level 2: The following is the level 2 data flow diagram of the project.

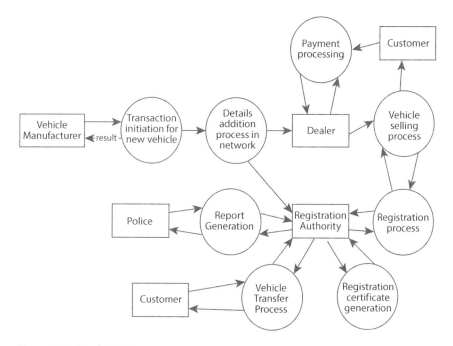

Figure 5.11 Level 2 DFD.

5.4.5.4.2   Activity Diagram

The following is the activity diagram showing the Login of the customer into the system.

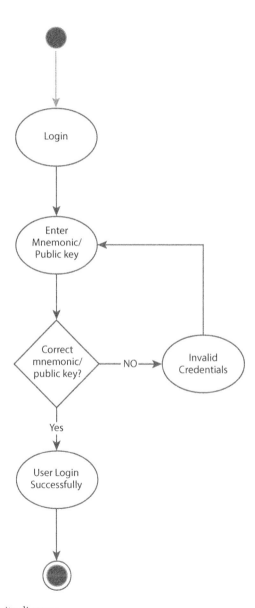

Figure 5.12 Activity diagram.

5.4.5.4.3 ER-Diagram

The following is the entity-relationship diagram for the system.

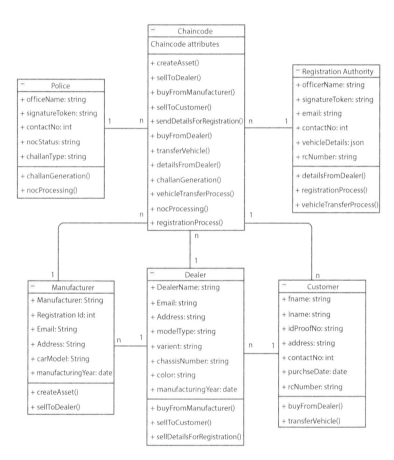

Figure 5.13 Entity relationship diagram.

5.4.5.4.4   Database Schema Diagrams

Hyperledger Fabric supports two types of peer databases: LevelDB is the default state database embedded in the peer node and stores chain code data as simple key-value pairs; and CouchDB is an alternate state database that supports advanced queries when modeling chain code data values as JSON (as per Figures 5.14 to 5.19).

1. **Assets:** The following is the schema for the asset data stored in the system.

```
{
    "$class": "org.driveloop.vehicle.Vehicle",
    "vin": "4242",
    "vehicleDetails": {
        "$class": "org.driveloop.vehicle.VehicleDetails",
        "make": "fvefvsd",
        "modelType": "svsvsd",
        "model": "svsds",
        "variant": "csdcsdc",
        "chassisNumber": "sdsdcsd",
        "engineNumber": "csdcsd",
        "colour": "sdcsdc",
        "manufacturingYear": "csdcsdc",
        "bodyWeight": "cdcsd"
    },
    "vehicleStatus": "UNDER_MANUFACTURER"
}
```

Figure 5.14 Schema for assets.

2. Manufacturer: The following is the schema for the manufacturer data stored in the system.

```
{
  "$class": "org.driveloop.participant.Manufacturer",
  "make": {
    "$class": "org.driveloop.participant.Make",
    "name": "BMW",
    "registrationId": "asj5w67dw87wgx87x8vw"
  },
  "participantId": "9192"
}
```

Figure 5.15 Schema for manufacturer.

3. RTO: The following is the schema for the RTO data stored
in the system.

```
{
  "$class": "org.driveloop.participant.RegistrationAuthority",
  "officerName": "Mr. Joe",
  "signatureToken": "43546756545",
  "participantId": "8753"
}
```

Figure 5.16 Schema for RTO.

4. **Dealer:** The following is the schema for the dealer data stored in the system.

```
{
    "$class": "org.driveloop.participant.Dealer",
    "dealerName": "Man Sales",
    "contact": {
        "$class": "org.driveloop.participant.Contact",
        "email": "mansales@gmail.com",
        "address": "south district"
    },
    "participantId": "3888"
}
```

Figure 5.17 Schema for dealer.

5. **Police:** The following is the schema for the police data stored in the system.

```
{
    "$class": "org.driveloop.participant.Police",
    "officerName": "Mr. Joe",
    "signatureToken": "43546756545",
    "participantId": "8753"
}
```

Figure 5.18 Schema for police.

6. Customer: The following is the schema for the customer data stored in the system.

```
{

    "$class": "org.driveloop.participant.Customer",

    "fname": "Anuranjan",

    "lname": "Singh",

    "contact": {

        "$class": "org.driveloop.participant.Contact",

        "email": "anuranjansingh@gmail.com",

        "address": "ballia"

    },

    "participantId": "9317"

}
```

Figure 5.19 Schema for customer.

5.5 Software and Hardware Requirements

5.5.1 Software Requirements

a) **Ubuntu 20.04:** Researchers' team has chosen Linux operating system for its best support and user friendliness for this project.

b) **Hyperledger Fabric v0.20:** It is used as a modular Blockchain structure, which serves as the basis for the development of Blockchain-based products, solutions and applications using plug-and-play components intended for use in private companies.

c) **Node JS v12.16.0-x64:** It is been used to write down the back end logic, i.e., Chain code for the automation of the transactions.

d) **Docker 19.03.8:** It is used as a service product that uses OS-level virtualization to deliver software in packages called containers.

e) **Postman 7.24.0:** It is used to create, share, test, and document APIs. This is achieved because users can create and save simple and complex HTTP/s requests and their responses. This results in more effective and less tiring work.

5.5.2 Hardware Requirements

a) **Processor:** Intel i5-6200U/Intel Core or better.
b) **GPU:** 2.30 GHz
c) **Ram:** 8 GB or more.
d) **Hard Disk:** 20 GB or more.
e) **Input Device:** Standard Keyboard, Mouse, and USB.

5.6 Implementation Details

Snapshots of interfaces 1are shown in Figures 5.20 to 5.27.

There are few snapshots from the project.

Figure 5.20 demonstrates the front page where the user can easily go to the platform and using the drive loop and different Blockchain techniques, it facilitates the user for automobile registration using authentic and transparent manner.

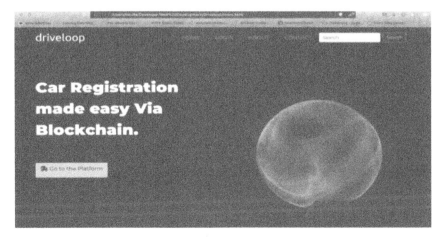

Figure 5.20 Front page.

Figure 5.21 depicts the main page on which user can upload the documents of automobile and can see the all parties which were involved earlier in whole transaction before the registration of this particular vehicle. It will be able to show the whole history of automobile.

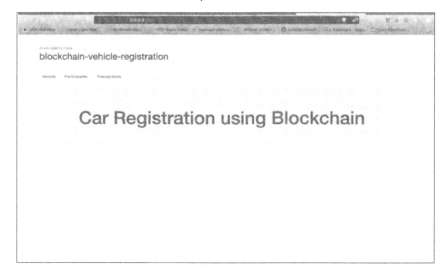

Figure 5.21 Main page.

Asset can be created by Figure 5.22 where the blocks will contain the records for automobile and whole details of all possible transactions will

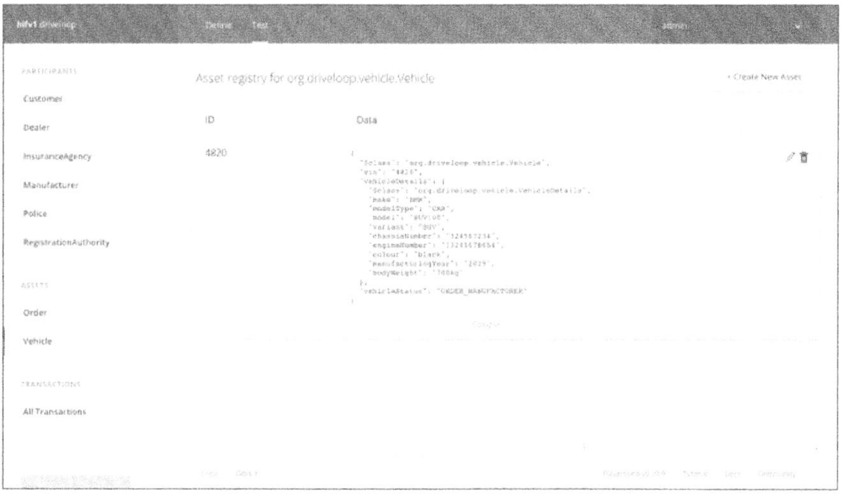

Figure 5.22 Asset creation.

be stored for future purposes. This asset will be base information and will be authenticated by all parties for transparency.

Figure 5.23 shows the model for manufacturer and displays the process of entering the unique and basic details of automobile by the manufacturer which will help to maintain the transparency and ease in smart contract and future transactions.

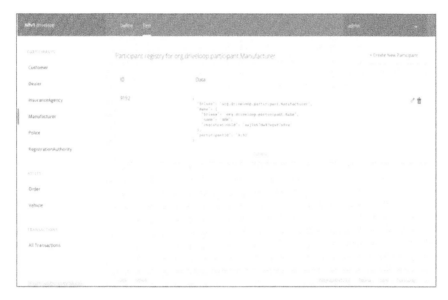

Figure 5.23 Model testing for manufacturer.

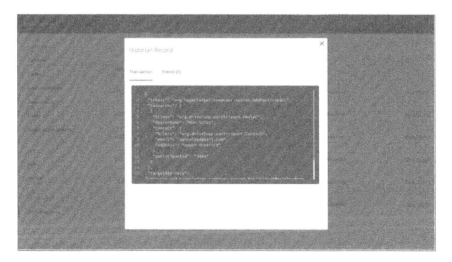

Figure 5.24 Transaction history.

In Figure 5.24, code in hyperledger shows the transaction history along with all necessary details for an automobile.

Figure 5.25 runs the possible test cases and checks the right functioning of the software.

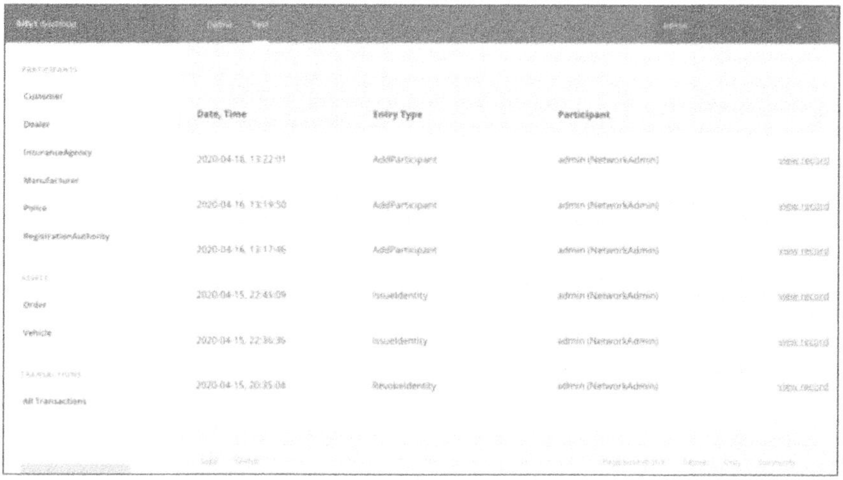

Figure 5.25 Process history.

Test Cases
To run the tests locally, we use a Docker file that builds our environment. The Docker file would be something like the following:

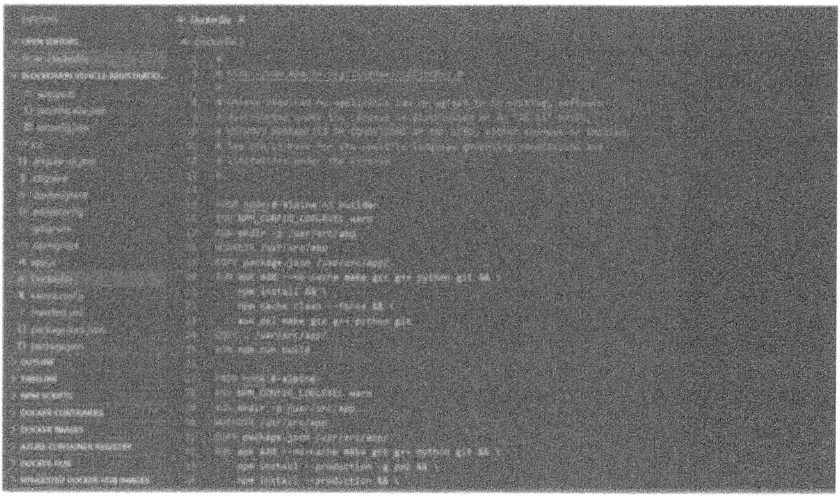

Figure 5.26 Docker file.

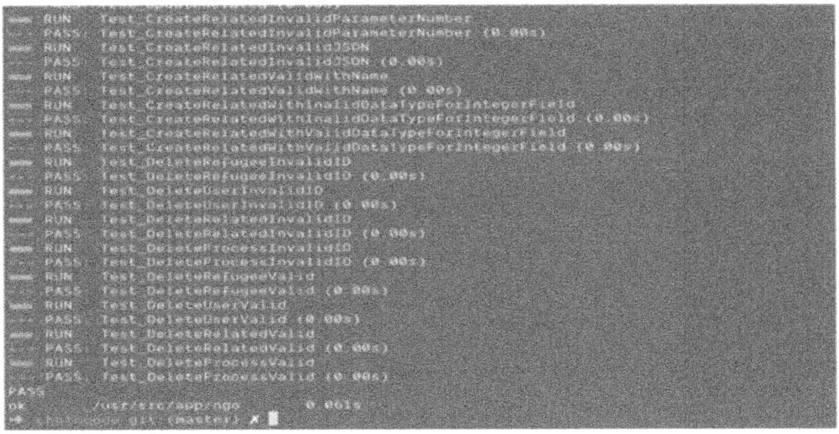

Figure 5.27 Test cases.

We will get a response like this if everything occurred nicely in Figure 5.27 after running all the test cases. The sample snippets are presented for the understanding of the readers.

5.7   Results and Discussions

DriveLoop enables all information to be accumulated into one place so that it can be easily accessed and managed. Vehicle registration, citations, insurance details, and everything else accruing to the vehicle in question are integrated on this platform. So, when you log in to find out something about one particular vehicle, what you will find is everything there is to know about it. A comprehensive, all-encompassing history is obtained. Anybody who is even remotely aware of the Blockchain technology will tell you how authentic it is.

It is structured in such a way that only authorized personnel can make entries or change records. Hence, there is no need to worry about any kind of tempering with the data or falsification of information.

From our research, we implemented the Blockchain technology to maintain trust, security, and clarity in the system. We used many technologies and one of the technologies is IoT, Ethereum. On the basis of latency of Blockchain, the throughput of Blockchain, and the accuracy of transactions, we tested our proposed idea.

For comparison with the existing state-of-the-art technologies, refer Table 5.1.

Table 5.1 Comparative analysis.

Carchain	DriveLoop (our application)
1 It is used to maintain the data for Rental cars.	1. It is an automated process for buying and selling of cars.
2. It uses the Ethereum platform.	2. It uses Hyperledger Fabric platform.
3. It is a public Blockchain.	3. It is a private Blockchain.

5.8   Novelty and Recommendations

Before we go on to talk about the problems of the process of vehicle registration, we first need to understand why vehicle registration is such an important aspect of automobile dealing. Car ownership of changes as many times as you can imagine. Whether you look at it in the terms of dealing in spare parts or in assembled vehicles, dealings by the middlemen or by the retailer who makes the final sale to a consumer, or in terms of the resale of a second-hand vehicle, there are a number of stakeholders who would very much want to know about all the history of the vehicle they are buying. Not to mention the insurance agencies, the police and other authorities, and, well, the government too needs to keep tabs on the automobiles for various reasons [9, 10].

The fact of the matter is that all these stakeholders need information about the vehicles, starting from its manufacturing story, covering its first sale, the accidents, if any, that it has been in, and any and all repairs and maintenance. This is crucial not just to maintain a track record of the vehicle in question to determine its market value but also for legal and insurance purposes [26].

The word automobile is derived from the Greek word auto which means "self" and the French word mobile which means "moving". The significance of automobile is as follows:

a)   The increase in the demand for automobiles such as cars and other vehicles increase the income of driver of the automobile industry.

b)   In this foster age, people need to reach destinations rapidly. So, automobiles help one over here and it became popular. With the help of automobile, people from all over the world can travel anywhere. Automobiles play a vital role in the country's socio-economic development.

c) There is also a worldwide sharing in automotive industry of cars, vehicles, parts, and accessories that ranges from 15% to 40% in US, South Korea, etc.

d) The automotive industry provides development of the taxable base and revenues of the state budget.

e) It also influences scientific and technical progress [11].

5.9 Future Research Directions

There is a huge transformation in the urban development in 21st century because of the advanced technologies and various services. Nowadays, research activities become common for growing smarter cities. Smart city is the demanding solution of sustainability and urbanization. Nowadays, corruption is common and mostly it is paid by the poor. It is like a cancer that eats away at a citizen's faith in the government. For example, smart cities may lead to injustice in the world where citizens or people are pushed to subaltern roles and it is regulated by technocratic governments. Increase in population in urban areas often leads to the problem of parking spaces and has been a big challenge for urban planners, architects, and administrators. So keeping all such views, an innovative solution is much more awaited and demanded [3].

There are few future remedies that can be carried out in this project.

a) We intend to add certain features like location detection through GPS and addition of some more services according to user requirements afterward.

b) We also intend to add an insurance party into our project.

c) We also intend to increase the scalability of this project worldwide, i.e., beyond our country [22, 23].

5.10 Limitations

The study was a good learning process and was a very satisfying experience. Yet there are several factors that limited this researchers' plan to study as every researcher desired limitations. Some are as follows:

a)   Access to documentation and information: The required data was not readily available. The process of documentation is not a continual practice.

b)   Automobile industry: Because of strict rules and many policies, the R&D and design executives are bound up in the automotive industry. Data sharing is very limited. To share the information openly and willingly is not considered good practice in the corporations.

5.11   Conclusions

The interesting parts, like fabricators, conventions, clients, and automobile agencies, can easily be facilitated for accrediting and updating the information of the vehicle in its secure function. The solution also guarantees that the information is more precise and completely sealed and transmits secure and economical form.

Performance Evaluation

a)   The performance of the service providers is based on ratings given to them by service users.

b)   The performance of the service users is based on ratings given to them by service providers.

c)   The performance of the overall website is based on feedback given to us by the users of the website.

d)   The reviews for the website will be taken from mentors, coordinators, and peers' students.

IoT, big data systems, and mobility are some of the services programmers of smart cities. Smart parking is the crucial parts of smart city. Connected automobile with its advanced technology reduces the chances of accident and help drivers save time and gasoline in their limits. More urban our planet becomes, smarter the cities have to be. In the coming days, due to the advanced technology, the smart cities would prone to the smarter cities.

References

1. Agarwal, A., Goel, D., Tyagi, A., Aggarwal, A., Rastogi, R., A Smarter Approach for Better Lifestyle in Indian Societies, in: *Progress in Advanced Computing and Intelligent Engineering., Advances in Intelligent Systems and Computing*, vol. 563, K. Saeed, N. Chaki, B. Pati, S. Bakshi, D. Mohapatra (Eds.), pp. 355–362, Springer, Singapore, February 2018, https://doi.org/10.1007/978-981-10-6872-0_33.

2. Aggarwal, S., Rastogi, R., Mittal, S., A Novel approach for Communication Among Blind Deaf and Dumb People, in: *Proceedings of 09th INDIACom; 2nd International Conference on Computing for Sustainable Global Development*, 11th–13th March, 2015, pp. 605–610, https://ieeexplore.ieee.org/abstract/document/7100321.

3. Arora, S., R., Goel, P., Maini, J., Mallick, P., Increasing Efficiency in Online Studies through Web Socket, in: *Proceedings of 3rd International Conference on Computing for Sustainable Global Development*, 16th–18th March, 2016, pp. 509–512, https://ieeexplore.ieee.org/document/7724316.

4. Goel, D., Agarwal, A., Rastogi, R., A Novel Approach for Residential Society Maintenance Problem for Better Human Life, in: *Communication and Power Engineering*, R. Rajesh and B. Mathivanan (Eds.), vol. 1, pp. 177–185, 2016a.

5. Goel, D., Agarwal, A., Rastogi, R., A Novel Approach for Residential Society Maintenance Problem for Better Human Life. *Int. J. Urban Design Ubiquitous Comput., IJUDUC*, 1–8, Sept.-2016b, affiliated to the National Library of Australia, Global Vision School Publication, Sandy Bay, Tasmania, Australia, 4.

6. Gupta, R., Rastogi, R., Singh, A., A novel approach for vehicle tracking system for trafficjam problem, in: *Proceedings of 09th INDIACom; 2nd International Conference on Computing for Sustainable Global Development*, 11th–13th March, 2015a, pp. 169–174, https://ieeexplore.ieee.org/document/7100240.

7. Gupta, R., Rastogi, R., Mondal, P., Aggarwal, K., G.A. Based Clustering of Mixed Data Type of Attributes (Numeric, Categorical, Ordinal, Binary, Ratio-Scaled). *BIJIT*, 7, 2, 861–866, Jan-June 2014, http://bvicam.ac.in/bjit/issues.asp?issue=14.

8. Kaul, U., Rastogi, R., Agarwal, S., Sharma, P., Jain, S., A Novel D&C Approach for Efficient Fuzzy Unsupervised Classification for Mixed Variety of Data, in: *Emerging ICT for Bridging the Future- Proceedings of the 49th Annual Convention of the Computer Society of India, CSI Volume 2. Advances in Intelligent Systems and Computing*, vol. 338, Springer, Cham, pp. 553–563, 2015, https://doi.org/10.1007/978-3-319-13731-5_60, https://link.springer.com/chapter/10.1007/978-3-319-13731-5_60.

9. Khanna, A. and Anand, R., IoT based smart parking system, in: *International Conference on Internet of Things and Applications (IOTA)*, IEEE, pp. 266–270, 2016.

10. Mejri, N., Ayari, M., Langar, R., Kamoun, F., Pujolle, G., Saidane, L., Cooperation versus competition towards an efficient parking assignment solution. *IEEE International Conference on Communications (ICC)*, pp. 2915–2920, 2014.

11. Nigam, A., Rastogi, R., Mishra, R., Arya, P., Sharma, S., Security of Data Transmission Using Logic Gates and Crypt Analysis. *CSI Communication 17*, Delhi, India, June-2015, http://www.csi-india.org/communications/CSI%20 June15%20Combine.pdf.

12. Nigam, A., Rastogi, R., Mishra, R., Arya, P., Sharma, S., Security of data transmission using logic gates and crypt analysis. *proceedings of 09th INDIACom; 2015 2nd International Conference on Computing for Sustainable Global Development*, 11th–13th March, 2015, pp. 101–105, https://ieeexplore.ieee. org/document/7100229.

13. Pham, T.N., Tsai, M.-F., Nguyen, D.B., Dow, C.-R., Deng, D.-J., A cloud-based smart-parking system based on Internet-of-Things technologies. *IEEE Access*, 3, 1581–1591, 2015.

14. Pilkington, M., *Blockchain technology: principles and applications, Research handbook on digital transformations*, SSRN Elsevier, Germany, p. 225, 2016.

15. Rastogi, R., Aggarwal, K., Mondal, P., An exhaustive review for infix to postfix conversion with applications and benefits, in: *Proceedings of 09th INDIACom;2nd International Conference on Computing for Sustainable Global Development*, 11th – 13th March, 2015, pp. 95–100, https://ieeexplore.ieee.org/document/7100228.

16. Rastogi, R., Agarwal, S., Sharma, P., Kaul, U., Jain, S., Unsupervised Classification of Mixed Data Type of Attributes Using Genetic Algorithm (Numeric, Categorical, Ordinal, Binary, Ratio-Scaled), in: *Proceedings of the Third International Conference on Soft Computing for Problem Solving. Advances in Intelligent Systems and Computing*, M. Pant, K. Deep, A. Nagar, J. Bansal (Eds.), vol. 258, Springer, New Delhi, pp. 121–131, 2014, https://doi. org/10.1007/978-81-322-1771-8_11.

17. Rhodes, C., Blewitt, W., Sharp, C., Ushaw, G., Morgan, G., Smart routing: A novel application of collaborative path finding to smart parking systems, in: *CBI*, (1), pp. 119–126, 2014.

18. Rungta, S., Srivastava, S., Yadav, U.S., Rastogi, R., A Comparative Analysis of New Approach with an Existing Algorithm to Detect Cycles in a Directed Graph, in: *ICT and Critical Infrastructure: Proceedings of the 48th Annual Convention of Computer Society of India- Vol. II*, vol. 249, Advances in Intelligent Systems and Computing Springer, Cham, pp. 37–47, 2014, https:// doi.org/10.1007/978-3-319-03095-1_5.

19. Sharma, R., Jain, A., Rastogi, R., A New Face To Photo Security Of Facebook, in: *Proceedings of the Sixth International Conference on Contemporary Computing, Jointly Organized by Jaypee Institute of Information Technology & University of Florida, IC3*, Aug. 8–10, 2013, pp. 415–420, https://ieeexplore. ieee.org/document/6612231.

20. Sharma, S., Rastogi, R., Kumar, S., A revolutionary technology to help the differently abled person, in: *Proceedings of 09th INDIACom; 2nd International Conference on Computing for Sustainable Global Development*, 11th–13th March, 2015, pp. 622–624, https://ieeexplore.ieee.org/document/7100324.

21. Sharma, P., Rastogi, R., Aggarwal, S., Kaul, U., Jain, S., Business Analysis and Decision Making Through Unsupervised Classification of Mixed Data Type of Attributes Through Genetic Algorithm. *BIJIT*, 6, 1, 683–689, Jan.-June, 2014, Special Issue of BIJIT on Fuzzy Logic.http://bvicam.ac.in/bjit/issues.asp?issue=11, Indexed in DBLP, published by Springer.

22. Shekhar, S., Rastogi, R., Mittal, S., Linear algorithm for Imbricate Cryptography using Pseudo Random Number Generator, in: *Proceedings of 09th INDIACom, 2nd International Conference on Computing for Sustainable Global Development*, 11th–13th March, 2015, pp. 89–94, https://ieeexplore. ieee.org/document/7100227.

23. Srivatava, S., Rastogi, R., Rungta, S., Yadav, U., A Methodology to Find the Cycle in a Directed Graph Using Linked List. *BIJIT*, 6, 2, 743–749, July-December, 2014, http://bvicam.ac.in/bjit/issues.asp?issue=12, Indexed in DBLP, published by Springer.

24. Wood, G., Ethereum: A secure decentralized generalized transaction ledger, *Ethereum Project yellow paper*, github.com, Istanbul, Turkey, vol. 151, pp. 1–32, 2014.

25. Wu, H., Li, Z., King, B., Miled, Z.B., Wassick, J., Tazelaar, J., A distributed ledger for supply chain physical distribution visibility. *Information*, 8, 4, 137, 2017.

26. Zheng, Z., Xie, S., Dai, H., Wang, H., *Blockchain challenges and opportunities: A survey*, Work Pap, Inderscience, Geneva, Switzerland, pp. 23–29, 2016.

27. Zyskind, G., Nathan, O. *et al.*, Decentralizing Privacy: Using blockchain to protect personal data, in: *Security and Privacy Workshops (SPW)*, IEEE, pp. 180–184, 2015.

28. Kumar, A., Payal, M., Dixit, P., Chatterjee, J.M., Framework for Realization of Green Smart Cities Through the Internet of Things (IoT), in: *Trends in Cloud-based IoT*, pp. 85–111, 2020.

29. Son, L.H., Jha, S., Kumar, R., Chatterjee, J.M., Khari, M., Collaborative handshaking approaches between internet of computing and internet of things towards a smart world: a review from 2009–2017. *Telecommun. Syst.*, 70, 4, 617–634, 2019.

6

Designing of Fuzzy Controller for Adaptive Chair and Desk System

Puneet Kundra[1], Rashmi Vashisth[3]* and Ashwani Kumar Dubey[2]

[1]Instrumentation and Control Engineering, Amity Institute of Engineering and Technology, New Delhi, India
[2]Electronics and Communication Engineering, Amity University, Noida, Uttar Pradesh, India
[3]Electronics and Communication Engineering, Amity Institute of Engineering and Technology, New Delhi, India

Abstract

The purpose of the adaptive chair and desk is to maintain a correct posture for humans of different physical stature while sitting and using a computer system. The fuzzy controller is a precise and economical controller for controlling this type of system. Posture is a very important aspect of physical and mental health, and most of the time, humans are sitting in the wrong posture while using computer systems. Thus, an adaptive system is required which will automatically adjust the chair and the desk on which the computer is kept according to the height of the person who is using the computer at that moment. The art of controlling processes with a degree of autonomy is dependent upon the quality of the intelligent control system being used and the quality of the data or information provided to the control system.

Keywords: Fuzzy logic control, adaptive chair and table, correct posture

6.1 Introduction

The computer has become an integral part of human life: In recent years, electronic games, the home computer system (personal computers), and

---

*Corresponding author: rashmiapj@gmail.com

Vishal Kumar, Vishal Jain, Bharti Sharma, Jyotir Moy Chatterjee and Rakesh Shrestha (eds.) Smart City Infrastructure: The Blockchain Perspective, (163–184) © 2022 Scrivener Publishing LLC

work stations became an important and fundamental part of our lives, as most of the people are working on personal computers or work stations to earn a livelihood, gain knowledge, and information, acquire new skills and learn new technologies, carry out their research work, play computer games, having video conferencing, and carrying out their businesses online, thus spending a lot of their time sitting in front of computer screens [1]. Also, according to Nicole Fisher's article in Forbes, an average American adult spends 12 hours a day in front of computer screens [2]. Therefore, it is very important to maintain a proper posture while working or sitting in front of computer screens for such a long period.

Most of the time human beings tend to sit in a wrong manner due to poor habits, chair and body dimensions mismatch, and lack of awareness of correct posture and weak spine which leads to change in humans' posture continuously after sitting in one posture for quite some time. Further, sitting in the wrong posture leads to a decrease in the blood circulation to the brain, development of carpal tunnel syndrome, lower back pain, a decrease in digestion function, decreases in work efficiency, an increase in fatigue, and creating a sense of negative mood [3].

The list of demerits of sitting in the wrong posture is quite long; these demerits motivate for the development and design of a system that can calculate the correct posture for humans of different statures, so that correct posture is achieved without enormous efforts from the person who is using the computer. With the implementation of an adaptive chair and desk system, the user need not to remind himself again and again that he or she has to sit in the right posture and all the demerits of the sitting in the wrong posture can be avoided.

The user is only required to enter details of his or her physical stature and the system will automatically adapt to the ergonomically specified recommendations for that particular stature using an intelligent control system. In this system, the fuzzy logic controller is employed as it is the knowledge-based control system which is quite comprehended thanks to linguistic terms and well-structured If-Then fuzzy rules. Fuzzy logic control can also employ learning algorithms that it can adopt from other technologies like neural networks or genetic algorithms.

The fuzzy controller is well known for its abilities in automating various conventional systems and processes. It gained success in Japan for its use in home electronic appliances, consumer goods, and automation of various industrial plants. Fuzzy logic minimizes the requirement of human operators (unlike conventional controllers) as human operator's or process engineer's knowledge that he has gained by his experiences has been already embedded in the Fuzzy controller in the form of rules, thus providing a higher degree of automation as compared to other conventional controllers at a comparatively lower cost. These features and advantages make the fuzzy controller the most suitable controller for the automation of the chair and desk system.

The knowledge base is the feature of the Fuzzy controller which is the main reason behind the boosted success of the fuzzy logic controllers. Therefore, most accurate knowledge is required about the process or the system which is to be controlled. This knowledge base will lead us to a higher degree of automation and a robust control system. To satisfy this requirement in the adaptive chair and desk system, the knowledge base has been defined by the data harnessed from various sources like U.S. Army Personnel-Anthropometric surveys, furniture designer's datasheets, office furniture ergonomic records, National Center for Health Anthropometric Reference Data, and records showing the relation between furniture parameters and human body's dimensions.

This effort has been done to obtain the most accurate data by averaging all the records available for each parameter. Parameters are the variables that define the adaptive chair and desk system. These parameters are varied to adapt according to the body dimension of the person using the adaptive chair and the desk system (desk on which the computer system is placed), achieving a higher degree of automation, a common controller module for each adaptive chair and desk system, and to serve to a much wider audience.

6.2   Time Spent Sitting in Front of Computer Screen

Detail analysis for posture while using computers requires good estimates of time spent by adults and teenagers on computers, so as to justify the requirement of this type of adaptive system. Data used for analysis is obtained from the research paper [1]. The data in Table 6.1 shows the variation in terms of social class, gender, and age.

Data from National Statistics of America was quoted by Nicole Fisher in her article that an average American adult spends 12 hours a day in front of screens. Alysaa Cimino stated that Americans devote more than 10 hours a day to screen time in IST110: Introduction to Information Sciences and Technology.

All these above-stated information reflects that a lot of time of human adults and teenagers is spent in front of screens. Maintaining posture throughout these long-duration periods is very difficult due to unawareness of posture maintenance, weak spine, and poor support from the chair.

Table 6.1 Average screen time spent by different age groups and gender.

Weekly usage measure	Teenage boys	Teenage girls	Adults boys	Adults girls
Percent active per week	58	44	37	35
Number of Internet sessions	5.30	2.93	1.41	1.45
Hours online	4	1.51	0.82	0.57
Session length in minutes	37.98	30.83	33.54	28.13
Hours on e-mail	1.70	0.84	0.25	0.22
Percent online time using email	43	56	61	47
Unique website visited	11.17	3.89	4.34	1.93

This became the principal cause behind the idea of developing a system that could adapt to the dimension or body stature of the person and provides a comfortable position and a correct posture to the person, who is sitting on the chair and using the computer placed on the desk.

6.3   Posture

It is the position assumed by the body or the manner in which the body positions itself whether characteristic or for a special purpose. State or condition is adapted by the body in the given time especially with respect to capability in particular circumstances. During the corona pandemic, every individual is performing his/her job online sitting in front of computer screens, be it, students or adults. Meeting of company personnel, classes of students, research conferences, training, and coaching of new skills and technologies have taken place using computers and the internet while sitting at home [3].

This adaptive system is all about maintaining the correct procedure while the person is sitting and working on the computer. It is a difficult task to constantly focus on your body posture while working or performing your job. An improperly constructed chair that was not designed considering the ergonomics leads to poor postural problems and week spine. This cannot be corrected easily as constant monitoring self posture is not possible. So, an adaptive chair and desk system is required which could adapt to the person's stature and automatically provides an ergonomic setup so a comfortable position with a perfect posture could be obtained.

6.3.1 Need for Correct Posture

- Reduction in pelvic pain.
- Increased efficiency at work due to better energy levels.
- Fewer tensions felt in the shoulders and neck due to less pressure on inner muscles.
- Risk of abnormal wearing of joint surface decreases.
- Increased lung capacity, thus better breathing.
- A sense of positivity.
- Improved circulation and digestion [3, 4].

6.3.2 Causes of Sitting in the Wrong Posture

- Mismatch of dimensions: Lack of proper fitting chair according to human stature.
- Poor postural habits: People do not maintain a correct posture and later on it becomes their habit.
- Psychological factors: Due to low self-esteem, humans tend to lose his or her posture.
- Awareness: People do not know the need to correct posture.
- Inflexible muscles: The range of the motion is affected.
- Muscle strength: The balance of the body gets affected.
- Lack of posture [4].

6.4 Designing of Ergonomic Seat

At an average 12 hours in a day is spent by Americans while sitting and most of them hate it doing but just do it for the sake of earning a livelihood. Thus, ergonomic chairs are required for a sitting so that workers can sit without pain. As ergonomic chairs are designed for providing immense comfort and help in increasing the efficiency of the person while performing a task [5, 6].

6.4.1   Considerate Factors of an Ergonomic Chair and Desk System

- **The Stature of the Person:** It is the input variable in this adaptive system, and the most important factor as the rest of the specifications is depending upon the stature only. All the adaptive measures are taken in respect of stature only [7, 8].
- **Seat Height Adjustment:** Stature varies from person to person, and thus, it plays a keen role in the designing of ergonomic chair which can adapt to persons of different statures. The criteria for obtaining an appropriate seat height depend upon popliteal height, the angle between thighs, and knee to toe, and for obtaining correct measurements, the knees should be kept lower as compared to hips level, while the feet should be placed flat on the ground [7, 9].
- **Seat Depth Adjustment:** As stature varies from person to person, the buttock to political length also varies from person to person. So, the seat depth is controlled as it provides a proper base to the person sitting on the chair and allows for a proper posture. The depth of the seat is obtained by maintaining 1 to 5 inches between the back of the person's knee and the seat's front edge. For this parameter, sinusoidal membership function has been used and data for this function was taken from US Army Personnel—Anthropometric Survey 1988 [8, 9].
- **Desk Height Adjustment:** Desk is the place where the computer is been kept on. So, the proper height of the desk depending upon stature is very important for posture maintenance and to prevent eye strain, headache, and pain. Standards have been defined for obtaining desk height for a particular height of a person [10, 11].
- **Swivel Base:** It provides the ability to turnaround while seating on the chair.
- **Armrest Height Adjustment:** This allows a proper position of armrest according to the person's stature, so as to provide optimum comfort and maintaining shoulders in a correct posture, thus avoiding pain due to pressure at shoulder level. It should be at level with the desk's height, as the person requires arms to keep on the armrest in such a way that hands can be appropriately placed on the keyboard so that arms and hands do not feel any kind of strain [12, 13].

- **Sitting Eye Height:** It is defined to provide an optimum view to the person depending upon the stature of that particular person. This will help in increasing the efficiency of the person and prevent eye strain [14, 15].

All the above explained parameters have been graphically shown in Figure 6.1. The data are shown in Table 6.2 is obtained by averaging data obtained by various research papers of ergonomics and various furniture

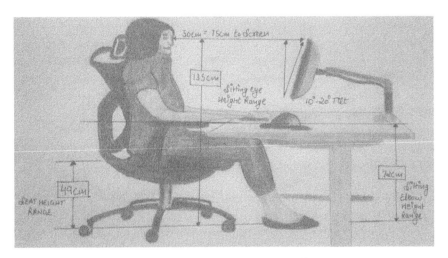

Figure 6.1 Parameters that are controlled by the fuzzy controller.

Table 6.2 Data of different parameters with respect to height of the person.

S. no.	Height of the person (cm)	Armrest height (cm)	Eye level height (cm)	Desk's height (cm)	Chair's height (cm)
1	130	19	100.5	52	35
2	140	21	103	56	38
3	150	22	106	60	40
4	160	24	110	65	43
5	170	25	118	69	46
6	180	27	126.5	73	48
7	190	28	135.5	77	52

companies that have designed the algorithms and created calculators for calculating appropriate position [7, 8, 11–16].

6.5   Fuzzy Control Designing

The chair and desk adaptive system works on the fundamental principle of fuzzy logic. Lotfia Zadeh has elaborated on the fundamentals of fuzzy logic [17]. He defined fuzzy logic as a method of filtering data by defining membership set instead of non-membership sets and observed that a fuzzy set induces a possibility distribution on the universe of discourse [18]. It was designed for representing and reasoning with some particular form of knowledge. The knowledge is expressed in a linguistic form and the whole process is operationally powerful; thus, computers are required for the processing [19].

The principle design specification of FKBC includes fuzzification, scaling factors, defuzzification membership function, and denormalization of the data with respect to rule base and data base [20].

The fuzzy controller's uniqueness is defined by the type of dataset upon which fuzzy controller logic is applied. It uses fuzzy sets formed by grouping data based on the relational function of each element of the fuzzy set which is termed as membership function. This membership function's value is always between 0 and 1 depending upon the degree of relation [21]. It is unlike conventional controllers that use crisp data values for their functioning.

Crisp input values are provided then normalization or scaling is done for the process of fuzzification which converts crisp values into fuzzy sets on the basis of the rule base.

The main aim is to adapt various parameters of chair and table as per the stature of the person, and this process is done with the help of fuzzy logic controller the parameters that help in correcting the posture of the person can be adjusted by entering the stature of the person. As various proportionality factors have been developed to find appropriate values for chair height, desk height, armrest height, seat depth using the height of the person, and various equations to find appropriate output values. The fuzzy logic decides at a certain period of time and produced different commands according to different inputs. In the below block diagram, a simple fuzzy logic system has been described for controlling seat parameters. Figure 6.2 shows the implementation of fuzzy logic controller for the ACD system and in Figure 6.3 block diagram representation of the system has been shown.

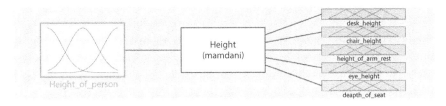

Figure 6.2 Input/output block in fuzzy logic control for adaptive chair and desk system.

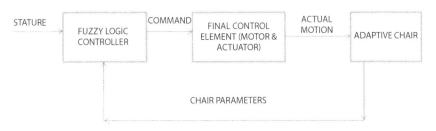

Figure 6.3 Block diagram of the fuzzy logic controller.

6.5.1   Fuzzy Logic Controller Algorithm [20]

Algorithm of the fuzzy controller with which it can adapt to the changing environment is shown in the Table 6.3.

Table 6.3 Algorithm of fuzzy logic controller.

S. no.	Processes involved
1	Linguistic variable definition
2	Membership function creation
3	Rule base definition
4	Conversion of crisp non-fuzzy values to fuzzy values on the basis of the membership function definition
5	Evaluating the rules
6	Combination of the results corresponding to a particular rule
7	Defuzzification, i.e., conversion of fuzzy values to crisp values

6.5.2   Fuzzy Membership Functions

Membership functions play a vital role in the process of fuzzification and defuzzification. Membership functions help in creating a relation between the crisp input values and fuzzy linguistic variables or terms [21]. It helps the controller to make precise decisions on the basis of appropriate crisp values provided as input.

In this process, real crisp values are translated into fuzzy values. After these translations, the possible outcomes are called linguistic terms. Membership functions make the fuzzy logic an adaptive and efficient learning controller [19].

Figures 6.4 to 6.8 and Tables 6.4 to 6.8 show the description of all the membership functions used in this system.

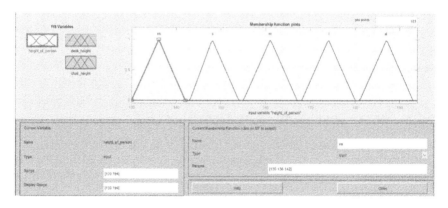

Figure 6.4 Membership function for the height of the person.

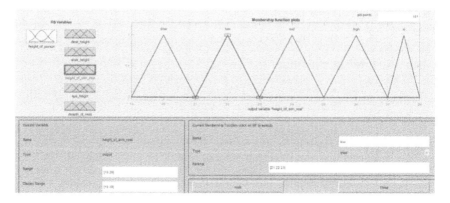

Figure 6.5 Membership function for the chair's height.

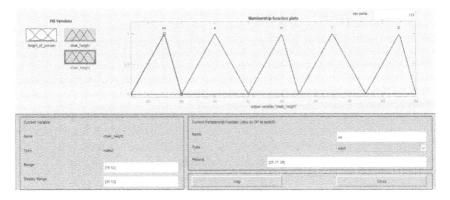

Figure 6.6 Membership function for the armrest height.

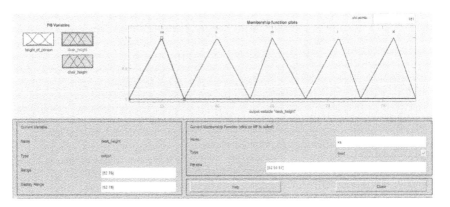

Figure 6.7 Membership function for the desk height.

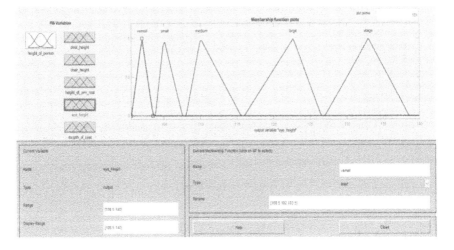

Figure 6.8 Membership function for the eye height level.

6.5.3   Rule Base

Once fuzzification is done, the next step is to make a decision or deciding what command or action is required to be taken for optimum manipulations to adapt to the varying stature of the person. The definition of rules is given by the "IF "and "THEN" approach [19].

The situation is depicted by the IF part is known as rule antecedent and the resulting reaction is defined by the THEN part which is known as the

Table 6.4 Membership function for the height of the person.

1	130 to 142	Extra Small (XS)
2	143 to 155	Small (S)
3	156 to 168	Medium (M)
4	169 to 181	Large (L)
5	182 to 194	Extra Large (XL)

Table 6.5 Membership function for the chair height.

S. no.	Crisp values for chair height (output)	Fuzzy linguistic value set
1	35 to 38	Extra Small (XS)
2	38 to 42	Small (S)
3	62 to 45	Medium (M)
4	45 to 49	Large (L)
5	49 to 52	Extra Large (XL)

Table 6.6 Membership function for the armrest height.

S. no.	Crisp values for armrest height	Fuzzy linguistic value set
1	19 to 21	Extra Small (XS)
2	22 to 23	Small (S)
3	23 to 25	Medium (M)
4	25 to 27	Large (L)
5	27 to 28	Extra Large (XL)

Table 6.7 Membership function for the desk height.

S. no.	Crisp values for desk height (cm)	Fuzzy linguistic value set
1	52 to 57	Extra Small (XS)
2	57 to 63	Small (S)
3	43 to 68	Medium (M)
4	68 to 73	Large (L)
5	73 to 78	Extra Large (XL)

Table 6.8 Membership function for the eye height level.

S. no.	Crisp values for eye height level	Fuzzy linguistic value set
1	100.5 to 103.5	Extra Small (XS)
2	103.5 to 107.5	Small (S)
3	107.5 to 115.5	Medium (M)
4	115.5 to 126.5	Large (L)
5	126.5 to 138.5	Extra Large (XL)

Table 6.9 Rule base for the adaptive chair and desk system.

S. no.	Fuzzy rules for the system
1	If (height_of_person is xs), then (desk_height is xs) (chair_height is xs)(height_of_arm_rest is vlow)(eye_height is vsmall)(deapth_of_seat is xs)
2	If (height_of_person is s), then (desk_height is s)(chair_height is s) (height_of_arm_rest is low)(eye_height is small)(deapth_of_seat is s)
3	If (height_of_person is m), then (desk_height is m)(chair_height is m)(height_of_arm_rest is mid)(eye_height is medium)(deapth_of_seat is MID)
4	If (height_of_person is l), then (desk_height is l)(chair_height is l) (height_of_arm_rest is high)(eye_height is large)(deapth_of_seat is l)
5	If (height_of_person is xl), then (desk_height is xl)(chair_height is xl)(height_of_arm_rest is xl)(eye_height is vlarge)(deapth_of_seat is XL)

rule consequent part. The Rule Base is the part of the knowledge block, which includes the knowledge base and rule base [22].

The rule base is present in the knowledge base. These If-Then statements are saved as fuzzy prepositions and whenever the controller finds an input similar to the antecedent part, it chooses the corresponding consequent part of the rule [23]. Table 6.9 shows the rule base used for the optimization of the adaptive chair and desk system.

6.5.4   Why Fuzzy Controller?

- Fuzzy controller is a real-time controlling mechanism in which employees process engineer's or human operator's knowledge, which he has obtained by his experiences [24]. This knowledge is implemented in terms of rules or situations and is not expressed easily in terms of differential equations or conventional controller parameters [22].
- In an adaptive chair and desk system, knowledge about various parameters on which the functioning of the system depends was available in abundance [25], thus fuzzy logic controller became the appropriate choice in comparison with other controllers because the whole process could be controlled with a few linguistic rules and provides a fast and real-time response.
- The fuzzy controller has attained a boosted success in controlling small, micro-controller bassed white goods and household appliances [23].
- The fuzzy logic controller is comprehensible due to its well structured If-Then rules and linguistic values and variables [22, 26]. This feature helps a lot in the controller designing process as the designer can easily understand the functioning of the controller unlike neural networks [27].
- Fuzzy logic due to its intellectual linguistic rules can be married to neural networks to form neuro-fuzzy (N-F) networks. N-F networks have both the intellectual linguistic structure and learning capabilities [28, 29].
- Genetic algorithms can also be used in conjugation for searching and optimization purposes [30].
- Fuzzy logic controller focuses on the state transitioning situations in a system that is under control rather than the processes involved in the system [30]. This became the major reason for its selection as a controller in the adaptive chair and control system, as in this system, the controller is

required to primarily concentrate on adapting to the body dimension which varies from person to person.

- In the mind of people of European countries and Japan, the name "fuzzy controlled" has positive sentiments attached with it; hence, a sense of security, safety, and longevity with respect to the product are observed in people while buying and using fuzzy controlled goods [31].

- Fuzzy controllers provide robust systems, as the controller mechanism can identify noises and prevents it from affecting the performance of the system [32].

- Designing and maintenance time is considerably less than other controllers due to the presence of two abstracted levels and both having linguistic terms that are understandable to the designers and also to the process engineer [33], thus saving time and money as the communication gap between control designers and process engineers is negligible thanks to the linguistic rules and values.

6.6 Result of Chair and Desk Control

The surface diagram of each parameter with respect to the height of the person is shown in Figures from 6.9 to 6.12. The height of the person in the case study is as follows:

Input:

Height of person = 182 cm
Membership function used = Extra Large (XL)

Output:

Membership function equiped = Extra Large
Height of chair = 50.5 cm
Height of desk= 75.5 cm
Height of arm rest = 27.5 cm
Height of eye level = 133 cm
Width of seat =44 cm

These outputs are shown in Figure 6.13.

6.7 Conclusions and Further Improvements

- In this paper, the fuzzy controller was trained to work similarly to the modernized chair and desk which can adapt

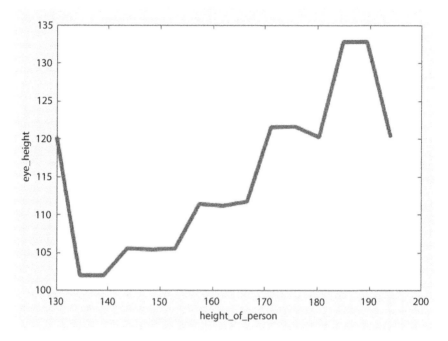

Figure 6.9 Surface view of eye height level.

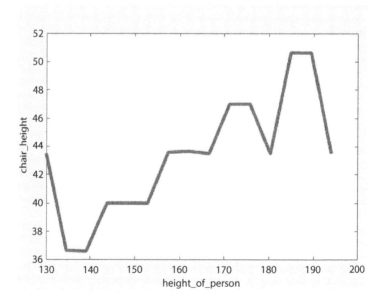

Figure 6.10 Surface view of chair's height.

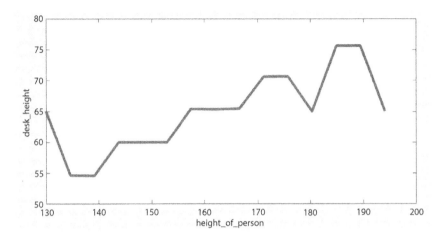

Figure 6.11 Surface view of desk height.

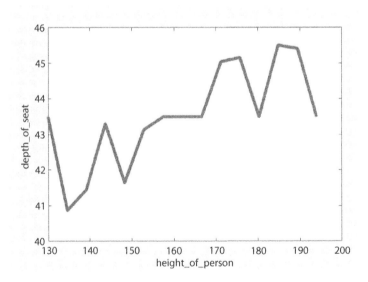

Figure 6.12 Surface view of seat depth.

according to the stature of the person who is currently occupying the chair and using the computer system which has been kept on the desk. Membership function plays an important role in a fuzzy control system; accurate and detailed membership functions help in reducing errors in the final trained model of the system.

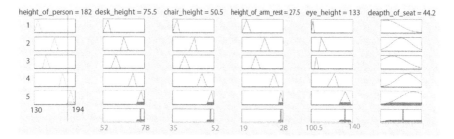

Figure 6.13 Rule view of the complete adaptive system, showing results for the person height (input) = 182 cm.

- Adaptive chair and desk systems are important for work-places because people of different statures use similar work station setups [34].
- The fuzzy controller is an intelligent controller and it works more efficiently as compared to conventional controllers due to the presence of fuzzification of inputs and outputs which allows the system to work upon complex functions and controller keeps adapting according to the ever-changing environment.
- The learning process of the adaptive system can be made continuous by encouraging users to enter the feedback after using the adaptive chair and desk system [31]. This feedback can be used for learning using N-F networks [32], thus improving the system throughout its life and providing the benefits of this system to a wider audience.
- Memory features can also be integrated into this system, similar to that of automobile seats, [35] which will enable the users to use this setup without providing inputs again and again rather they can simply assign a number to a user, and the system will remember the settings related to the user number.
- The performance of the fuzzy logic controller in the adaptive chair and desk system is quite accurate but not perfect.
- The main reason behind some cases of failure in this adaptive system is that the length of human body parts varies in humans. For example, buttock_ popliteal length may vary in two humans even if those two humans have the same stature.
- Demerits of the wrong posture could be corrected using adaptive chairs which works upon the data collected from

various surveys to find an appropriate table and chair height for people of different heights. Awareness of correct posture should be made so that people can inherently improve their postures.

- People should try to decrease their on-screen times as it is increasing at an alarming rate, and it is hazardous for personal health and mental hygiene and for the whole society.
- This work can even be extended to cars, buses, and trucks for obtaining correct postures for drivers, i.e., adaptive driving seats, designing ergonomic driving seats for pregnant women.
- In this research paper, we have come to a conclusion that the automatic system works quite well, but still, manual adjustment options should be provided, as sometimes, the automatic system may adjust the chair in a way that user could find the position to be too upright and the lengths of body parts varies even if stature is similar.

References

1. Subrahmanyam, K., Greenfield, P., Kraut, R., Gross, E., The impact of computer use on children's and adolescents' development. *J. Appl. Dev. Psychol.*, 22, 1, 7–30, 2001, https://doi.org/10.1016/S0193-3973(00)00063-0.

2. Roberts, N., How Much Time AmericansSpend In Front Of Screens Will Terrify You, Forbes Media, Washington Blvd, Jersey City, NJ 2019, January, https://www.forbes.com/sites/nicolefisher/2019/01/24/how-much-time-americans-spend-in-front-of-screens-will-terrify-you/?sh=2143793a1c67.

3. BURT, *Chiropractic Care and Correction of a Bad Posture*, United States, Burt Chiropractic Rehabilitation Center, San Leandro, CA, 2016, http://www.burtchiropractic.com/2016/03/08/chiropractic-care-and-bad-posture/.

4. Healthbeat., *Why good posture matters*, Boston, MA, United States, pp. 1–2, Harvard Health, 2018, https://www.health.harvard.edu/staying-healthy/why-good-posture-matters.

5. Mitchell, K.B., Choi, H.J., Garlie, T.N., *Anthropometry and range of motion of the encumbered soldier*, U.S. Army Natick Soldier Research, Development and Engineering Center Natick, Massachusetts, 2017, April 2012.

6. Saba, B., Yesus, G.G.G., Singh, A.P., Woyessa, G.K., Seid, S., Ergonomics Assessment of Passenger Seats of Minibuses in Ethiopia. *Global J. Res. Eng. Ind. Eng.*, 13, 1, 7, 2013.

7. humanSolution., *Ergonomic Office Desk, Ergonomic Chair, and Keyboard Height Calculator*, n.d., Human Solution & Uplift Desk Showroom (Office

Furniture), Austin, TX https://www.thehumansolution.com/ergonomic-office-desk-ergonomic-chair-and-keyboard-height-calculator/.

8. Ismaila, S.O. and Akanbi, O.G., Relationship between Standing Height and Popliteal Height. *International Conference on Industrial Engineering and Operations Management, 2008–2011*, 2012.

9. LifeSpan., *Treadmill Desk and Standing Desk Ergonomics*, Lifespan US, 2014, https://www.lifespanfitness.com/workplace/resources/articles/treadmill-desk-ergonomics.

10. Fryar, C.D., Gu, Q., Ogden, C.L., Flegal, K.M., Anthropometric Reference Data for Children and Adults: United States, 2011-2014. *Vital Health Stat. Ser. 3*, Analytical Studies, 39, 1–46, 2016.

11. Fryar, C.D.C., Gu, Q., Ogden, C.L., Flegal, K.M., McDowell, M.A., Fryar, C.D.C., Ogden, C.L., Flegal, K.M., Anthropometric Reference Data for Children and Adults: United States. *Vital Health Stat.*, 11, 251, 2007–2010, 2010, http://www.ncbi.nlm.nih.gov/pubmed/19642512%0Ahttp://www.ncbi.nlm.nih.gov/pubmed/25585443%0Ahttp://www.ncbi.nlm.nih.gov/pubmed/28437242%0Ahttp://www.cdc.gov/nchs/data/series/sr_11/sr11_252.pdf.

12. Tr-, N., Gordon, C.C., Mcconville, J.T., Tebbetts, I., Walker, R.a., Anthropometric Survey Of U.S. Army Personnel, in: *INC. Yellow Springs*, United States Army Natick Research, Development and Engineering Center, Natick, Massachusetts, 1988.

13. Flexispot, Ergonomic Calculator, FLEXISPOT US, Livermore, CA, https://www.flexispot.com/ergonomic-calculator.

14. Baharampour, S., Nazari, J., Dianat, I., Asgharijafarabadi, M., Student's Body Dimensions in Relation to Classroom Furniture. *Health Promot. Perspect.*, 3, 2, 165–174, 2013, https://doi.org/10.5681/hpp.2013.020.

15. Kim, D., Cho, M., Park, Y., Yang, Y., Effect of an exercise program for posture correction on musculoskeletal pain. *J. Phys. Ther. Sci.*, 27, 6, 1791–1794, 2015, https://doi.org/10.1589/jpts.27.1791.

16. Ansari, S., Nikpay, A., Varmazyar, S., Design and Development of an Ergonomic Chair for Students in Educational Settings. *Health Scope*, In Press (In Press), 7, 4, 2018, https://doi.org/10.5812/jhealthscope.60531.

17. Zadeh, L.A., Fuzzy Sets. *Sci. Direct*, 8, 3, 33–353, 1965, https://doi.org/10.1016/S0019-9958(68)90211-8.

18. Driankov, D., Hellendoorn, H., Reinfrank, M., *An Introduction to Fuzzy Control*, NAROSA PUBLISHING HOUSE, Delhi Medical Association Road Daryaganj, New Delhi, India, 1996.

19. Braae, M. and Rutherford, D.A., Theoretical and linguistic aspects of the fuzzy logic controller. *Automatica*, 15, 5, 553–577, 1979, https://doi.org/10.1016/0005-1098(79)90005-0.

20. Zadeh, L.A., Fuzzy algorithms. *Inf. Control*, 12, 2, 94–102, 1968, https://doi.org/10.1016/S0019-9958(68)90211-8.

21. Klir, G. and Yuan, B., *Fuzzy Sets and Fuzzy Logic:Theory and Applications*, Pearson, Hudson in New York City, New York, 1995.

22. Bernard, J.A., *Fuzzy Sets and Fuzzy Logic:Theory and Applications*, The Springer International Series in Engineering and Computer Science book series (SECS, volume 457) Springer Nature Switzerland AG, 1988.

23. Ciliz, K., Frei, J., Isik, C., Practical Aspects of the Knowledge-based control of a mobile robot motion. *30th Midwest Symp. on Circuits and Systems*, 1987.

24. Yen, J. and Reza, L., *Fuzzy Logic: Intelligence, Control, and Information*, Pearson, Hudson in New York City, New York, 1999.

25. Omron, *Fuzzy Guide Book*, Omron Publishing, OMRON Corporation Industrial Automation Company Heita Nada Shiokoji Horikawa Kyoto, Japan, 1992.

26. Zimmermann, H.-J., Fuzzy Set Theory—and Its Applications, in: *Fuzzy Set Theory—and Its Applications*, 2001, https://doi.org/10.1007/978-94-010-0646-0

27. Ogata, K., Modern control engineering, in: *Modern Control Engineering*, Prentice-Hall of India, Rimjhim House, Patparganj Industrial Estate, Delhi - India, 1977, https://doi.org/10.1201/9781315214573.

28. IEEE Transactions on Systems, Man, and Cybernetics Fuzzy_Logic_Control_Systems_II_Lee_1990.pdf, 20, 2, 1990.

29. Maiers, J. and Sherif, Y.S., Applications of fuzzy set theory. *IEEE Trans. Syst., Man, Cybern.*, SMC-15, 1, 175–189, Jan.-Feb. 1985.

30. Chai, Y., Jia, L., Zhang, Z., Mamdani model based adaptive neural fuzzy inference system and its application in traffic level of service evaluation. *6th International Conference on Fuzzy Systems and Knowledge Discovery, FSKD 2009, 4*, January 2009, pp. 555–559, 2009, https://doi.org/10.1109/FSKD.2009.76.

31. Guiffrida, A.L. and Nagi, R., Fuzzy set theory applications in production management research: A literature survey. *J. Intell. Manuf.*, 9, 1, 39–56, 1998, https://doi.org/10.1023/A:1008847308326.

32. Li, X. and Huang, T., Adaptive synchronization for fuzzy inertial complex-valued neural networks with state-dependent coefficients and mixed delays. *Fuzzy Sets Syst.*, 2020, https://doi.org/10.1016/j.fss.2020.05.013.

33. Mirzal, A., Approximation and Compensation of Delay in Analog Control Plant. *June, Proc. Japan Society for Precision Engineering*, Sapporo, Japan, 2015.

34. Taifa, I.W. and Desai, D.A., Anthropometric measurements for ergonomic design of students' furniture in India. *Eng. Sci. Technol., Int. J.*, 20, 1, 232–239, 2017, https://doi.org/10.1016/j.jestch.2016.08.004.

35. Berenji, H.R., Fuzzy Logic and Neural Networks for Control Systems. *IEEE, Educ. Act., Vis. Mater.*, 3, 5, 1992.

7

Blockchain Technology Dislocates Traditional Practice Through Cost Cutting in International Commodity Exchange

Arya Kumar

KIIT School of Commerce and Economics, Kalinga Institute of Industrial Technology, Deemed to be University, Bhubaneswar, Odisha, India

Abstract

A Blockchain is a ledger that exists digitally and can be easily traceable by any public or private body. The records of all the transactions are being maintained through cryptography that is distributed through computer networks worldwide. The present paper considers the soybeans trading from the Indian export market, i.e., Madhya Pradesh to Brazil FOB. The result provides that this technology brings down the cost by 3.2% and a further reduction of 38% in total cost that includes the time for transit and documentation per bushel of soybeans. Detailed analysis of risk factors through value-at-risk models suggests a reduction of 2.9% per bushel of Soybeans. This result might not be significant for any financial sector but for the agro-business; these amounts of reduction impact a large for the farmers and other stakeholders by implementing the technology of Blockchain in international commodity trading.

Keywords: Blockchain technology, commodity trading, international agro trading, soybeans

7.1 Introduction

The most distinctive trading activity is the agricultural food products because of its nature of perishability. This nature brings an earnest practice

Email: aryantripathy@yahoo.com
ORCID-0000-0002-8203-361X

Vishal Kumar, Vishal Jain, Bharti Sharma, Jyotir Moy Chatterjee and Rakesh Shrestha (eds.) Smart City Infrastructure: The Blockchain Perspective, (185–204) © 2022 Scrivener Publishing LLC

in maintaining the smooth flow of the supply chain, i.e., farm to market. When this exercise is implemented in international trading, this tends to be more difficult due to several documents, strict transactions, bulk operations, banking, and international trade approvals, that not only raise the cost but also the price of the commodity.

The agro-food product always follows three distinctive conceptions that are efficiency, transparency, and traceability. Among these three the primary need is maintaining the transparency of the product movements. Many customers feel safe and secured to know details about the products, i.e., how they are being transported, whether the commodities are still in better condition what documents are maintained in the process and the important is the source of origin. In absence of such the movement of products decelerates from days to weeks and it gets tough to get the information about the origin of the products and the chain that the product is experiencing [1]. Apart from this issue, the major issue in today's practice is the certificate of phytosanitary and certain similar form of a certificate that needs due approval from the origin country. The first company that used the Blockchain technique to electronically tracking of its shipments was the Maersk by using the customer process [1]. The most usable platform for Blockchain was for oil and energy trading that needs a systematic tracking due to the huge amount of trading [2]; now, this is also used during the trading of grains (as discussed below).

The second most important content is the traceability of the commodity, i.e., updating about the food products that whether it contains any contamination since from the origination. For instance, in the United States, nearly five deaths cases and nearly 200 illnesses were recorded in April 2018, and it was confirmed due to the presence of romaine lettuce in the food products [3]. This issue could have identified, but due to improper tracking, the Centre for Disease Control and Prevention able to confirm after several weeks of this mishap that the origin was from a farm of Yuma, i.e., from Arizona [4].

The last important element was maintaining the efficiency in wastage or spoilage of food products until it is delivered to the end user. So, any activities that are imperfect during international trading may detour the movement of the shipments or reject the partial documents that, in return, cause a huge financial and time loss.

The suitable way for dealing with all the above three challenges in a single effort is the implementation of Blockchain technology. This technique allows the digitization of all kinds of ledger, bills, and documents that can be viewed at any time all over the world no matter it is an individual, organization, and public or private firm. This document follows cryptography to maintain all transactions by following the computer network that avoids any alterations [5]. The supply chain consists of a wide range of parties, i.e., buyers; entities or traders that get the opportunity of understanding the commodities characteristics through Blockchain technology. Blockchain technology can be a blessing for all the participants, i.e., farmers, the national buyer, any intermediaries, the authority of export, the bankers, the importers, and the final users (the soybean crushers' that extracts the soy oil).

In this trend, many large participants tried to experience the benefits of Blockchain technology in various fields. For instance, a Blockchain Food Safety Alliance was formed under the collaborations of Walmart, IBM, Jingdong, and Tsinghua University to bring transparency in the movement of the agricultural supply chain [6]. In recent days the Blockchain is about to automate the post-trade process for agro products, i.e., oilseeds and grains under the guidance of Archer Daniels Midland, Bunge, Cargill, and Louis Dreyfus Co. [7, 8]. Latter on, one of the largest companies of food and agriculture, i.e., COFCO International joined in the group and develops the platform of Blockchain [9].

A great change was experienced by [10] where Mercuria Energy Group and Macro Dunand used to spend minimum forty days in transferring the documents from Africa to China and due to the use of Blockchain technology; it only needs four days that, in return, helped in saving a large number of costs.

The present paper considers the advantage of using Blockchain technology for agricultural products mainly the soybean for international trading. The present study highlights the inefficient and costly affairs international supply chain process where the exporters are the seller of agro products of India and the importer are the foreign countries. A comparison is made between the documentation maintained for the supply chain in the traditional form of commodity trading and between the Blockchain technologies. The present study makes an effort to understand the effect of Blockchain technology by considering a hypothesized soybean shipment from Madhya Pradesh, India, to Brazil FOB by implementing the Monte Carlo technique. Lastly, it includes other application of Blockchain technology in the food industry.

7.1.1 Maintenance of Documents of Supply Chain in Commodity Trading

The practice of digitization development in commodity trading has increased work performance and cost reduction by 26% which is the most significant growth in performance and cost reduction for oil and grains trading [10].

The development is not so significant in comparison to other equities or commodities due to Blockchain technology but this has developed the motive behind the growth of this method in the oil and energy sector slowly.

This particular part of the study focuses on the traditional international trade from the point of origin, i.e., A, and the point of consumption, i.e., B, that follows a lot of time, cost, documents, certificates, clearance, and etc., that are tracked by the banks and various authorizing agencies at very next steps. For instance, if a farmer sells its goods on an international platform, then they need a certificate or clearance to sell, the banks, the financial institutions, and further the government office bearers for smooth flow of the commodity.

Figure 7.1 demonstrates the traditional flow of commodities from the farmers of India to any other country. However, the present content illustrates the domestic channel but the main discussion of the paper revolves with international trading.

In Figure 7.1, it is sufficient enough to describe how the farmer follows various stages before trading the goods at an international platform. Primarily, the farmers store their grains or commodity in local storage or

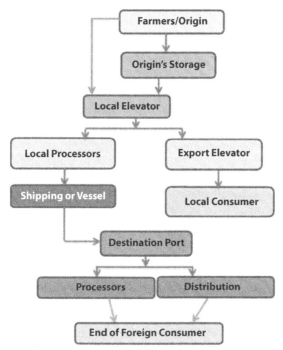

Figure 7.1 Traditional pattern of commodity flow from domestic to international platform. *(Source: Author's Creation).*

transfer the same to local elevators after cultivation. After that, the farmer starts trading the same as per the demand of the foreign markets or the agro firms, i.e., the export elevators contact the local elevators with a price quotation. If the price is found to be suitable, then the contract for the transaction settles between the export elevator and the local elevator. As the contract is settled the goods are transferred from local to the export elevator through barge or rails. Then, the commodities are either shipped or stored in a vessel for delivery as per the contract between the parties.

The contract terms may contain any one of the following, i.e., cost, insurance, and freight (CIF); cost and freight (CF); or freight on board (FOB) (see Table 7.1). As the commodity reaches the port, then it is immediately forwarded to the point of destination, i.e., to the end users of the foreign country via the local distribution centers or through the processors.

The above categories of contract define the payment option that is supposed to pay the said amount along with the shipping cost from point of the port. Table 7.1 depicts the structure of such a payment option where the contract between buyer and seller is based on the FOB and then the seller is responsible for all payment and fees till the point of loading and rest will be borne by the buyer to collect the same. In case the contract is of CIF or CF, then the seller is responsible for all the payment that includes transportation and marine insurance for the commodity.

In any foreign trade, the buyer and seller agree to settle the transaction by following certain modes of payment, fees, and quality and quantity of the commodity. Here, the seller from India makes an agreement with any foreign countries on this basis, and when the agreement is completed, the very next step is that the seller will ask the local elevator for the required details of the commodities and the buyer asks its local bank to generate the letter of credit (as per the terms of the contract). This, in turn, allows the foreign local bank to contact the exporters advising the bank for the

Table 7.1 Structure of contract payment.

Characteristic or nature	CIF	CF	FOB
Cost of loading and discharge	Seller	Seller	Buyer
Import documents	Buyer	Buyer	Buyer
Marine insurance	Seller	Buyer	Buyer
Vessel at port	Seller	Seller	Buyer

Source: Author's compilation from Slabotzky (1984).

approval of a letter of credit to buy the commodity [11]. The seller then asked with the letter of credit through the advising banks, and as soon as it is cleared, then there is a possibility of early transaction. In some cases, if there is an international presence, then both the banks, i.e., local or advising banks, may be the same.

Authors in [11] stated that as soon as the letter of credit is generated the advising allows a period of a minimum of 10 days to load its commodity at the port's vessel. The condition is made so that the seller should not start its process of loading before the confirmation from the buyer regarding the letter of credit.

The foremost duty of the seller is to gather all kinds of documents as per the commodity, the contract's term, and the destination point. In day-to-day practice, a third party authorized to prepare the handover of the documents all the required papers like phytosanitary certificate, the certificate of protein to the seller and the buyer in the appropriate language prescribed in the contract [11]. It is also required in the part of the seller to generate a certificate of stowage that defines about the ship or the vessel was cleaned before the loading of the commodity [11].

Previously, the large consignments with huge shipments on undifferentiated commodities of the practice of marketing system were developed and worked efficiently. During those days, every transaction was relying upon the CAD, i.e., cash on documents and that used to be prepared from the point of the origin. Such CAD is normally submitted at the bank for the payment before the loading. In case such a document is not released and submitted on time, then the amount, i.e., demurrage needs to be paid by the shippers [12].

At present, a new method is evolved for easy and quick access, i.e., the CAMR (cash against mate's receipt). In this process, after the receipt of the documents from the importer's bank, the shipper gets its payment immediately. The consignment needs a minimum of 14 days to deliver at

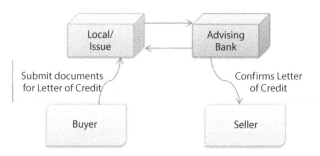

Figure 7.2 Generation of letter of credit from banks to firms. *Source: Author's Creation.*

the destination point. Normally, it further takes a week or two to a maximum a month for the preparation of the documents even in the same country. It is often experienced that the time required for the delivery of the documents may cross the specified time or till the consignment reaches the destination point, in such a condition the seller generates a letter of indemnity that can protect both buyer and seller from imposing the demurrage or the penalties (see Figure 7.2).

This process is considered as one of the efficient practices for any international trading until the development of the Blockchain system as it helps to make the process faster, safer, and suitable for wide distribution. This not only limits its work with the following attributes but also helpful in tracing, transparency and beneficial in cost reduction associated with transactions.

7.2   Blockchain Technology

It is a medium of maintaining traceable, time, and transferable ledger documents by any private or public body through a computerized network all over the world. This a database centrally located where the distributed documents will be passed from every station or location along with an approved copy to the end user. The approvals of the documents are made through cryptography it means verification through cryptographically, which means all the information will be recorded automatically that comes in the supply chain process [13]. Since after the commencement of the digital currency Bitcoin, the incorporation of Blockchain technology increased rapidly. Since after the successful acceptance of digital currency trading, i.e., Bitcoin the Blockchain technology got its mileage not only in the financial sector rather in every sector and at present it is considered as a boon for the agro-based industries.

One of the major elements that surround with the Blockchain technology is considering the issues and developing significant ways to handle such issues through Blockchain technologies. The present study considers the "smart contracts" through Blockchain and tries to reduce the inefficiencies that arise in international trading and support for the smooth running of the trading.

7.2.1   Smart Contracts

In several international trading, the documents require the details of the proprietors along with the quantity, prices, and margins [14]. As a result, customized and private Blockchain is accepted as more appropriate. This allows a few participants to verify or check after due permission that can be introduced in Blockchain technology.

In certain cases, it is a tedious activity of transforming documents from one party to another. This is done effectively by considering all stakeholders to a single platform through smart contracts which were first used during 1994 [15].

An advanced way of the ledger was developed known as Ethereum which is an open Blockchain method through DApps, i.e., decentralized application where the user has a benefit of restricting the participants to view the information [16]. This app holds and prepared with many complicated computations through EVM, i.e., Ethereum Virtual Machine [16].

In general, this holds two separate account types, i.e., CAs (contract accounts) and EOAs (external owned accounts). CAs use contract codes to access and identify the details while EOAs uses a private key to know the details that can be accessed by the network participants only.

As per the contract formation, various events or conditions are imposed in the smart contracts. As per the present study, only a few elements are considered as triggers, i.e., during shipment the letter of credit, during vessel loadings triggers full documents and final payment needs proof to the sellers.

Figure 7.3 specifies the ledger that distributes the triggers as per the needs of the stakeholders at international platforms. Normally, it needs permission and approval from both buyer and seller. For instance, with mutual consent, a consignment is to be delivered and the payment is to be made accordingly. Here, the buyer prefers to follow the EOA and provides a detailed update about the transaction through a smart contract which can be tracked and traced by all participants where it asks the local bank to transfer the amount to the advising bank; then, it is confirmed that the transaction is over [17]. As this process passes through several nodes, so the use of EVM helps to connect all nodes to maintain harmony in the Blockchain. In general, it confirms that all the process of the transaction is well executed.

As per the above process, the financial institutions are considered as one of the costly affairs. These intermediaries required a strict elimination through which the parties prefer to settle the agreement through cryptocurrencies. However, many parties feel reluctant to consider the way of payment as cryptocurrencies are found to be highly volatile. So, they prefer to settle the prices through US dollars and this needs a trusted mediator like a bank for both the buyer and sellers.

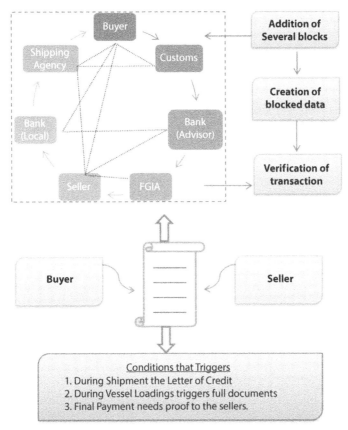

Figure 7.3 International trading of commodity through blockchain technology. *Source: Author's Creation.*

7.3   Blockchain Solutions

Many shipments accepted that several documents are necessary for efficient shipping. This excessive document requires costs, time, and risks and when such shipments are for any differentiated agro commodities like grains and oilseeds; then, it needs more detailed and additional documentation that may take several weeks to prepare and may need more time to generate a letter of credit.

To have control over such a rise of documentations and allow the information to be accessed in real-time, the "smart contract" along with Ethereum Blockchain with the facility of accessibility of participants can be more appropriate and significant. Blockchain technology is the best solution for the confirmation of the above-said issues. Here, the smart contracts play a crucial role in reducing the time and cost between both parties. For instance, the past international trading on soybean was carried on by Louis Dreyfus Company in early January 2018 and the buyer as Shandong Bohi Industry Company and banks. They all observed that this processing consume several weeks to settle [18]. But due to this technology, it has reduced the cost by 25% to 30%.

7.3.1   Monte Carlo Simulation in Blockchain Solution - An Illustration

Blockchain technology brings low cost and time and adds value to its process in the international market. Without the interference of centralized authority, it was able to provide cost and time reduction along with a rise in inefficiencies.

Authors in [19] said that Blockchain technology has reduced the process of documentation and supply chain processes to a marginal level that is confirmed through the Monte Carlo simulation model by referring to @Risk Microsoft Excel. The study considers two scenarios:

1. To understand the supply chain movement of soybeans from Madhya Pradesh, India, to Brazil FOB without Blockchain technology.
2. To comprehend the supply chain movement of soybeans from Madhya Pradesh, India, to Brazil FOB with Blockchain technology.

The study comprises the cost as Indian currency, i.e., dollar per bushel and time frame into no. of days.

a.   Distribution of Cost:
The cost incurred in the supply chain process of soybean on FOB basis is considered. The cost includes from origin to the end user that includes storage handling cots, elevation, refining, sorting, drying, segregation, warehousing, and rail loadings. Looking toward the rail, it includes several costs, i.e., rail transport tariffs and luggage charges, that fluctuates frequently. It includes several different charges, i.e., brokerage charges. The surcharge for fuel, demurrage charges is applicable when the origin or exporters makes a delay in placing the documents or luggage as per the scheduled time.

The cost of handling for both the origin and the export facilities seems to be similar but few exceptions like rail cars unloading, elevators, and ocean loading (see Figure 7.4). So, it can be accepted that the cost of origin is always higher than that of export location. The costs for demurrage are

Figure 7.4 Presentation of cost associated with FOB in soybeans export supply chain. *Source: Author's Creation.*

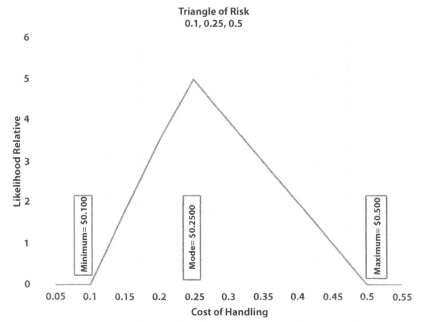

Figure 7.5 Representation of cost of handling in a triangular distribution through @Risk. *Source: Author's Creation.*

also accepted as similar only if the delay arises due to loading out is placed in vessel rather than in railcars.

In the structure of the Monte Carlo model of simulation, a representation is made in Figure 7.5, i.e., the triangular presentation of the cost incurred in handling. The representations of the cost are normally done into three categories, i.e., minimum, mode, and maximum.

Table 7.2 Distribution of cost and various sources of assumptions.

Phase	Parameters	Sources*	Distribution triangle ($ per Bushel)		
			Minimum	Mode	Maximum
1.	Handling Charges Origin	Wilson 2017	0.10	0.25	0.50
2	Primary Market (Rail)	Wilson 2017	0.0001	0.0002	0.0003
3.	Secondary Market (Rail)	NPI**	(0.0987)	(0.0987)	1.1366
4.	Tariff	NPI***	1.4498	1.3662	1.4112
5.	Demurrage (Origin)	Wilson 2017	-	0.0326	0.2380
6.	Surcharge (Fuel)	NPI#	-	-	0.3133
7.	Documentation Charges (Export)	Industrial responses###	-	-	-
8.	Handling Charges Export	Wilson 2017	0.0366	0.0999	0.1322
9.	Demurrage (Export)	Wilson 2017	-	0.0043	0.0065
10.	Ocean Shipping	NPI##	0.3692	0.2556	2.4463

* Calculation as per 4.323 bushels of soybeans in each rail car [20].

** NPI- Transportation data base from www.india.gov.in [21].

*** Using linear trend for calculation as per @Risk Benefit application from April 2000 to March 2018.

Best fit implementation in trend and using trend line projection.

Industrial responses and affected as per time frame.

Ocean freight from origin to destination [21].

Table 7.2 shows the parameters and the cost incurred at each level using the Monte Carlo simulation model. It is observed that the costs for the export documents are based on the time of preparation no as per the fixed-rate stated by participants.

b.   Distribution of Time:

The elapsed time frames are considered in at every stage of the supply chain process, to analyze the time PERT is used (see Figure 7.6). The parameters used for the analysis include the lower time, almost like time, and maximum time.

A flow chart of the whole supply chain process of soybeans along with the PERT distribution is represented in Figure 7.7. The parameter includes all the documentation stages for exporting suggested by Wilson [22]. The stages considered for the analysis are developed after consulting the officer in the Import General Manifest (IGM). The total cost is valued for the elapsed time by following the flow chart in Figure 7.7. The time elapsed in the process are divided with 365 days to convert in the number of years and multiplied with the annual rate of interest, i.e., 11.25% and further multiplied with the price of soybeans Rs. 27,845.65 (as of June 2020).

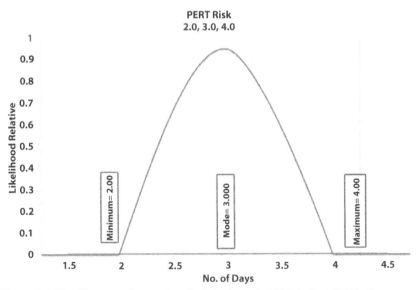

Figure 7.6 Handling stage from point of origin through @Risk in Pert distribution. *Source: Author's Creation.*

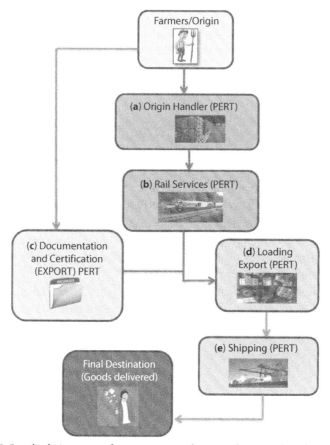

Figure 7.7 Supply chain process for exporting soy beans with PERT identifications.
Source: Author's Creation.

For instance, if the time is considered as 60 days, then the total cost would be Rs. 514.95 per bushel, i.e., $\frac{40}{365}$ x 0.1125 x 27,845.65.

Interview with the officers and the participants confirmed that the Blockchain implementation has a positive effect on reducing the cost mainly through elapsed time for documentation. As a result, the PERT stages of documentation tend to reduce after implementing the Blockchain technology up to 20% with a minimum as 4.2, mode of 5.5, and a maximum as 6.8 days. The same is compared with the base time and cost without Blockchain technology to identify the significant amount of savings by implementing Blockchain technology.

c.   Results of Monte Carlo Simulations:

A test of t-statistic is conducted using a two-sample one-tailed test with N, i.e., total sample of 2,300 with a hypothesis at 95% of confidence that the mean cost of the base is higher than the mean cost of Blockchain technology. A significance of 99% is considered for the meantime elapsed using the same information.

The simulation analysis after implementation of Blockchain analysis confirmed that there is a significant reduction in the change of price of soybeans up to 2.1 cents per bushel or 0.6% on an average. The elapsed time frame is further examined to be a reduction of 40%, i.e., 15.21 days from Madhya Pradesh, India, to Brazil. By implementing t-test statistics at a 5% level of significance confirms that the mean cost is lower than that of the base price. This result might not seem to be significant but for the agro-industry, that relays on export activities that make a huge difference in aggregate.

7.3.2   Supporting Blockchain Technology in the Food Industry Through Other Applications

The meat industry takes a sincere effort in upgrading to the Blockchain technology that will solve various challenges, i.e., trading, tracing, and trading at the international platform [23]. For instance, Cargill tried to introduce a Blockchain technology that supports the buyers to trace a farmer dealing with the Honeysuckle White brand. This Blockchain has a way that represents the details regarding the turkey from where it is purchased. This contains the information of the turkey along with the picture that the buyer has purchased which also states how the turkey was raised from which particular farm [24].

While trading with Auvergne Chickens by Carrefour stores a customized Blockchain technology was introduced where it says about hatcher, processor, producer, and consumer from every point through which the consignment passes and any tampering to the chicken or its packets can easily be traced at any point [25].

A contrary approach was made by authors in [26, 27] where they confirm that several other applications are available that are more advanced and provide better information than Blockchain technology as it gets restricted with farm source management, quality of the commodity, and farming process when it is made useful for agricultural products.

But many researchers still agree that Blockchain technology has changed the dimension of the traceability, transparency, and efficiencies [28].

Table 7.3 Costs and time elapsed by Monte Carlo simulation.

Test parameters	Cost incurred in $/Bushel			Time elapsed		
	Basic	Blockchain	Diff.	Basic	Blockchain	Diff.
Maximum	3.896	3.692	−0.204	52.3	31.06	−21.24
Minimum	2.228	2.103	−0.125	41.09	37.69	−3.4
Mean	3.624	3.603	−0.021	38	22.79	−15.21
Percentile 5th	2.396	2.108	−0.288	39.23	22.89	−16.34
Percentile 10th	2.691	2.632	−0.059	39.77	26.13	−13.64
Percentile 90th	4.332	4.316	−0.016	44.98	27.22	−17.76
Percentile 95th	4.692	4.663	−0.029	51.69	31.02	−20.67
Standard Deviation	0.4332	0.4331	−1E−04	3.1	1.8	−1.3

The United States has experienced a food-borne illness that cost the nation from $55.5 to $93.3 billion per year that was easily traced through Blockchain. Returning of food products has always been a costly affair unless the reason is traced or identification of fault handling at which particular stage. Authors in [29] stated that normally a food manufacturers experience recalling of 77% in case of food beverages that approximately cost around $30 million per recall. This recalls occurs due to a lack of identifying valid information [30] or source identification on the spot [31]. This recalls increased the burden of buying additional insurance to protect this loss [32].

Table 7.3, clearly depicts that blockchain technology is the best alternative to deal with such recalls. This, in return, supports both buyers and sellers in cost reductions and saves maximum time. So, it can be confirmed that Blockchain can be a valuable addition to every participant and can support the regulator in large.

7.4   Conclusion

The present study highlights the technology, i.e., blockchain practice in the agro-industry for commodity export. The commodity exchange in the international market holds a strong settlement mechanism but the implementation of Blockchain technology helps in tracing, is transparent, and accelerates the settlement process. The overall finding states (1) a reduction in the 0.6% per bushel; (2) a reduction of 40%, i.e., 15.21days for the time frame; (3) a further reduction of cost VaR by 2.1 Rupees per bushel.

In general, it is cleared after the success story of Blockchain technology in the financial sectors that the international market and the practitioners are more likely to depend and follow the practice of this traceable and transparent method to avoid the chances of risk.

Apart from that, this brings a practice of following specified documentation formats for sales contracts which were not possible earlier. If the products are heterogeneous in nature then Blockchain technology can be the best solution in dealing with the inappropriate documentation and certification for every product in trading. So, this technology brings a decent method of practice that can be easily traceable and referred at every stage of the supply chain.

7.5   Managerial Implication

This is an advanced technology so it needs due approval of all the stakeholders, i.e., farmers, warehouse keepers, bankers, shipping agents, and buyers distributors. But this technology will indeed cut down the cost of the transaction, risk of operation, and cost as a whole. But this may cause the small players at a large in respect to shifting from traditional to modern technology [12].

7.6   Future Scope of Study

It is true to state that the agro-industry has not accepted the Blockchain technology wholeheartedly as it holds a few challenges [12]. Some of the challenges are as follows: (1) it needs to be more industry-specific as per needs; (2) the practice needs to more homogenous no matter how far the product, the parties or the supply chain are heterogeneous in nature; and (3) Blockchain technology need to be segregated in respect to the level of investment, operation, and practice as per the commodity and parties specific where the transparency and traceability are essential. These are some of the areas that can be considered for further analysis to convert this technology as a more effective way for any international trading activities.

References

1. Hackett, R., Why big business is racing to build blockchains. *Fortune Magazine*, https://fortune.com/2017/08/22/bitcoin-ethereum-blockchain-cryptocurrency/, 2017.
2. Payne, J., Blockchain Platform Goes Live for North Sea Crude Oil Trading. *Reuters*, November, https://www.reuters.com/article/us-blockchain-oil-trading-idUSKCN1NY0X6, 2018.
3. Phillips, Kotller, Five Dead, Nearly 200 Sick in E. coli Outbreak from Lettuce and Investigators are Stumped, *Washington Post*, https://www.washingtonpost.com/news/to-your-health/wp/2018/06/02/five-dead-nearly-200-sick-in-e-coli-outbreak-from-lettuce-and-investigators-are-stumped/, June, 2018
4. Baber, Influenza Season Wrap-up–Jill. Multistate Outbreak of E. coli O157: H7 Infections Linked to Romaine Lettuce. (2018): I-II.
5. Carson, B. and Higginson, M., Blockchain Explained: What It Is and Isn't, and Why It Matters, *McKinsey*, https://www.mckinsey.com/business-functions/mckinsey-digital/our-insights/blockchain-explained-what-it-is-and-isnt-and-why-it-matters, September, 2018.
6. Forbes, IBM & Walmart Launching Blockchain Food Safety Alliance in China With Fortune 500's JD.com, https://www.forbes.com/sites/rogeraitken/2017/12/14/ibm-walmart-launching-blockchain-food-safety-alliance-in-china-with-fortune-500s-jd-com/?sh=4b48a5367d9c, 2017.
7. Plume, K., ABCD quartet of grain traders partner to digitize global trades. *Reuters*, October, https://www.reuters.com/article/global-grains-traders-idUSL2N1X50Y7, 2018.
8. World-Grain, From the Editor: A revolutionary development for grain trading, https://www.world-grain.com/articles/11397-from-the-editor-a-revolutionary-development-for-grain-trading, 2018.
9. AP-NEWS, COFCO International Joins Initiative to Modernize Global Agricultural Commodity Trade Operations, https://apnews.com/press-release/pr-businesswire/a2af8a797dd549ea90e9d2c08cf8179d, 2018.
10. Financial Times, Commodity trading enters the age of digitisation, https://www.ft.com/content/8cc7f5d4-59ca-11e8-b8b2-d6ceb45fa9d0, 2018.
11. Slabotzky, Albert. *Grain contracts and arbitration*. Lloyd's of London Press Ltd., https://agris.fao.org/agris-search/search.do?recordID=US201300395311, 1984.
12. Ehmke, T., Blockchain in Agricultural Commodity Trading: Dream or Reality? CoBank, https://www.uswheat.org/wheatletter/blockchain-in-agricultural-commodity-trading-dream-or-reality , June, 2019.
13. Burniske, C. and Jack T., *Cryptoassets: The innovative investor's guide to bitcoin and beyond*. New York: McGraw-Hill Education, https://www.oreilly.com/library/view/cryptoassets-the-innovative/9781260026689/, 2018.

14. McKinsey & Company, Blockchain technology for supply chains—A must or a maybe?, https://www.mckinsey.com/business-functions/operations/our-insights/blockchain-technology-for-supply-chainsa-must-or-a-maybe, 2017.
15. Szabo, N., Smart contracts. https://www.fon.hum.uva.nl/rob/Courses/InformationInSpeech/CDROM/Literature/LOTwinterschool2006/szabo.best.vwh.net/smart.contracts.html, 1994.
16. Ethereum community. Revision, Ethereum Homestead Documentation, https://ethdocs.org/en/latest/, 2016.
17. Sekar, P., Can Blockchain Disrupt Energy and Commodity Trading?, 2019.
18. Reuters, U.S. soy cargo to China traded using blockchain, https://www.reuters.com/article/grains-blockchain-idUSL8N1PG0VJ, 2018.
19. Palisade, *@Risk: Advanced Risk Analysis for Microsoft Excel and Project*, Palisade Software, https://www.palisade.com/risk/default.asp, 2019.
20. Government of India, agmarket, retrieved from https://agmarknet.gov.in/., 2020.
21. Government of India, *Ministry of statistics and programme implementation*, download reports, retrieved from https://www.india.gov.in/topics/transport, 2020.
22. Wilson, W.W., *Supply Chain Functions and Costs: North Dakota Soybeans to Asia*, Presentation to North Dakota Soybean Council, https://www.google.com/url?sa=t&rct=j&q=&esrc=s&source=web&cd=&cad=rja&uact=8&ved=2ahUKEwjbsaLIjbvyAhUBdCsKHWV7B7sQFnoECAMQAQ&url=https%3A%2F%2Fwww.ndsu.edu%2Ffileadmin%2Fagecon%2Fbio_march_20__002_.pdf&usg=AOvVaw0ret4KVhajuaFtM2EdzUuM, 2017.
23. Amen, T. and Ehmke, T., Blockchain: Change Is Coming to Agricultural Supply Chains, CoBank, https://www.google.com/url?sa=t&rct=j&q=&es rc=s&source=web&cd=&cad=rja&uact=8&ved=2ahUKEwjatoWEj7vyAhVO73MBHawHAF8QFnoECAMQAQ&url=http%3A%2F%2Fwww.uwyo.edu%2Fagecon%2Fabout-us%2Ffacultystaff%2Ffaculty-pages%2Fcehmke%2Fblockchain.pdf&usg=AOvVaw25eU6wXc0rD5I19svdQIVm, May, 2018.
24. Bricher, J.L., MIT Technology Review, In blockchain we trust, https://www.technologyreview.com/2018/04/09/3066/in-blockchain-we-trust/, 2018.
25. Bloomberg , Yes, These Chickens Are on the Blockchain, https://www.google.com/url?sa=t&rct=j&q=&esrc=s&source=web&cd=&cad=rja&uact=8&ved=2ahUKEwjikujzj7vyAhWe8HMBHaCBBdsQFnoECAUQAQ&url=https%3A%2F%2Fwww.bloomberg.com%2Fnews%2Ffeatures%2F2018-04-09%2Fyes-these-chickens-are-on-the-blockchain&usg=AOvVaw2okvmCNFR2SzLhwG_JdQRJ, April, 2018.
26. Belt, A. and Steven K., A Reality Check for Blockchain in Commodity Trading. *Boston Consulting Group*, September, https://www.bcg.com/en-in/publications/2018/reality-check-blockchain-commodity-trading, 2018.

27. AgFunder Network Partners, Blockchain is Coming for Agriculture and You Might Not Even Notice, https://agfundernews.com/blockchain-is-coming-for-agriculture.html, 2018.

28. Yahoo Finance, Food Recalls Cost Millions — and Companies Aren't the Only Ones Paying the Price, https://finance.yahoo.com/news/food-recalls-cost-millions-companies-185622514.html , 2018.

29. Scharff, R.L., State Estimates for the Annual Cost of Foodborne Illness. *J. Food Prot.*, 78, 6, 1064–71, 2015.

30. FDA, Commissioner Scott Gottlieb, M.D. and FDA Deputy Commissioner Frank Yiannas on new findings and updated consumer recommendations related to the romaine lettuce E. coli O157:H7 outbreak investigation, https://www.fda.gov/news-events/press-announcements/statement-fda-commissioner-scott-gottlieb-md-and-fda-deputy-commissioner-frank-yiannas-new-findings, 2018.

31. New York Times, From Farm to Blockchain: Walmart Tracks Its Lettuce, https://www.nytimes.com/2018/09/24/business/walmart-blockchain-lettuce.html, 2018.

32. Insureon, *Should Your Business Purchase Product Recall Insurance?*, https://www.insureon.com/small-business-insurance/product-liability/product-recall, 2018.

8

InterPlanetary File System Protocol– Based Blockchain Framework for Routine Data and Security Management in Smart Farming

Sreethi Thangam M.[1*], Janeera D.A.[2], Sherubha P.[3], Sasirekha S.P.[4], J. Geetha Ramani[5] and Ruth Anita Shirley D.[2]

[1]*VLSI Design, Sri Eshwar College of Engineering, Coimbatore, India*
[2]*Department of ECE, Sri Krishna College of Engineering and Technology, Coimbatore, India*
[3]*Department of IT, Karpagam College of Engineering, Coimbatore, India*
[4]*Department of CSE, VSB College of Engineering and Technical Campus, Coimbatore, India*
[5]*Department of ECE, SNS College of Technology, Coimbatore, India*

Abstract

The rapid emergence of the technologies has almost redesigned every industry including agriculture. Nowadays, agricultural practices are done by statistical and quantitative approaches. It is important to protect the data which are collected in the agricultural sector. Blockchain is one of the promising technologies that are used for the data encryption. Blockchain is used to store the transaction data. A huge amount of data is stored in IPFS, which ensures scalability and data confidentiality. It also ensures data privacy with the data sharing mechanism. The data collected from the agricultural sectors like moisture content of the soil, temperature, and crop status that are obtained from the IoT sensors on the agricultural land, other details such as previous year agricultural records, details of the agricultural land, yield, logistics, and so on are passed to the blockchain and so that the data cannot be used for malpractices. These data are helpful for the farmers to cultivate the crops according to their land conditions. This data can also be analyzed so that the farmer can get an estimate from the government and insurance organizations

Corresponding author: sreethinishasps@gmail.com

Vishal Kumar, Vishal Jain, Bharti Sharma, Jyotir Moy Chatterjee and Rakesh Shrestha (eds.) Smart City Infrastructure: The Blockchain Perspective, (205–224) © 2022 Scrivener Publishing LLC

to meet his needs. InterPlanetary File System (IPFS) is used for secure storage of this large quantity of information. This chapter presents a completely secure blockchain-based framework for smart farming using IoT sensors and a farmer support system to meet certain necessities of the farmer.

Keywords: Smart farming, IoT, IPFS, blockchain, data management

8.1 Introduction

India is one of the largest agricultural nations in the world. The Indian economy highly depends on agriculture. It is important to protect the voluminous data generated from the smart sensors used in agricultural sector [1]. In case of war, the border sharing countries may easily target the food productivity of our country by means of this big data. To overcome the data security drawbacks, the data collected from the agricultural sector can be stored in blockchain so that the data cannot be accessed by unauthorized users. With the evolution of technology, several innovative developments are made for reducing the efforts of labor, reducing the resources, and improving the yield in agriculture. However, matching the demand and supply has been a boundless challenge with the continuous increase in population.

Based on certain statistics figures, in 2050, the global population is expected to rise to 9.8 billion which is 25% higher than the current numbers [2]. A large portion of this rise in population is expected in developing countries. With urbanization increasing at an accelerated pace, 70% of the world population is expected to be urban in 2050, whereas currently, it is 45%. As a result, the demand for food will increase in the developing countries. This increasing demand has caused the quality and quantity of the supplies to be affected, which also leads the customers toward change their preferences to legumes and meat. To provide enough supplies to the urban population, production should rise to double the figure in 2050. Especially, the production of the food should increase to equal demands. So, more cereal and meat production should be done to fulfill the demand of the upcoming population rise.

The total area for cultivation in 1991 was about 19.5 million square miles. But as years go by, the area for cultivation has reduced to 18.6 million square miles in 2013 [3]. As time passes, there is more demand for the food supplies which is not a good sign. Every crop has unique characteristics and these characteristics are defined by the quality and quantity. These crops depend upon the area of cultivation and other factors like soil type and materials used in the area of cultivation. Even if the same crop is cultivated on a huge area, its produce differs from season to season and along the width of the field [4]. To match the demands in the future the farmers need to upgrade the equipment and with the help of technology, we can make the farming work easier too.

Farmers have to visit their lands frequently to understand the status on crop conditions. A smart farming scheme has been introduced for this purpose as farmers need more time to monitor their lands and crop quality. Through this smart scheme, farmers can know the nature of the environment, details of the land, and the events related to it. Recently, a solution has been devised to detect crop events through sensory skills and technology so that farmers can detect crop conditions and its quality without visiting the land. It also allows farmers to detect pests, crop diseases, and damage to crops [5]. Farmers can view everything from crop yield to harvest through a smart program created by combining various cutting edge technologies like IoT, cloud computing, big data analytics, and blockchain. Complaints and information in sensor technology can be detected at short time intervals.

A wide variety of machinery is currently used in the agricultural industry. Further, the sensors accurately detect the levels of crop quality and inform the farmer [6]. Sensor technology is becoming more and more useful to farmers today and gives us accurate information regarding crop conditions, and soil quality details. In the present era, IoT has started to affect the agriculture sector, health sector as well as the communication sector. There is a tremendous probability that IoT is going to play a major role in agriculture and various sectors in the near future [7]. So, we can put the telecommunication information and sensor capabilities through IoT to provide optimal solution in smart farming technology. However, with the implementation of these technologies, maintaining the safety of this voluminous data is crucial to avoid data security issues. For this purpose, we propose a combination of blockchain and IFPS providing secure agricultural data management.

8.1.1   Blockchain Technology for Agriculture

Transactional records of public from multiple databases termed as "chain" is stored in the blockchain structure termed as "block" in a network connected through peer-to-peer nodes. Typically, this storage is referred to as a "digital ledger". This ledger contains all the transactions and accounts of all participants [8]. It is a trustful source for investors and contracts in agriculture, where the collection of data and information that are become expensive.

Data provenance is the field of recording the history of data, from its inceptions to various stages of the data lifecycle. Blockchain technology tracks the provenance of food and also helps to develop a reliable bond between consumers and producers. As a reliable data source, it makes strategic decisions based on data analysis and interpretation to make better and smart farming. By using smart contracts in blockchain, it is easy for payment transaction to the stakeholders without third party intervention [9]. Any changes that appear in the blockchain data are easily traceable thereby improving the data security level.

8.2   Data Management in Smart Farming

A wide range of data is involved in smart farming like soil and moisture data, food safety, supply chain, and quality management. As the time progress, there have been several changes in the field of data management. There is a massive impact on the performance and profitability in agricultural operation. Figure 8.1 shows some of the prominent domains in smart farming where blockchain technology is used [10]. The demand for agricultural data and produce is high. This could make a huge difference to farmers who are involved in marketing and selling their produce. Smart farming involves dealing with the information and communication for farming requirements.

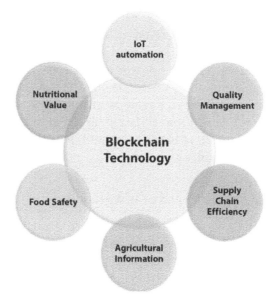

Figure 8.1 Blockchain in smart farming.

In future, the role of robots and artificial intelligence (AI) in smart farming is high. These technologies assist in making the farm work easier and faster. This section provides a detailed understanding of the data involved in smart farming and efficient management of the data.

8.2.1   Agricultural Information

From farmer to manufacturer to grocery store and the consumer, block-chain is reshaping the food production industry in conjunction with IoT. Blockchain is set to transform agriculture into a sustainable practice by improving agricultural resources [11]. From soil sampling, irrigation, fertilizer, crop disease, pest management, yield monitoring, forecasting, to harvesting, smart sensors are used for gathering the complete agricultural information [12]. Usually, farmers get counseling and support regarding crop health and sales from various sources. They are given priority depending on whom they are getting advice from. Demand for this support has grown significantly which has led to several corporate scandals.

Depending on the condition of the farm, the crop quality and reliability can be estimated. The proposed data management scheme allows farmers to rely on its ability to accurately locate farm information and display the information graphically. On that map, the farmer can accurately identify the crop quality and its statistics. Farmers can pay for the drone system and get information about the field from the image processing console and the sensors placed at various locations in the field [13]. This allows viewing of information accurately and mapping is done based on the quality of crop at every segment of the field. Several mathematical models are used for improving the accuracy of the algorithm in estimating the plant quality. Farmers can identify crop growth and pest infestations. This data can be shared with agronomists and researchers based on the farmers interest. The farmer can consult with them to improve the quality of crops based on the advice of experts for the cultivation of the crops.

8.2.2   Supply Chain Efficiency

A variety of tasks such as harvesting, winnowing, threshing, packaging, transportation, storing, processing, and trading must be undergone by the agricultural commodities before reaching the market. Economy of the world is greatly influenced by agriculture. However, various factors a like the supply chain member roles, coordination, technology, government policies, market availability, culture techniques, seed quality, and weather changes affect the agricultural products [14]. The coordination across the supply chain that ensures increasing profitability and ensuring value for consumers decides the measure of success of the supply chain. The most common use of blockchain in food and agricultural supply chains is to improve detectability. This allows agriculturists to quickly track unsafe products to their source and see where they are distributed elsewhere. The billing systems, supply chains, and consumer databases are used for tracking this information in an efficient manner.

8.2.3   Quality Management

Advances in the technology of data acquisition and control systems can benefit based on the quality of agricultural products. Ensuring the freshness of the produce, elimination, or minimization of biological and chemical hazards and providing marketable quality pest free products are the key aspects of quality management [15]. Other than acquiring the product quality information, quality control must also ensure that the defective products are screened at the initial level itself, and does not reach the consumer. The credence and experience characteristics of food products cause concerns when the consumers purchase food products. It is essential to meet the quality standards of food products while meeting the demands and requirements of the consumers.

Grading of food products based on their features, like color and size of fruits, is performed during packaging. This process can be automated using an image processing model. Several cutting edge tools and algorithms can be used for this purpose involving AI, machine learning, deep learning, and so on. This enables efficient quality management of agricultural produce, offers inspection parameter flexibility, reduces time consumption, overcomes errors in human inspection, and contributes toward improving the efficiency and effectiveness of the inspection process.

8.2.4   Nutritional Value

Agriculture and nutrition share a common entry point: "food". The main effect of agricultural activities is food. It is also the main input for good nutrition. There is little food or nutrition without agriculture, but getting food from agriculture does not guarantee good nutrition [16]. General knowledge dictates a strengthening relationship between the two sectors of agriculture and nutrition, but in reality, there is often a significant disconnect. This report makes a strong connection between agriculture and nutrition. Malnutrition remains a global challenge and a stubborn barrier to ending poverty [17]. Nutritional status of mankind is improved by the introduction of nutrition-smart farming. The productivity and profits are increased while achieving the objectives of agricultural business and improving the nutritional status. Modern biotechnology, conventional plant breeding, or agronomic practices are used for improving the nutritional quality of seeds providing biofortified seeds leading to the growth of biofortified crops. These crops satisfy the preferences and tastes of the consumers while being resistant to crop diseases and pests providing increased productivity.

8.2.5   Food Safety

Quantity, diversity, and quality of the food we consume are the constituents of food safety. Every year around 10 million people die of nutrition insufficiency. Malnutrition due to lack of iron, vitamin A, iodine, and such micronutrients and protein maybe caused when food with inadequate nutrients are consumed on a regular basis. The immune system is weakened leading to long term and permanent impairment of cognitive as well as physical development of children, heart diseases, measles, and pneumonia. Experts view nutrition as the realm of health traditionally. Farmers and health care professionals have to work together to overcome the challenges of food safety. Blockchain technology helps to find information in the food supply chain, thus improving food security. It provides a secure way to store and manage data, facilitating the development and application of data-driven innovations for smart farming and smart index-based agricultural insurance [18].

8.2.6   IoT Automation

Smart farming is a growing concept because IoT sensors are capable of providing information about agricultural sectors and then operating on the basis of user input IoT (Internet of Things) refers to the use of sensors, cameras and other devices in the agricultural environment [19]. IoT helps in achieving improved efficiency of crop production. IoT-based hydroponic models and greenhouses enable closed-cycle smart farming system to grow food even in urban areas and buildings. IoT helps in optimization of agricultural resources, enables an organic and cleaner process, increases process agility, and improves the quality of produce. It has multiple applications such as livestock monitoring, monitoring climatic conditions, greenhouse automation, crop monitoring, and drones.

8.3 Proposed Smart Farming Framework

Figure 8.2 provides the block diagram representation of the proposed IPFS blockchain-based smart agriculture management system.

This model incorporates several IoT sensors for obtaining data from the farmland regarding the soil quality, seed quality, and farm atmosphere. The data regarding the farmland, crop and farmer's health insurance is also obtained along with the logistics, warehouse, market demand and price data. All these information are processed by the IPFS blockchain technology and is stored in the cloud environment for access by the farmer on a mobile interface. Each block of the architecture is explained in detail.

8.3.1 Wireless Sensors

With the availability of all the materials and tools required for smart farming, the demand for wireless sensors is continuously increasing. The quality of the crop and its conditions can be accurately detected by wireless sensors. Wireless sensors are used separately where needed in various modern machines [20]. Sensors can detect environmental conditions, seed quality, soil condition, plant growth rate, need for pesticides and insecticides, and weather conditions. Sensors can monitor accurate operation of agricultural machinery and equipment, correct assessment of agricultural

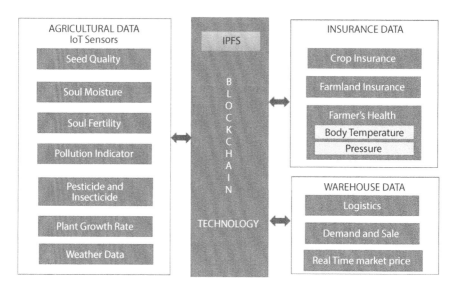

Figure 8.2 Proposed IPFS blockchain-based smart agriculture management system.

data, and the condition of logistics, warehouse, and market. Mobile Data Saving system enables the users to manage crop and adjust to the soil variation and to gather information about it. Through this system, information can be collected and the operational condition of the farm machines and equipment can be detected. It can be used to determine soil quality, seed quality, yield, temperature, pest infestation, wind speed, humidity, and weather. This information can be sent to the manager and analysts to diagnose any problems with the data and get advice from them to fix it.

Appropriate sensors are used to measure the temperature of the farmland as well as to measure the moisture content in the soil and the atmosphere. The sensor that measures temperature is called the temperature sensor and the sensor that measures the humidity is called the dew sensor. Humidity sensors are used to detect the humidity level of the air. Sensors are used to measure the amount of water available for irrigation for optimal management of water resources. It is very helpful to measure the water quality in the yielding land. It is very suitable for all irrigation types. The soil moisture sensor is used in all areas of the farmland. Sensors are also used to detect environmental conditions, climate, and agricultural produce. Sensors can detect microorganisms and bacteria in the soil [21]. Plant infections are diagnosed using a variety of modern tools, such as amplifier processors. The details of the disease are sent to the farmer through the mobile service. Electrochemical sensors are used to detect nutrient conditions so that the most accurate soil salinity can be detected. This telematics enhances communication. Thus, the farmers can obtain all the information statistically.

8.3.2   Communication Channels

Communication is considered important as it provides crucial information and calculations of agricultural data in a timely manner. Communication integrates all information so that there is quality and secure transfer of data. If IoT is to be implemented in the agricultural sector, it has to provide the necessary security measures. Services can only be linked to one site when the network service is low [22]. Normally, this service is not connected to the site over a long distance. Multiple information are detected through the network and communicated to the agricultural organization. Eventually, data is used based on the network size and the need for applications. Appropriate communication channel is used based on the size of the farm and the number of sensors used. 4G and 5G communications would be appropriate in the current era. Network services are very limited in rural areas. Another method by which data can be exchanged is by exchanging information via satellite. But this method would be more expensive. It may not be suitable for poor farmers. Communication used by sensors is done on some farms. But the sensors should have long life and battery life. So, we can use it on low power using low-power wide-area network (LPWAN) network. It is suitable for middle class people as it has long battery life and affordable. LPWAN network plays a very important role in agricultural data transfer [23].

Zigbee is used to communicate between very long and wide systems. These modules are designed to meet the needs of the application. It is also designed to replace any existing non-standard technologies. Zigbee has a diverse network range and is used to meet the needs of agriculture with network character. Zigbee Communication technology can work to detect and report the sensor data. Through the Zigbee process all information is sent to farmers through the mobile service. Through this, the farmers can understand the condition of the crops. In smaller level farms, Bluetooth can be used as the significant wireless communication device. This is used to transmit information over short distances. These are simple to use and inexpensive [24]. Bluetooth is used in its smart farming and various IoT systems. Sensors are used by the BLE to detect and communicate the humidity and temperature of the garden. These are developed according to the weather and the environmental conditions in the farm. LoRa (Long Range Radio) wireless transmission is also commonly used in IoT data transmission. It is a long range communication process. It is designed to be much more effective than Bluetooth or wireless. LoRa wireless sensors are used for surveillance in most places. These can be parked in small objects and can penetrate complex buildings. It enables connectivity of people, animals, devices, machines, gateways, and sensors to the cloud wirelessly.

8.3.3 IoT and Cloud Computing

India is the most important producer of all food commodities like grains. However, the farmers still use old and redundant techniques that are not suitable to match the growing demands. They are less likely to use new and modern mechanized practices. Thus, the supply of goods and the fulfillment of needs are lagging. Thus, the country is still lagging in terms national income. These problems can be fixed with the new technologies like IoT and cloud computing. The cloud allows the complete information regarding the crops to be stored in one place, so that farmers and researchers can obtain all the essential information collected by the IoT sensors at any given time.

Temperature, humidity, and other factors are monitored using sensors in smart farming via IoT [25]. Various actions can be performed using the information obtained from these sensors and irrigation can be automated. Farmers can know the condition of their crops and the environment from anywhere through this. Now, several smart projects are implemented in the agricultural sector. In emerging civilization, agriculture can be made prosperous through various technologies. Treatments, input optimization, and water usage efficiency can be improved using IoT in smart farming, thereby overcoming the environmental issues. Information from tools like weather stations, satellite images, and soil sensors are aggregated in the cloud that aids farmers to analyze the farmland.

The global market is extensively covered by the cloud computing technology. However, the Indian agricultural sector has not been sensitized with the benefits of this technology. Cloud technology [26] offers various benefits like low setup cost, efficient information management, data availability, reduction of urban rural migration, and promotion of agricultural product circulation, which are very beneficial especially to the Indian market.

8.3.4   Blockchain and IPFS Integration

Blockchain technology is combined with InterPlanetary File System (IPFS) for management of agricultural data presenting a query and data storage mechanism. In applications and computing devices that involve voluminous data storage, IPFS enables connectivity between the devices with the same file system on a global scale. Blockchain and IPFS are initially used as a data storage model [27]. Sensor information, images, and video data that are uploaded automatically encapsulated and analyzed using this model. IPFS model stores the data and blockchain stores the consequent hash addresses of the data. A database is used for storage of the blockchain transaction hash values. When the sensor information is required by the user, the blockchain transaction content can be accessed for data retrieval.

Figure 8.3 provides the architectural design of the agricultural product information system where blockchain, IPFS, IoT sensors, and vision system is interfaced for easy analysis and tracking. Sensors are used for obtaining the real-time information along with the picture and video information from the field level to processing, packaging, and logistics. This data is processes, encapsulated, and stored in the IPFS. Validation of the information in IPFS is done by generating a hash for the data which is further stored in the blockchain. This data can be used for various applications to achieve optimization in the field of agriculture and manufacture of food products.

Figure 8.4 provides an Ethereum framework of blockchain along with IFPS open source model for data storage and management.

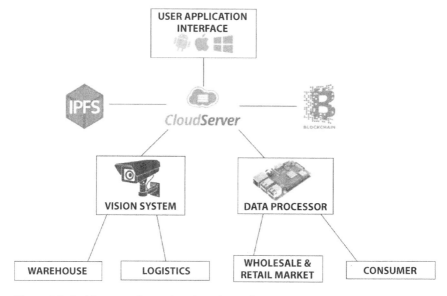

Figure 8.3 Architecture of agricultural product information system.

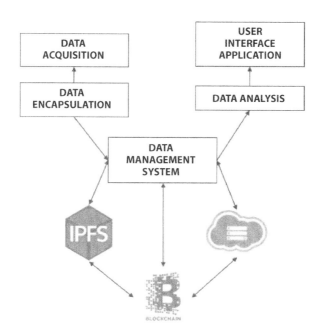

Figure 8.4 Data management model.

Data management is performed on analysis of the encapsulated data in this model. The sensor, picture, and video data are encapsulated with the corresponding crop data. Blockchain and IPFS interact with the data management module. Blockchain stores the content with respect to transaction as hash addresses that are obtained from the encapsulated data of agricultural product available in the IPFS. This enables easy tracing of the information [28]. Provenance packets are generated for storing the information. During data extraction, the transaction hash available in the blockchain is accessed by the system to query transaction and obtain the hash address of IPFS. Further, data is obtained from the IPFS. The application is built using the analyzed information obtained by the data management system.

8.4   Farmers Support System

Smart farming is about strengthening agriculture and the agro-industrial system. It is also to increase productivity and monitor production-related information. Digital agriculture is pushing agriculture to a new level.

Figure 8.5 Android application interface for farmers.

As represented in Figure 8.5, a farmer support system interface is developed where the farmer can obtain all the information regarding the crop, field, sales, logistics, warehouse, and insurance and also add additional info that he needs to keep track of [29]. The support system allows the farmer to type the query or to send it as a voice note for which response will be given by the chatbot or a customer support executive. The model facilitates farmer to upload images of the plant or pest so as to get better clarity and inputs. The support system is also made available in regional languages so that the technology is introduced to the farmer community without any glitches.

8.4.1   Sustainable Farming

Performing agriculture in a sustainable manner, catering to the demands of the society without negative impacts on the future production is termed as sustainable farming. Agricultural sustainability can be improved in multiple ways. It is crucial to understand the services of the ecosystem [30]. Flexible farming practices and business schemes must be developed when sustainable practices are incorporated in agriculture. Deforestation, land degradation, water scarcity, climate change, and other environmental processes are impacted due to agriculture. Sustainability of mankind depends on sustainable development of food systems. This also enables mitigation of climate changes. Despite the varying environmental conditions, sustainable agriculture offers optimal solutions to feed the continuously increasing population.

Climate-smart agriculture (CSA) and environment-smart agriculture (ESA) can help overcome the uncertainties and negative impacts on environment enabling friendly farm practices to maximize yield. Negative impacts on multiple dimensions are generated leading to the depletion of natural ecosystem and contamination of agricultural environment when farm chemicals are used extensively to increase the crop yield [31]. The farmers and government should work collectively for implementing ESA despite various challenges. The negative environmental impact can be reduced to a greater extent if the mitigation and adaptation responsibilities are shared by the farmers. Sensitization of farmers regarding the use of modern technologies in farming and chemical inputs is essential. ESA can be affected due to the farmer's lack of awareness, depletion of vegetation, and soil and exploitation of the agricultural environment.

At farm level, the constraints and environmental impacts of ESA implementation are measured using a proxy index. Further, for minimizing the negative impacts on the environment and mitigating cost, damage cost approach is used in a conventional agriculture setup. Then, the relationship between the environmental factors and behavior can be analyzed using directed graph approach. This offers an efficient platform for ESA implementation.

8.5   Results and Discussions

Agricultural products and their traceability are analyzed using an application. Every 10 minutes, the real-time agricultural data obtained by the sensors are uploaded to the system. During transportation of produce to the storage system, image and video data is captured by the system. This helps the user to trace the produce using the corresponding product ID.

As shown in Figure 8.6a, seven parameters are monitored using IoT sensors, namely, soil moisture, temperature, humidity, fertility, seed quality, plant growth rate, and plant health. For experimental purpose, the average data for three consecutive days are considered. Figure 8.6b represents the histogram of temperature on ThingSpeak and MATLAB environment that helps the farmer in deciding the right time for cultivating the right crop and managing the water resources. Figure 8.6c represents the humidity of the soil as well as the atmosphere. Figure 8.6d offers the analysis of temperature vs. humidity in the field on ThingSpeak platform. Figure 8.6e analyzes the temperature and wind speed, while Figure 8.6f is the consolidation of all the atmospheric parameters with respect to time. Based on the time duration and corresponding parameters selected by the farmer, an analysis report is presented that aids the farmer from cultivation to harvest.

8.5.1   Benefits and Challenges

One out of every nine people faces food shortage on a global scale which sums up to around 800 million people according to the WHO (World Health Organization) release. The international community and UN are working toward sustainable development since 2015 to end hunger by the year 2030. Poor diet and shortage of food is leading to early death of around 11 million people annually [32]. To overcome these challenges, the production of food and cash crops has to increase. Rubber and cotton production also should be increased to meet the growing demand of ethanol and other bioenergy products. However, despite the development of cutting edge solutions and innovative farming schemes like aquaponics, hydroponics, and vertical farming, the rural community and farmers are unwilling to use them as they are accustomed to the traditional ways of farming.

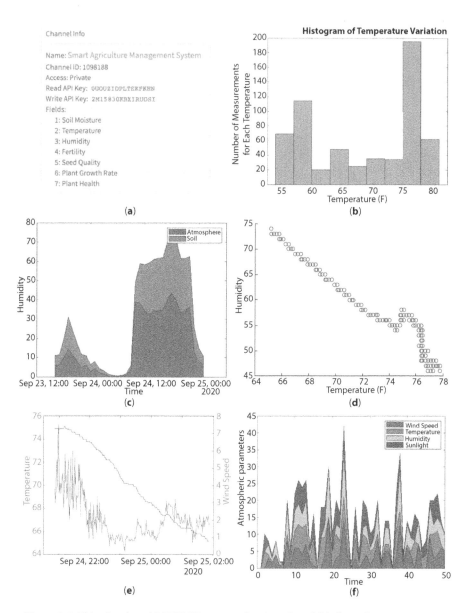

Figure 8.6 ThingSpeak and MATLAB output of various data fields from the smart farm environment. (a) Channel information, (b) Temperature variation histogram, (c) Humidity variation with time, (d) Temperature vs. humidity, (e) Temperature variation with time, and (f) Variation comparison of atmospheric parameters with time.

Sensitizing the farmers and providing them with the technological inputs has been a challenge. The user interface application has been developed in regional languages that help in overcoming a certain extent of this issue [33].

8.6   Conclusion

In a shrinking agricultural industry, more emphasis needs to be placed on meeting the demands of the growing population by producing better crop resources. Through the intervention of technology, young people are becoming more interested in the agricultural industry. It is considered as a significant profession. Various new technologies are used to improve agriculture. All of these technologies are being efficiently used to meet future food requirements. IoT is used in agriculture to meet a variety of needs and is a prominent cause for the revolution in agricultural industry. Complete information of the field from the wireless sensors is stored in the cloud platform. Data regarding consumers, retailers, suppliers and farmers, nutrition and safety labeling, crop growth, soil fertility, seed quality, farm insurance, and so on are managed efficiently using this model. Communication technologies, cloud computing, blockchain, and wireless sensors are discussed thoroughly. Integration of blockchain technology with IFPS offers the highest level of security for the agricultural data. For increasing the produce in agriculture, every bit of the farmland is crucial. Optimal use of these technologies with adequate data security leads us toward a hunger free planet.

8.7   Future Scope

The interconnected systems in agriculture are expected to revolutionize the industry with big data and AI technologies. Management of farm machinery from planting the seeds to forecasting production can be combined into a single unit. AI, big data, cloud computing, agricultural robots, drones, IoT, wireless sensors, and other cutting edge technologies with smart farming techniques like vertical farming, hydroponics, and aquaponics help in achieving a sustainable agricultural ecosystem. The environmental impact is reduced along with resource consumption and labor while the productivity is increased using these technologies. Precise and wise utilization of the resources of the planet is enabled by the sensible use of technologies. A clear and prosperous agricultural sector leads to a healthy society. Advanced technologies discussed in the paper helps toward achieving this goal to a great extent.

References

1. Aryal, J.P., Sapkota, T.B., Rahut, D.B., Jat, M.L., Agricultural sustainability under emerging climatic variability: the role of climate-smart agriculture and relevant policies in India. *Int. J. Innov. Sustain. Dev.*, 14, 2, 219–245, 2020.

2. Hunter, M.C., Smith, R.G., Schipanski, M.E., Atwood, L.W., Mortensen, D.A., Agriculture in 2050: recalibrating targets for sustainable intensification. *Bioscience*, 67, 4, 386–391, 2017.

3. Willer, H. and Lernoud, J., *Organic Agriculture Worldwide: Key results from the FiBL-IFOAM survey on organic agriculture worldwide 2013. Slide collection*, Frick, Switzerland, 2013.

4. Balafoutis, A.T., Beck, B., Fountas, S., Tsiropoulos, Z., Vangeyte, J., van der Wal, T., Pedersen, S.M., Smart farming technologies–description, taxonomy and economic impact, in: *Precision Agriculture: Technology and Economic Perspectives*, pp. 21–77, Springer, Cham, 2017.

5. Blok, V. and Gremmen, B., Agricultural technologies as living machines: toward a biomimetic conceptualization of smart farming technologies. *Ethics, Policy Environ.*, 21, 2, 246–263, 2018.

6. Viani, F., Experimental validation of a wireless system for the irrigation management in smart farming applications. *Microw. Opt. Technol. Lett.*, 58, 9, 2186–2189, 2016.

7. Wiseman, L., Sanderson, J., Zhang, A., Jakku, E., Farmers and their data: An examination of farmers' reluctance to share their data through the lens of the laws impacting smart farming. *NJAS-Wagen. J. Life Sci.*, 90, 100301, 2019.

8. Akram, S.V., Malik, P.K., Singh, R., Anita, G., Tanwar, S., *Adoption of blockchain technology in various realms: Opportunities and challenges*, p. e109, Security and Privacy, Wiley Online Library, 2020.

9. Sarri, D., Lombardo, S., Pagliai, A., Perna, C., Lisci, R., De Pascale, V., Vieri, M., Smart Farming Introduction in Wine Farms: A Systematic Review and a New Proposal. *Sustainability*, 12, 17, 7191, 2020.

10. Usery, E.L., Pocknee, S., Boydell, B., Precision farming data management using geographic information systems. *Photogramm. Eng. Remote Sens.*, 61, 11, 1383–1392, 1995.

11. Iftikhar, N. and Pedersen, T.B., Flexible exchange of farming device data. *Comput. Electron. Agric.*, 75, 1, 52–63, 2011.

12. Rao, N.H., Big Data and Climate Smart Agriculture-Status and Implications for Agricultural Research and Innovation in India. *Proc. Indian Natl. Sci. Acad.*, 84, 3, 625–640, 2018.

13. Muangprathub, J., Boonnam, N., Kajornkasirat, S., Lekbangpong, N., Wanichsombat, A., Nillaor, P., IoT and agriculture data analysis for smart farm. *Comput. Electron. Agric.*, 156, 467–474, 2019.

14. Kamble, S.S., Gunasekaran, A., Gawankar, S.A., Achieving sustainable performance in a data-driven agriculture supply chain: A review for research and applications. *Int. J. Prod. Econ.*, 219, 179–194, 2020.

15. Jian, M.S., Xu, H.Y., Sheen, J.F., Ye, Y.L., Cloud based agriculture safety inspection with multiple standard sources, in: *2018 20th International Conference on Advanced Communication Technology (ICACT)*, IEEE, pp. 201–206, 2018, February.

16. Sarker, M.N.I., Wu, M., Alam, G.M., Islam, M.S., Role of climate smart agriculture in promoting sustainable agriculture: a systematic literature review. *Int. J. Agric. Resour., Gov. Ecol.*, 15, 4, 323–337, 2019.

17. Bryan, E., Theis, S., Choufani, J., *Gender-Sensitive, Climate-Smart Agriculture for Improved Nutrition in Africa South of the Sahara*, Washington, DC: IFPRI, 2017.

18. Agrimonti, C., Lauro, M., Visioli, G., Smart agriculture for food quality: facing climate change in the 21st century. *Crit. Rev. Food Sci. Nutr.*, 61, 6, 1–11, 2020.

19. Bu, F. and Wang, X., A smart agriculture IoT system based on deep reinforcement learning. *Future Gener. Comput. Syst.*, 99, 500–507, 2019.

20. Wang, N., Zhang, N., Wang, M., Wireless sensors in agriculture and food industry—Recent development and future perspective. *Comput. Electron. Agric.*, 50, 1, 1–14, 2006.

21. Abbasi, A.Z., Islam, N., Shaikh, Z.A., A review of wireless sensors and networks' applications in agriculture. *Comput. Stand. Interfaces*, 36, 2, 263–270, 2014.

22. Malhan, I.V. and Rao, S., *Agricultural knowledge transfer in India: A study of prevailing communication channels*, p. 200, Library Philosophy and Practice, Lincoln, Nebraska, 2007.

23. Wu, Q., Liang, Y., Li, Y., Liang, Y., Research on intelligent acquisition of smart agricultural big data, in: *2017 25th International Conference on Geoinformatics*, IEEE, pp. 1–7, 2017, August.

24. Ray, P.P., Internet of things for smart agriculture: Technologies, practices and future direction. *J. Ambient Intell. Smart Environ.*, 9, 4, 395–420, 2017.

25. Gondchawar, N. and Kawitkar, R.S., IoT based smart agriculture. *Int. J. Adv. Res. Comput. Commun. Eng.*, 5, 6, 838–842, 2016.

26. Mekala, M.S., Viswanathan, P., A Survey: Smart agriculture IoT with cloud computing, in: *2017 international conference on microelectronic devices, circuits and systems (ICMDCS)*, IEEE, pp. 1–7, 2017, August.

27. Salah, K., Nizamuddin, N., Jayaraman, R., Omar, M., Blockchain-based soybean traceability in agricultural supply chain. *IEEE Access*, 7, 73295–73305, 2019.

28. Javed, M.U., Javaid, N., Aldegheishem, A., Alrajeh, N., Tahir, M., Ramzan, M., Scheduling Charging of Electric Vehicles in a Secured Manner by Emphasizing Cost Minimization Using Blockchain Technology and IPFS. *Sustainability*, 12, 12, 5151, 2020.

29. Bachuwar, V.D., Shligram, A.D., Deshmukh, L.P., Monitoring the soil parameters using IoT and Android based application for smart agriculture, in: *AIP conference proceedings*, vol. 1989, No. 1, AIP Publishing LLC, p. 020003, 2018, July.

30. Walter, A., Finger, R., Huber, R., Buchmann, N., Opinion: Smart farming is key to developing sustainable agriculture. *Proc. Natl. Acad. Sci.*, 114, 24, 6148–6150, 2017.

31. Tripicchio, P., Satler, M., Dabisias, G., Ruffaldi, E., Avizzano, C.A., Towards smart farming and sustainable agriculture with drones, in: *2015 International Conference on Intelligent Environments*, IEEE, pp. 140–143, 2015, July.

32. Elijah, O., Rahman, T.A., Orikumhi, I., Leow, C.Y., Hindia, M.N., An overview of Internet of Things (IoT) and data analytics in agriculture: Benefits and challenges. *IEEE Internet Things J.*, 5, 5, 3758–3773, 2018.

33. Chatterjee, J.M., Kumar, A., Rathore, P.S., Jain, V. (Eds.), *Internet of Things and Machine Learning in Agriculture: Technological Impacts and Challenges*, vol. 8, Walter de Gruyter GmbH & Co KG, Berlin, Germany, 2021.

A Review of Blockchain Technology

Er. Aarti

Dept. of Computer Science and Engineering, LPU, Punjab, India

Abstract

Blockchain has much more to it than just cryptocurrencies because of its flexible nature. It is one of the most imaginative advances and troublesome too, which is the central perpetual, decentralized, ledger of records. Undoubtedly, it is a revolution in systems of record. As blockchain innovation re-architects our digital framework, it additionally reformulates the security condition and also promises to revolutionize the management of smart cities. They can have a large number of users everywhere throughout the world as they are distributed networks. Cryptography is used to secure the whole data residing in the blockchain where each client can add information. It can be done by utilizing an arrangement of three keys (public, private, and the receiver's key) that permit individuals to check the integrity of the information. Blockchain network does not have a central authority. This innovation has already rooted into the finance and banking areas by its uncommon straightforwardness, adaptability, and security that encourage the management of exchanges in a decentralized way. Features like distributed and peer-authentication empower it to span across auxiliary areas like smart grids, government public services, reputation systems, smart cities with IoT, and security services. However, it can change different enterprises, including logistics, healthcare, supply chain, insurance, and considerably more. Well-known enterprises like Samsung and IBM are likewise embracing blockchain innovation to attempt imaginative solutions and approaches to enterprises and new businesses.

Nowadays, the fastest-growing skill on the platform is blockchain, who is leaving behind the skills like TensorFlow and Machine Learning as well as led to an increase in demand for developers of blockchain. Solidity, Geth, Mist, Remix, and Metamask are the different blockchain advancement tools. Various

Email: rti_aaa@yahoo.co.in

Vishal Kumar, Vishal Jain, Bharti Sharma, Jyotir Moy Chatterjee and Rakesh Shrestha (eds.) Smart City Infrastructure: The Blockchain Perspective, (225–246) © 2022 Scrivener Publishing LLC

blockchain technologies are public blockchain, consortium or federated block-chains, and private blockchains. Ethereum, BigchainDB, HydraChain, and Corda are some of the examples of blockchain platforms. Whereas, Ethereum is considered as one of the best open-source blockchain platforms, which helps in running smart contract and gives distinctive tools for programming to make them. The blockchain applications are the recent pattern in the computerized world. It has the capability to change customary organizations. But to ride the rush of their fame, knowledge regarding the usage of tools and technology is must to create a perfect product. This chapter highlights the major characteristics, architecture, and taxonomy of blockchain technology. Furthermore, it also provides an insight into the various consensus algorithms and main application areas in the blockchain technology.

Keywords: Blockchain, cryptocurrency, distributed, consensus, public blockchain

9.1   Introduction

Blockchain is a period stepped adjustment of unchanging archives of data that is overseen by a cluster of PCs, instead of any single element. It may likewise be seen as a public record [2]. It consists of a sequence of blocks. Various cryptographic standards are used to secure and bound each block of information with the other, in this way, framing a chain. This network has no central expert or authority [4]. It is increasingly similar to a democ-ratized framework with a universal and unchanging record, with the information open for the general public's viewing pleasure [16]. Anything fabricated utilizing blockchain innovation is extremely straightforward from its nature, and everyone associated with it is responsible for their activities [6]. Blockchain innovation can upgrade the fundamental admin-istrations that are basic in exchange money [3]. It is more strong and secure than the restrictive, by its tendency [14]. It has brought together central-ized models which is at present utilized in the biological exchange system [15]. At its center, blockchain depends on a decentralized, digitalized, and disseminated record model.

Blockchain innovation makes a suitable, decentralized record of exchanges—the appropriated record—which permits the substitution of a single ace database [9]. It keeps a permanent record of all things considered, back to the starting purpose of an exchange. It is also called the provenance, which is needed in exchange fund, permitting budgetary establishments to survey all exchange steps and decrease the risk of misrepresentation [7].

As blockchain innovation re-engineers our advanced framework, it likewise reformulates the security condition [8]. A fundamental interpretation of blockchain is that it tends to be applied to any action that needs a database and to handle data management issues, it follows that blockchain software brings to bear tools, especially around protection, security, and validation [12]. Not to make any changes in information is the most fundamental property of one of dispersed record innovations. Adjustment and falsification are not possible in case when a log is made of transaction or an activity [17]. It offers an unheard of degree of straightforwardness and, finally, security. Moreover, network administrators never approach to clients' password, which means there is no path for them to control or make a change in clients' information. Instead, they get just a preview of the identities of individual clients because of the utilization of private key authentication [5].

Blockchain is notable for supporting digital types of money, for example, Ethereum and Bitcoin; however, it can possibly change different businesses, including logistics and supply chain, healthcare, financial, insurance, and substantially more [13]. To offer inventive arrangements and approaches to ventures and new companies, these well-known companies like IBM and Samsung are likewise adopting this innovation [10]. Blockchain is by all accounts the quickest developing expertise on the platform, deserting the abilities like TensorFlow and Machine Learning [11]. It has prompted an expanding interest for blockchain developers [1].

9.1.1   Characteristics of Blockchain Technology

Different remarkable features of a blockchain that have made it a favored innovation in the market are as follows in Figure 9.1.

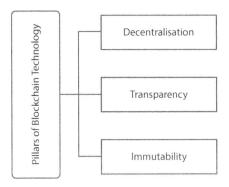

Figure 9.1 Characteristics of blockchain technology.

9.1.1.1 Decentralization

Before the appearance of Bitcoin, a model was already in much use through which exclusively interaction with a centralized entity taken place that put away all the information to extricate whateverinformation is required. No doubt, such incorporated frameworks do have a couple of vulnerabilities related to them, such as being hard to redesign, distinct objectives for hackers, etc. While thinking about this, the idea of decentralized frameworks was presented [18]. The data is not put away by a singular entity in such contexts. Everybody is the proprietor of the data in the system. On the off chance that the main party of the structure needs to associate with the subsequent one, both can straightforwardly connect without the mediator third centralized entity [19]. On account of Bitcoin, cash can be transferred to anybody on the chain without a need of a bank.

9.1.1.2 Transparency

It is considered as one of the most misunderstood aspects of blockchain innovation. A few of us comprehend that it gives security, whereas others think about it as transparent. Everybody's character is masked by sophisticated encryption in blockchain and also represented by public address only. While considering an individual's exchange history in a blockchain, it would not see something like "Bob sent US$ 100" however rather, and it will be something like 1MF1bhsFLkBzzz9vpFYEmvwT2TbyCt7NZJ sent $100. With these lines, while the individual's genuine character is not uncovered, a look can take place at all the exchanges that individual has done utilizing their public address. This degree of transparency never exists within any money-related framework. The public address of a client can simply be popped in an explorer, according to a digital money perspective [20]. Location of a client can be popped simply, and a list of all the transactions can be seen that the individual has engaged in, provided that the public address is already known. This is the thing that forces various organizations utilizing this innovation to be completely honest.

9.1.1.3 Immutability

It states that once something is gone into the blockchain cannot be changed. This property is supported by the blockchain as it stores information by utilizing the cryptographic hash function. Hashing alludes to the way toward considering an information string of any length but yield a static length string [21]. If there should be an occurrence of digital forms of cash like Bitcoin, then various exchanges are considered as information sources, and afterward, go through a particular hash calculation that produces a result of fixed length. It makes the blockchain so incredibly stable [22].

Advantages of Blockchain Technology

1. Data integrity and immutability
2. Security
3. Reliability
4. High availability and accessibility
5. Transparency and consensus
6. Decentralization
7. Automation
8. Processing Time

Disadvantages of Blockchain Technology

1. Cost issues
2. Latency issues
3. Data malleability issues
4. Wasted resources
5. Integration concerns
6. Immaturity of the technology

9.2   Related Work

Despite the fact that blockchain is sensibly new innovation, a plethora of literature overview is accessible from different sources like sites, organization, and whitepapers distributed by different associations executing and testing in the blockchain. Zibin *et al.* have explained about consensus and also discussed different taxonomy of blockchain [49]. Nasti *et al.* have accomplished work on Bitcoin mining [50]. Tschorsch *et al.* surveyed on decentralized digital currencies including Bitcoin. Comparing to [51], the focus is on blockchain innovation rather than digital currency.

9.3   Architecture of Blockchain and Its Components

The blockchain is a computerized, decentralized (circulated), and changeless record that tracks all exchange that happens over a shared organization.

It is also an arranged collection of blocks, where every block holds a whole list of exchange records like regular public record. It is an interlinked and persistent block of records put away safely over the organization. Each block is remarkably associated with the last block by means of the computerized signature, as it contains a hash portrayal of the last block. Such an ordering helps recorded exchanges in this innovation not be erased or modified without discrediting the chain of hashes. This joined with additional computational imperatives that make blockchain permanent. The primary block of a blockchain is known as the genesis block that has no parent block. The main thought here is setting the trust not in a main position like a government, a bank, or a global company rather in the organization.

Inward subtleties of an individual block are clarified underneath. Each block comprises of the body and the header.

Specifically, the header of block incorporates:

i.   Block variant: 4-byte long version number that demonstrates the convention version utilized by the hub for block approval rules to be followed.
ii.   Merkle tree root hash: It contains the hash value of the apparent multitude of exchanges in theblock.
iii. Timestamp: It stores the current time as seconds in the universal time since January 1, 1970.
iv.   nBits: target limit of a legitimate block hash.
v.   Nonce: a 4-byte field that stores an arbitrary number which as a rule begins with 0 and increments for each hash figuring. Any change made to hinder information will change the whole block hash.
vi.   Parent block hash: a 256 - bit hash value that focuses to the last block.

The body of block comprises of an exchange counter and set of exchanges. The most extreme countof exchanges, a specific block can contain relies upon the block size and the size of every exchange.

Validation and approval of exchanges in this innovation are guaranteed with the computerizedsignature dependent on asymmetric cryptography.

The major components of Blockchain are as follows:

A.   Consensus
B.   Distributed Ledger
C.   Cryptography
D.   Smart contract

9.4   Blockchain Taxonomy

Various types of blockchain technologies are public blockchain, consortium or federated blockchains,and private blockchains.

9.4.1   Public Blockchain

These conventions depend on the PoW consensus algorithm and are accessible as open-source [1]. Public blockchains do not discriminate in terms of who can participate in the network. Anyone can take an interest in these without authorization. They are also called the permissionless blockchain. Downloading the code and then run any of the public nodes can be done by everyone on their nearby gadget to approve different exchanges in the network [23]. This procedure helps in deciding the condition of various blocks that get added to the chain.

Transactions can be done by anyone at anywhere in the world through this network and can hope to see them remembered in the blockchain on the off chance that they are legitimate. Additionally, transactions can read by anyone on a public block explorer. All the exchanges are straightforward, however, unknown [24]. A lot of framework cost does not acquire by this procedure. For instance, Ethereum and Bitcoin fall under a public blockchain classification.

9.4.2   Consortium Blockchain

Consortium or federated blockchains consistently work heavily influenced by a group. It is the combination of both permissionless and permissioned blockchain [25]. In contrast with a public blockchain (Figure 9.2), they do

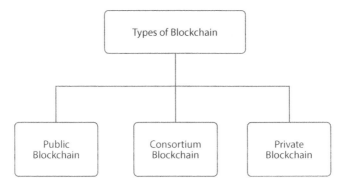

Figure 9.2 Types of blockchain.

not permit any individual with internet access to involve in the procedure of exchange check [26]. They are progressively adaptable, quicker, and even give more exchange security. They are generally utilized in the financial sector.

The consensus procedure is in the control of a pre-chosen set of nodes. The right to read the complete blockchain might be open or might be confined uniquely to the pre-chosen members. To reduce the data redundancies and the related exchange costs, this sort of blockchain is used, henceforth streamlining the record dealing with the process. It additionally assists in disposing of the semi-manual consistency methods. For instance, R3 (in banking) and EWF (from the vitality division) fall under the consortium classification.

9.4.3 Private Blockchain

Based on access control, they are also called permissioned blockchain. It contains various members and groups who can check different exchanges inside without much of a stretch. In just one organization, write consents, keep centralized while read authorizations may be open or confined to a limited degree. For example, auditing applications and database management are always inward to a solitary organization, so open comprehensibility may not be essential by any means, in specific cases. Open review consents might be wanted in some cases. They are essential for their effectiveness and protection from misrepresentation inside different budgetary foundations. Due to the smaller number of participants, it is easy to change the rules for a group. Scalability is one of its advantages. They are most commonly utilized by companies to transfer information among themselves and additionally with their sub-organizations. For instance, Multichain, Hyperledger, and MONAX are private blockchains [1]. The comparison between the different types of blockchain is specified in Table 9.1.

Table 9.1 Comparison between different types of blockchain.

Characteristics	Public blockchain	Consortium blockchain	Private blockchain
Participation	Public	Selected	Restricted to organization
Identity	Anonymous	Known	Known
Efficiency	Low	High	High
Consensus Process	Permissionless	Permissioned	Permissioned
Centralized	No	Partial	Yes
Example	Bitcoin	R3	MONAX

9.5   Consensus Algorithms

The consensus mechanism is a set of rules which used to perform this immensely significant task that helps in deciding the contributions in blockchain done by the various participants. Utilization of consensus algorithms is optimal for a better output. There are a lot of things common in the blockchain and function in the same way, yet one of the way by which blockchain can be one of a kind in which transactions are valid and added. Different consensus mechanisms are used in blockchain to achieve this. As, this method is fault-tolerant that can be utilized in blockchain frameworks and computer to attain the significant deal to a solitary information value or a solitary status of the system among distributed processes, for example, cryptocurrency. To make balance and fairness in the digital world, the techniques utilized are blockchain consensus models. The accord framework used for this consent is called a consensus theorem. Such models are substantially more reliable and fault-tolerant. These algorithms are an effective procedure for a group, where people of the group support and build the choice that works best for the rest of them. These mechanisms are protocols that ensure all nodes considered as a device on the blockchain to be synchronized with each other that keeps up the processes transactions and blockchain and also agreed upon addition and transactions which are legitimate too in the blockchain. These mechanisms are considered to be significant to work effectively for a blockchain. Everybody ensures the usage of the same blockchain. Everyone submits things which added to the blockchain, so regular checking of all the transactions and evaluation of all nodes done by the blockchain is mandatory. The consensus mechanism is the center of this distributed ledger system because the blockchain network has no central expert or authority [4]. Blockchain is at risk of different attacks in the absence of suitable consensus mechanisms. Various categories of consensus algorithms work on different principles. Some variants are PoW, PoS, Proof of Capacity, Proof of Activity, Proof of Burn, and many more. No doubt, versatility in the nature of the blockchain system is due to the accord algorithms. The beauty of this blockchain is the continual change for improvement. The consensus method is needed to make the framework completely decentralized, which is the main idea of blockchain technology.

9.5.1   Functions of Blockchain Consensus Mechanisms

Blockchain innovation's consensus systems intended to encourage the dynamic procedures of a gathering of clients. Consensus conventions empower a blockchain's clients to produce fairly, and decision on choices that influence the whole system. Choices can go from everyday information preparing like which node the opportunity to deliver the following block, to administration issues gets relating to updates to the blockchain's genuine engineering [27].

The functions are as follows:

- Looking for Agreement
  The consensus is characterized as an understanding by a larger part of a number of individual from a gathering. Looking for understanding is considered as the primary target of a consensus system is to realize understanding by at least the most of the individuals, this keeping up group solidarity.
- Coordinated effort
  The second target of a consensus convention is to maintain an understanding of the ideological opinions relevant to the gathering's proposed exercises. The agreement empowers clients to team up more legitimately without a third party.
- Egalitarianism
  For consensus to happen, votes of individual members from a gathering should hold equivalent weight and none ought to be, under any conditions, be viewed as being progressively significant.
- Comprehensiveness
  The voting procedure on a blockchain should not support certain individuals over others and be available to whatever number contestants as would be prudent, advancing cooperation by all individual.

9.5.2   Some Approaches to Consensus

There are different approaches of consensus methods which work on various standards.

9.5.2.1   Proof of Work (PoW)

PoW is the cryptocurrency accord method presented in the blockchain system [28]. This consensus model is used by many blockchain technologies to validate all the exchanges and produce appropriate blocks to the network series [28]. It is developed and designed by Satoshi Nakamoto, who is a Bitcoin maker. It is developed to remove the Byzantine shortcomings, which permits the formation of Bitcoin as a Byzantine Fault Tolerant system.

It implies that the Bitcoin blockchain is exceptionally impervious to mal-functions because of the dispersed system as well as on account of the PoW algorithm [29], for example, the 51% attack is a situation when a client or a gathering of clients controls most of the mining power. The attackers get sufficient capacity to rule most of the occasions in the system. They can consume the creation of new blocks and get awards to keep different diggers for completing the blocks. Transactions can be reversed. Fifty-one percent of attack is not a gainful choice, as it requires a huge measure of mining power [30].

In digital money, PoW is a framework that utilizes hard-to-compute, however, simple to confirm capacities to confine taking points of interest of cryptographic money mining. It is the oldest as well as the most commonly utilized accord method in the blockchain [56].

The PoW idea was created in 1993 to take care of digital attacks as Distributed Denial of Service (DDoS) [29]. PoW idea is needed to clarify an expensive PC computation, known as mining which created to confirm the validity of a transaction or ignore a method called Double-spending [29]. The PoW idea is as follows:

- Transactions aggregated like blocks.
- Miners affirm transactions inside the blocks as authentic.
- The miners handle a mathematical problem known as the PoW.
- A reward is then given to the primary individual to tackle the issue.
- The public blockchain network used to store the verified transactions.
- The oldest and most widespread and known method [31]

9.5.2.2   Proof of Stake (PoS)

The stake is the digital money which a client claims and vows to participate in approval. Proof of Stake is a kind of accord method wherein clients of a blockchain-based system need to stake some portion of coins or tokens, in order to get an opportunity at checking exchanges in a block [29]. When a client is picked to approve a block and can check all transfers in that block, at that point, a client remunerated with a specific measure of digital money for its work. PoS is practically identical to the PoW algorithm in which the two of them need their system members to arrive at a dispersed consensus. Likewise, the main target of consensus mechanisms like PoS is to safe a blockchain system. A client that checks exchanges is known as a miner in PoW, however as indicated, alluded to as a falsifier in PoS. This method is not about mining but is about the validation of transactions in blocks [14]. There are numerous crypto coins hoping to change over to PoS framework as it is substantially more to bring together and vitality effective over the large haul and extremely captivating to a new financial specialist with more up to date idea. Common PoS coins are Navvcoin, Neo, PivX, Reddcoin, and Dash. Some variants of the PoS algorithm are Delegated PoS and Leased PoS.

9.5.2.3 Delegated Proof of Stake (DPoS)

It depends on PoS framework where a client's stake decides casting a ballot power, but DPoS clients stake their coin possessions to choose nodes to add new blocks to the system and vote on proposed system redesigns. Similar cartel-like conduct predominant in PoW and PoS systems has been seen in systems running Delegated Proof of Stake (Figure 9.3). The discussions are encompassing the administration of EOS being a portion of the issues emerging from DPoS [32].

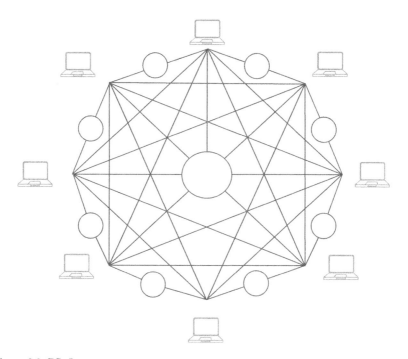

Figure 9.3 DPoS.

An intriguing kind of PoS called DPoS. EOS is using this method to scale up to an enormous number of trades each second. Anyone can participate in the block generator political race, and they will be given an opportunity to make blocks proportionate to the total votes they get concerning each and every other generator. If they can truly pull it off, by then, they will have the DPoS to thank. DPoS was first introduced by Bitshares [33] blockchain that is why considered as the backbone of it [34].

9.5.2.4   Leased Proof of Stake (LPoS)

It is a leading variant of the PoS mechanism. It permits the network to make a unified network inside a decentralized platform. By and large, in the PoS algorithm, each node holds aspecific measure of digital money and is appropriate to include the following block into the blockchain. But, with LPoS, clients can rent their balance to full nodes. The higher the sum that is rented, the better the chances are that the full node will be chosen to create the following block.

On the off chance that the node is chosen, the client will get some portion of exchange charges thatare gathered by the node. In LPoS, smallholders easily get an opportunity of staking. The Waves platform is used to help the small-time investors who never get an opportunity like others which highlights the transparency of this algorithm [35]. Waves and NXT [36] network deals with LPoS consensus algorithm combined with the Waves-NG convention, taking into account a high level of versatility, exchange throughput and less amount of power consumption [29].

9.5.2.5   Practical Byzantine Fault Tolerance (PBFT)

This method solves the Byzantine Generals' Problem by having members affirm messages sent to them by running a computation to decide its choice about the message's legitimacy [37]. A Byzantine shortcoming is a situation when various eyewitnesses get various indications. A Byzantine disappointment is any sort of framework administration loss because of a Byzantine fault [11]. It couldendure up to 1/3 malevolent byzantine copies [2]. In every round, a new block is resolved.

In each cycle, an essential would be chosen by certain standards, and it is liable for requesting the exchange. It has five phases wherein the main node advances the message to the next three nodes. Regardless of whether one node crashes, different nodes must finish a series of agreement, guaranteeing strong consistency and practicality for the network [2]. The three main phases of the whole process are pre-prepared, prepared and commit [8]. So, the knowledge of each other is required in the system. The party at that point communicates its choice to different nodes that at that point process a choice on it [41]. An ultimate choice relies upon the choices returned by different nodes. It is a lightweight algorithm, as it relies upon the number of nodes as restricts a high hash-rate to arrive at a consensus. Ripple and Stellar, as well as Hyperledger [42], utilize PBFT algorithms. Ripple is closed source, centralized, and the third-largest cryptocurrency [43].

Consensus without mining or PoW is through a consensus method such as Hyperledger that is based on PBFT [44]. Stellar gives the option to individuals to pick which set of different participants to accept [4]. Antshares [45] has implemented its DBFT based on PBFT.

9.5.2.6   Proof of Burn (PoB)

The PoB consensus method accomplishes its target by having clients trade the estimation of single cash to create hinders by expecting clients to reason produced "unspent locations" in return for local digital currency. It is one of the fairest [46], manageable, democratic, and beneficial method. Slimcoin applies PoB alongside a blend of different consensus conventions. Value of single computerized money can be traded then onto the following through the PoB system. It suggests a node participatesin a lottery to pick the status of the blockchain by consuming worth they starting at now hold, as cryptographic cash, for instance, Bitcoin or Ether [47]. To find the accompanying block, the node moves Bitcoin, Ether, or some other advanced money to an unspent location.

Consequently, the node gets compensation in the coins neighborhood to the blockchain it supports to continue. The primary blockchain to viably apply the PoB method for mining was Slimcoin. In contrast to PoW, energy

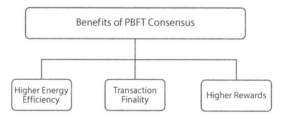

Figure 9.4 Benefits of PBFT.

is not wasted in this consensus method [29]. The genuine processing power is not basic to evade control. For this situation, the nodes demolish or consume their tokens in the event that they need to make the following blocks and get a prize. This method is normally utilized to commence new coin projects as a way to give reasonable dissemination initially.

This can be viewed as an alternative scheme where the estimation of the new coins originates from the way that already a specific number of coins have been demolished [10] (Figure 9.4).

9.5.2.7   Proof of Elapsed Time (PoET)

It is frequently utilized mainly on permissioned blockchain network where permission is required before accessing the network. They need to determine the mining rights or voting principles on the network. It uses a particular strategy to cover the transparency [28] into the network and ensure the smooth conduct of each node. It also ensures a secure login into the system, as the network demand reorganization of the client before they are permitted to join. It understands the client commission issues brought about by PoS consensus algorithms by adequately guaranteeing each node has an equivalent chance to create a block. PoET [52] permits all nodes to create blocks for a predetermined measure of time and then rests for a particular amount of time while other nodes add blocks to the system [48]. This consensus algorithm uses a fair way to select the winners.

9.6   Challenges in Terms of Technologies

The blockchain innovation is getting predominant in multidisciplinary applications, shortcomings, and difficulties ought to involve concern. Talked about underneath were simply the difficulties that the innovation has brought forth [53].

1. Maintain the consistency with this present reality
2. Correction of data
3. Appropriate utilization of an individual advances that led disruption to existing industrypractices
4. Particular check of the impacts of cost reduction
5. Management of security and protection

9.7   Major Application Areas

9.7.1   Finance

Blockchain innovation has its underlying foundations in account and banking area. A huge assortment of cryptocurrencies is already in usage. Different varieties are in tax collection, the key credits of blockchain specifically provenance, straightforwardness, and recognizability meet the specific need of present day tax assessment plans.

9.7.2   Education

This innovation is also useful in education area, where the instructive records of the student's credentials can be placed safely and imparted them to the partner's by appropriate consent system. Likewise, it diminishes the requirement of verification as the records are accessible whenever and substantial. It is also needed to give award to the significant kids for their overall development. By utilizing blockchain, the award framework can be managed which guarantees that the correct youngster will get the correct award at right time. Likewise the progressions are done straightforwardly.

9.7.3   Secured Connection

A blockchain-based security system is suggested in [54], to empower safe delivery of data in a smart city. This innovation gives numerous unique highlights like assistance in improving dependability, adaptability, support faster, and proficient activity with adaptation to internal failure ability, and it is strong against numerous dangers.

9.7.4   Health

A solitary electronic well-being record for the residents can be created by utilizing blockchain innovation. It is more adaptable, secure and reliable for the patients just as well-being suppliers. Such records are decentralized and no compelling reason to convey various well-being records with them while visiting the expert. They are made accessible whenever. Likewise, enlisting the professionals and offices of care suppliers is also possible. It guarantees better control on clinical specialist organizations in the city just as on the approved experts. Healthcare area is getting increasingly more digitalized after some time as it helps in getting inter-medical services between nations. Clinical information is assorted and tremendous and requires no modifications [55].

9.7.5   Insurance

A disseminated organization of different gatherings, for example, medical clinics, insurers, and the recipient, can frame the hubs of the blockchain. This setup will accelerate the whole strategy included and furthermore assists with eliminating frauds.

9.7.6   E-Voting

The prerequisites of electronic voting, for example, secrecy, permanence, and public evidence, are appropriate for incorporating blockchain innovation.

9.7.7   Smart Contracts

It is proposed to perform the exchange electronically between the gatherings without outsider inclusion. The exchanges are identifiable and irreversible. They have the option to confirm the performance of exchange whenever required. They are helpful for such circumstances including the money-related and lawful processes like crowd funding agreements, property law, insurance premiums, and budgetary administrations.

Blockchain innovation is utilized to build up a more grounded and available agreements, just the gatherings those are associated with the agreement could hold the real information on it; however, the genuineness of the equivalent could be confirmed by the outsider by utilizing the overall safety efforts which includes hashed crypto keys.

9.7.8   Waste and Sanitation

One of the significant challenges in the advancement of smart city is the administration of waste and sanitation. To manage this, proficient and better waste administration techniques are required to precisely follow the waste creation level or disbursal. Such a technique can be actualized by consolidating IoT-based arrangement with blockchain innovation. Such frameworks likewise accommodating in charging the punishments or awards to the waste administration organizations in the event that they neglect to give better time-based administrations.

9.8 Conclusion

Nowadays, Blockchain technology is one of the most fascinating thoughts for many researchers to work on it and suggesting various solutions in different areas. In this chapter, a comprehensive review of Blockchain technology with its architecture is discussed. The key characteristics of blockchain technology, architecture, taxonomy, and various consensus algorithms are also explained. The challenges and major application areas of blockchain innovation are also provided. Comparison is also done between various types of blockchain. It can be seen that blockchain innovation has high worth and great possibilities in settling issues of preventing fraud, improving transparency, upgrade security, and data integrity, and establishing trust and privacy. Blockchain innovation has a gigantic potential in presenting imaginative solutions, contingent upon the zone or the area of its execution, since monetary proficiency and social advantages can be accomplished through specialized advancement and applications. More concentrated research in this area of Blockchain technology is important to propel the development of this field, since it is still in the exploratory stage and there are numerous specialized issues to be settled.

References

1. Staff, C., *9 Key Tools and Technologies to Develop and Test Blockchain Applications*, 2020, January 23, Retrieved from https://www.coinspeaker.com/tools-technologies-blockchain-applications/.
2. Ahmed, I., Shilpi, Amjad, M., Blockchain Technology A Literature Survey. *Int. Res. J. Eng. Technol. (IRJET)*, 5, 10, 1490–1493, 2018.
3. Dorri, A., Steger, M., Kanhere, S.S., Jurdak, R., BlockChain: A Distributed Solution to Automotive Security and Privacy. *IEEE Commun. Mag.*, 55, 12, 119–125, 2017, https://doi.org/10.1109/mcom.2017.1700879.
4. Zheng, Z., Xie, S., Dai, H., Chen, X., Wang, H., An Overview of Blockchain Technology: Architecture, Consensus, and Future Trends. *2017 IEEE International Congress on Big Data (BigData Congress)*, pp. 557–564, 2017, https://doi.org/10.1109/bigdatacongress.2017.85.
5. H., *The Role of Blockchain in Data Security*, 2018, November 9, Retrieved from https://www.infosecurity-magazine.com/opinions/role-blockchain-data-security/.
6. Zou, Y., Meng, T., Zhang, P., Zhang, W., Li, H., Focus on Blockchain: A Comprehensive Survey on Academic and Application. *IEEE Access*, 8, 187182–187201, 2020. https://doi.org/10.1109/access.2020.3030491

7. Belin, O., *6 Essential Blockchain Technology Concepts You Need To Know*, 2020, March 26, Retrieved from https://tradeix.com/essential-blockchain-technology-concepts/.

8. Ali Syed, T., Alzahrani, A., Jan, S., Siddiqui, M. S., Nadeem, A., Alghamdi, T. A Comparative Analysis of Blockchain Architecture and its Applications: Problems and Recommendations. *IEEE Access*, 7, 176838–176869, 2019. https://doi.org/10.1109/access.2019.2957660

9. *Corda|Open Source Blockchain Platform for Business*, 2020, April 29, Retrieved from https://www.corda.net.

10. Bashir, I., *Mastering Blockchain*, Van Haren Publishing, Zaltbommel, Netherlands, 2017.

11. Tinu, N.S., A Survey on Blockchain Technology - Taxonomy, Consensus Algorithms and Applications. *Int. J. Comput. Sci. Eng.*, 6, 5, 691–696, 2018, Retrieved from https://www.ijcseonline.org/pdf_paper_view.php?paper_id=2044&112- IJCSE-03588.pdfMay 2019. E-ISSN: 2347 – 2693.

12. Panarello, A., Tapas, N., Merlino, G., Longo, F., Puliafito, A., Blockchain and IoT Integration: A Systematic Survey. *Sensors*, *18*, 8, 2575, 2018, https://doi.org/10.3390/s18082575.

13. *Blockchain Tutorial for Beginners: Learn Blockchain Technology*, 2020, May 2, Retrieved from https://www.guru99.com/blockchain-tutorial.html.

14. Singhal, B., Dhameja, G., Panda, P.S., *Beginning Blockchain*, Apress, Berkeley, CA, 2018, https://doi.org/10.1007/978-1-4842-3444-0.

15. *Advantages and Disadvantages of Blockchain Technology | Redbytes*, 2018, July 26, Retrieved from https://www.redbytes.in/advantages-and-disadvantages-of-blockchain- technology/.

16. *Blockchain Explained - Intro - Beginners Guide to Blockchain*, 2019, August 29, Retrieved from https://blockchainhub.net/blockchain-intro/.

17. Rosic, A., *What is Blockchain Technology? A Step-by-Step Guide For Beginners*, 2020, May 3, Retrieved from https://blockgeeks.com/guides/what-is-blockchain-technology/.

18. Dhanalakshmi, S., Charles, G., Babu, G.C., An Examination of Big Data And Blockchain Technology. *Int. J. Innov. Technol. Explor. Eng. (IJITEE)*, 8, *11*, 3118–3122, 2019, Retrieved from https://www.ijitee.org/wp-content/uploads/papers/v8i11/K24970981119.pdf.

19. Kang, J., Xiong, Z., Niyato, D., Wang, P., Ye, D., Kim, D.I., Incentivizing Consensus Propagation in Proof-of-Stake Based Consortium Blockchain Networks. *IEEE Wirel. Commun. Lett.*, 8, 1, 157–160, 2019, https://doi.org/10.1109/lwc.2018.2864758.

20. C., *Blockchain and big data use cases: Challenges and opportunities with blockchain and data science*, 2019, February 22, Retrieved from http://cloudconsultingcompanies.com/2019/02/22/blockchain-and-big-data-use-cases- challenges-and-opportunities-with-blockchain-and-data-science/.

21. Jayasinghe, U. and Lee, G.M., MacDermott, Á., Rhee, W. S., TrustChain: A Privacy Preserving Blockchain with Edge Computing. *Wirel. Commun. Mobile Comput.*, 2019, 1–17, 2019, https://doi.org/10.1155/2019/2014697.

22. Zheng, Z., Xie, S., Dai, H.N., Chen, X., Wang, H., Blockchain challenges and opportunities: a survey. *Int. J. Web Grid Serv.*, *14*, 4, 352, 2018, https://doi.org/10.1504/ijwgs.2018.095647.

23. 999, T.B., *Some Basic Blockchain Techniques*, 2018, September 16, Retrieved from https://medium.com/kriptoa/some-basic-blockchain-techniques-2d4c09c4d76a.

24. Jayachandran, P., *The difference between public and private blockchain*, 2020, February 12, Retrieved from https://www.ibm.com/blogs/blockchain/2017/05/the-difference-between- public-and-private-blockchain/.

25. Admin., *5 Tools Everyone in the Blockchain Technology Industry Should Be Using*, 2018, August 31, Retrieved from https://www.enukesoftware.com/blog/5-tools-everyone-in- blockchain-industry-is-using.html.

26. *Blockchain Advantages and Disadvantages*, 2020, January 19, Retrieved from https://www.binance.vision/blockchain/positives-and-negatives-of-blockchain.

27. Salimitari, M., Chatterjee, M., Fallah, Y. P., A survey on consensus methods in blockchain for resource-constrained IoT networks. *Internet of Things*, 11, 100212, 2020. https://doi.org/10.1016/j.iot.2020.100212

28. Anwar, H., *Consensus Algorithms: The Root Of The Blockchain Technology*, 2020, March 2, Retrieved from https://101blockchains.com/consensus-algorithms-blockchain/.

29. *Blockchain Consensus Algorithms & Mechanisms: Startup Guide For Beginners*, Retrieved from https://www.developcoins.com/blockchain-consensus-algorithms.

30. Tar, A., *Proof-of-Work, Explained*, 2019, December 11, Retrieved from https://cointelegraph.com/explained/proof-of-work-explained.

31. Miguel, C. and Barbara, L., *Practical byzantine fault tolerance (1999). Proceedings of the Third Symposium on Operating Systems Design and Implementation, 99,* USENIX Association, New Orleans, USA, pp. 173–186, 1999, https://doi.org/10.5555/296806.

32. *Hyperledger – Open Source Blockchain Technologies 2021, August 25,* Retrieved from https://www.hyperledger.org.

33. Admin, N. *Proof-of-Stake Variants Explained. NOBI Blog.* 2021, January 21, https://usenobi.com/blog/proof-of-stake-variants-explained/.

34. *BitShares - Delegated Proof-of-Stake Consensus|BitShares*, 2019, May 13, Retrieved from https://bitshareshub.io/delegated-proof-of-stake-consensus/.

35. Anwar, and H., *Consensus Algorithms: The Root of The Blockchain Technology*, 2020, March 2, Retrieved from https://101blockchains.com/consensus-algorithms-blockchain/.

36. *Categorizing*, 2018, Retrieved from https://tokens-economy.gitbook.io/consensus/categorizing-consensus.

37. Kravchenko, P., *What is Consensus Algorithm in Blockchain and Why Do We Need it?*, 2018, June 28, Retrieved from https://cryptovest.com/education/what-is-consensus-algorithm- in-blockchain-and-why-do-we-need-it/.

38. Perera, S., Nanayakkara, S., Rodrigo, M., Senaratne, S., Weinand, R. Blockchain technology: Is it hype or real in the construction industry? *J. Ind. Inf. Integration*, 17, 100125, 2020. https://doi.org/10.1016/j.jii.2020.100125

39. Monrat, A. A., Schelen, O., Andersson, K., A Survey of Blockchain From the Perspectives of Applications, Challenges, and Opportunities. *IEEE Access*, 7, 117134–117151, 2019. https://doi.org/10.1109/access.2019.2936094

40. Naz, S. and Lee, S. U. J., Why the new consensus mechanism is needed in blockchain technology? *2020 Second International Conference on Blockchain Computing and Applications (BCCA)*. Published. https://doi.org/10.1109/bcca50787.2020.9274461

41. Miguel, C. and Barbara, L., Practical byzantine fault tolerance. *(1999). Proceedings of the Third Symposium on Operating Systems Design and Implementation, 99*, New Orleans, USA, pp. 173–186, 1999, https://doi.org/10.5555/296806.

42. Cachin, C., Architecture of the hyperledger blockchain fabric, in: *Proceedings of the Workshop on distributed cryptocurrencies and consensus ledgers*, 2016.

43. Gates, M., *Blockchain: Ultimate Guide to understanding blockchain, bitcoin, cryptocurrencies, smart contracts and the future of money*, Wise Fox, United States, 2017.

44. Swan, M., *Blockchain: Blueprint for a New Economy*, 1st ed., O'Reilly Media, Sebastopol, USA, 2015.

45. F., *Antshares, Digital Assets for Everyone*, 2016, December 23, Retrieved from http://ftreporter.com/antshares-digital-assets-for-everyone/.

46. Correos, E.D., *How DPoS Benefits Blockchain: ABBC Consensus Explained*, 2020, January 6, Retrieved from https://abbccoin.com/blog/how-dpos-benefits-blockchain-abbc-consensus-explained/.

47. Anurag, *8 Famous Blockchain Consensus Mechanisms and their Benefits*, 2020, April 18, Retrieved from https://www.newgenapps.com/blog/8-blockchain-consensus-mechanisms-and- benefits/.

48. Shraddha, S. , Consensus Mechanisms in Blockchain Technology: A Review. *Int. J. Sci. Res.*, 9, 2, 1513–1518, 2020. https://www.ijsr.net/archive/v9i2/SR20222152735.pdf

49. Zheng, Z., Xie, S., Dai, H., Chen, X., Wang, H., An Overview of Blockchain Technology: Architecture, Consensus, and Future Trends. *IEEE 6th International Congress On Big Data*, pp. 557–564.

50. Nasti, S.M., Nasti, S.J., Bashir, R., Butt, M.A., Bitcoin: Surveying First Revolutionary Cryptographic Virtual Currency. *Int. J. Comput. Sci. Eng.*, 6, 1, 101–103, 2018.

51. Tschorsch, B., Scheuermann, Bitcoin and beyond: A technical survey on decentralized digital currencies. *IEEE Commun. Surv. Tutor.*, 18, 3, 464, 2016.

52. Kaur, S., Chaturvedi, S., Sharma, A., Kar, J., A Research Survey on Applications of Consensus Protocols in Blockchain. in: *Security and Communication Networks*, D. He (Ed.), 1–22, 2021. Hindawi Limited. https://doi.org/10.1155/2021/6693731 and cite in 9.5.2.7 main text

53. Zheng, Z., Xie, S., Dai, H.-N., Chen, X., Wang, H., Blockchain Challenges and Opportunities: A Survey. *International Journal of Web and Grid Services*, 2017.

54. Biswas, K. and Muthukkumarasamy, V., Securing Smart Cities Using Blockchain Technology, in: *2016 IEEE 14th International Conference on Smart Cities*, pp. 1392–1393.

55. Gurpreet, k. and Manreet, S., IOT Survey: The Phase Changer in Healthcare Industry. *Int. J. Sci. Res. Netw. Secur. Commun.*, 6, 2, 34–39, 2018.

56. Gupta, C. and Mahajan, A., Evaluation of Proof-of-Work Consensus Algorithm for Blockchain Networks. *2020 11th International Conference on Computing, Communication and Networking Technologies (ICCCNT)*, 2020 Published. https://doi.org/10.1109/icccnt49239.2020.9225676

10

Technological Dimension of a Smart City

Laxmi Kumari Pathak[1†], Shalini Mahato[1*†] and Soni Sweta[2]

[1]Department of Computer Science and Information Technology, Amity Institute of Information Technology, Amity University, Jharkhand, India
[2]Department of Computer Science and Engineering, Amity School of Technology, Amity University, Mumbai, India

Abstract

In this era of development, people from rural areas are moving to toward cities in a huge number. The increasing population in cities and the fast rate of urbanization are now forcing the cities to switch to smart cities. In smart city, Information Technology is performing a huge responsibility in building smart cities and the implementation is supported by Big Data, Artificial Intelligence (AI), and Internet of Things (IoT). Purpose of smart city is to create a smarter city in terms of sustainability, efficiency, and living conditions. The chapter discusses about the mechanisms that makes a city smart. The chapter also discusses about the different dimension of smart city, the problem domain along with the various challenges faced in smart city development. Generally, there are numerous problems in any city, such as improper waste management, pollution, traffic congestion, outdated homes, huge energy consumption, and wastage of electricity that can be dealt through smart city.

Keywords: Artificial Intelligence (AI), smart city, big data, Internet of Things (IoT), sensors

10.1 Introduction

Smart cities help to efficiently manage all the services of the city using Information and Communication Technologies (ICT), machine learning (ML), cloud computing, Internet of Things (IoT), and big data. Smart cities are focused in effectively managing population growth, enhancing the level of living and economic growth of the individual, providing ease as well as

---

*Corresponding author: swarup.shalini@gmail.com
†Both authors contributed equally as the First Author to this chapter

Vishal Kumar, Vishal Jain, Bharti Sharma, Jyotir Moy Chatterjee and Rakesh Shrestha (eds.) Smart City Infrastructure: The Blockchain Perspective, (247–268) © 2022 Scrivener Publishing LLC

efficiency to people in solving real-time problem. USA has the highest number of smart cities. The "smart" term refers to the city being more focused to be eco-friendly, better waste management, and thus converting to green city [1].

In an environment of urban areas, modern cities across the globe are progressively moving their composition and economic role. The continuously increasing movement of people from rural to urban locations influences the growth of cities [2]. Developing sustainable and smart towns has always been a worldwide movement over recent years. To overcome dynamic issues and challenges in contemporary cities, the smart city idea is emerging [3]. The strategic planning of a smart city is mainly based on the incorporation of various ICT approaches to leverage the infrastructure of the city [4]. Cities ought to be managed in a way that drives sustainable prosperity and ensures social stability and environmental protection. Smart living encompasses a range of initiatives that enhance life style of people, such as activities related to culture, tourism, and educational events, and emphasize on the healthcare service quality [5].

The below are some of the main characteristics of a smart city: i) environment and climate friendly; ii) dynamic is nature; iii) helps in making life sustainable; iv) efficient use of resources; v) adds innovations in the field of application; vi) improves quality of life; vii) helps in decision-making; and viii) works in integrated manner.

There are many advantages of smart city [7]. Some of major points are as follows:

    i.   More efficient utilization of all the available resources.

    ii.   A large number of responsibilities of workplace and home are completed automatically.

   iii.   Less wastage of time in proper decision-making.

   iv.   City can more efficiently and easy adapt to uncertain scenarios.

    v.   A large amount of useful information is generated and stored that can be later analysed for decision-making.

   vi.   All the smart cities would be connected to each other in an integrated manner.

  vii.   Economic and social prospects would increase a lot.

The basic components of smart city are [29]:

    i.   Smart economy which is related to enhancing the efficiency by implementation in industrial sector.

    ii.   Smart people which is related to enhancement in education sector.

iii. Smart governance which related to E-democracy which increases transparency of decision-making

iv. Smart mobility which is related to efficient movement of goods and infrastructure.

v. Smart environment deals with sustainability and reduction pollution and waste management.

vi. Smart living is linked to an increase in the standard of living as well as taking into concern the security aspect of it.

The smart city idea is primarily based on Big Data and IoT, but Artificial Intelligence (AI) is also the backbone for complete automation of services. The most commonly accepted system levels in development of smart city are as follows:

i. Sensor Level: This layer mainly comprises of interconnected sensors in IoT devices which communicates with each other. These sensors constantly scrutinize the parameters and are the markers of the smart city situation.

ii. Data Level: All the data generated from numerous IoT devices are collected, processed, and stored in database, which further helps in analysing the scenario and decision-making.

iii. Business Level: In this level, data modeling is done for analysis and visualization and for understanding the metadata, semantics, and business logic.

iv. Application Level: This level contains the applications for the people, municipal, government, and public and private organization.

The "degree of accuracy" of solution provided by the smart city remedy is also an important feature of smart city which specifies the degree of reliability.

10.2 Major Advanced Technological Components of ICT in Smart City

ICT is there to plays a significant role in decision-making, implementation, and the ultimate productive services. ICT makes the smart city connected, efficient, intelligent, secure, and energy efficient with the help of the core components of it. Major components of ICT are i) IoT, ii) Big Data, and iii) AI.

10.2.1 Internet of Things

The IoT is a huge step forward in the development of the Internet. It is expected that IoT impact every field of life in next 5 to 10 years and would significantly change the society. The number of connected wireless devices would increase drastically [30]. IoT makes everyday objects intelligent and context aware with the aid of wireless communication network and embedded sensor that are also wireless. The commonly used devices in our day-to-day life, e.g., clothes, coffee maker, and water sprinkler, all will become intelligent with the help IoT. Thus, all the commonly use devices would become intelligent, context aware, and would be able to communicate with each other and would be having the decision-making capability. This would drastically improve every field of life and make life easy [31].

10.2.2 Big Data

Implementation of IoT would lead to generation of large amount of information at every second. This information further requires to be stored and analysis needs to be done to understand the pattern which would further help decision-making and prediction. The data is generally stored in cloud or smart city server. The processed data helps in developing services for smart traffic control, smart hospital, smart energy management, smart home, smart parking, and many more.

10.2.3 Artificial Intelligence

Implementation AI makes the smart cities object context-aware and pseudo intelligent. The object can learn from a situation and has decision-making capability. There is a huge range of application of AI in almost every field. Some of the implementation of AI are recommendation system, self-driving car, and industrial robots [8].

10.3 Different Dimensions of Smart Cities

Immense amount of work has been done in various facets of smart city. Table 10.1 shows the present state of art in different facets of smart city. Figure 10.1 also shows the different dimensions of smart city.

10.4 Issues Related to Smart Cities

There are several issues in implementation of smart city. The major issues includes i) system interoperability among different kind of devices, ii) cost-efficient technology which could be used among large number of devices, and iii) privacy and security of data which generated by the devices.

Table 10.1 Present state of art in different dimension of smart cities.

Sl. no.	Application area	Problem domain	Reference	Solution/Methodology
1	Smart Waste Management System	In the current situation, it is frequently found that the trash bins or garbage bins being put in public areas in the cities. It produces unhygienic environments for individuals and produces a poor smell all over the locality, adding to the spread of certain dangerous viruses and human illness. Waste disposal is a significant public operation in which substantial costs are involved. Challenges in waste management are highly concerning areas.	[9]	The authors define the configuration of the paths and schedules of vehicles for accumulating the solid waste in cities in eastern Finland. A newly established directed variable neighborhood produces the solutions. A meta-heuristic level that is tailored to address challenges in the processing of real-life garbage. A few strategies to execution to accelerate the process and memory consumption reduction are addressed.

(Continued)

Table 10.1 Present state of art in different dimension of smart cities. (*Continued*)

Sl. no.	Application area	Problem domain	Reference	Solution/Methodology
2			[10]	Authors intend to build "IoT-Based Waste Management System for Intelligent Cities". In this suggested form, there are many dustbins in the town filled with low-cost devices, each equipped with an integrated tracker that helps monitor the garbage bins' level, as well as a unique ID. It is quite helpful to pinpoint which trash compacter is loaded. When the level crosses the top of the maximum level, the computer, together with the unique level, will move the level as well as the assigned unique ID. The related authorities can use the data with an active Internet connection; hence, a prompt step can be taken to empty the trash bins.

(*Continued*)

Table 10.1 Present state of art in different dimension of smart cities. (*Continued*)

Sl. no.	Application area	Problem domain	Reference	Solution/Methodology
3	Air Pollution Monitoring	Air pollution is a significant component of global warming and the emphasis is increasingly on resolving this issue. Local societies trying to take advantage of Information Technology (IT) and communication systems to enhance the monitoring of pollution and noise from the atmosphere contamination. The goal is to increase understanding health-threatening hazards in regard to effects of vulnerability to air pollution.	[11]	The authors created an online array of GPRS sensors with a mobile data acquisition unit and a static internet-enabled pollution monitoring server to track air pollution. The system is embedded with a microcontroller having a single-chip, air pollution sensor array, a GPRS modem and a GPS module. It has a high-tech pollution server having Internet connection. The mobile-DAQ collects air pollutants levels (like CO, SO_2, and NO_2), and combines all of these in a packet with GPS location, date and time. This packet will be sent to the GPRS modem and then to the server of pollution through the network of mobile. The level of pollutants is stored in database server. The pollution server is connected to Google Maps to view current pollution levels and their positions in cities.

(*Continued*)

Table 10.1 Present state of art in different dimension of smart cities. (*Continued*)

Sl. no.	Application area	Problem domain	Reference	Solution/Methodology
4			[12]	The authors discuss the main problems of real-time emissions in this paper. Tracking devices include cameras, networking standards for the Internet of Things, and data capture and communication via channels of communication, and also data protection and security. The protection standards stick to the guidelines and best practices that guarantee reliability. The system use predictive analytics to analyze the gathered data to generate maps of pollution. It can be integrated with traffic management system so that vehicles can be diverted to other routes when the pollution level of a particular area rises.

(Continued)

Table 10.1 Present state of art in different dimension of smart cities. (*Continued*)

Sl. no.	Application area	Problem domain	Reference	Solution/Methodology
5	Noise Pollution Monitoring	Most of the world population now stays in cities that will rise up to 60% in 2030. It is the main challenge regarding noise pollution that can cause serious health hazards. At this time, an intelligent solution is needed to deal with noise pollution before it crosses the risk levels in the cities.	[13]	Authors gave a unique technique to measure noise pollution with their prototype called noise tube by enabling the people with the ability to track their individual level of exposure to noise in their day-to-day life. GPS-enabled smartphones were used as sensors for this approach. The data gathered at individual level can be sent automatically to share with other people online, so that the collective mapping of noise can be done.
6			[14]	A unique IoT-based architecture is proposed by the authors that can detect the polluted areas with noise and can inform the same and new areas of city can also be predicted. Authors developed an intelligent noise pollution monitoring system that can identify the areas, time, and the noise level with the help of data mining techniques. It can also detect the rush hours of a particular area so that time of high noise levels can be detected. In this study, Support Vector Machine and Random Forest were to generate a model that can predict noise pollution before its occurrence.

(Continued)

Table 10.1 Present state of art in different dimension of smart cities. (*Continued*)

Sl. no.	Application area	Problem domain	Reference	Solution/Methodology
7	Traffic Congestion Monitoring	In the present scenario, traffic congestion at peak hours are one of the main problems of day-to-day life.	[15]	Authors proposed a vehicle-based sensor system for monitoring the traffic. They tested their system in Shanghai, China, by installing the sensors in almost 4,000 vehicles. The link-oriented and vehicle-oriented status-estimation algorithms were given and analyzed. They found quite satisfactory and accurate results.
8		In some emergency conditions, like flood and storm, vehicles get slowdown in jams. In these conditions, some emergency services cannot be delivered because the vehicles are not equipped to cope with this situation that can cost so many lives.	[16]	In this paper, authors have introduced a self-ruling two-level framework. It can recognize emergency vehicles. The structure is IoT-based and it can monitor and manage the traffic situation efficiently and in a continuous manner.

(*Continued*)

Table 10.1 Present state of art in different dimension of smart cities. (*Continued*)

Sl. no.	Application area	Problem domain	Reference	Solution/Methodology
9	Smart Traffic Management System	In the present scenario of smart city, the traffic scenes are very congested in the market and industry areas, especially at the high times of business in the day. As the increasing rate of population and rising numbers of vehicles, people staying at cities and populated areas encounter with a lot of problems at some specific points. It causes delayed commutation and also pollution. In urban areas, smart traffic management is the only solution to this problem.	[17]	The author found that instant and accurate traffic detection by analyzing the performance of road network is much needed to control or prevent the situation. In this paper, authors have given CoTEC (COperative Traffic congestion detEction), that is a new cooperative method based on vehicle-to-vehicle (V2V) communications. They used fuzzy logic to detect the traffic congestion on road without the installing any sensors. The concept is able in truthfully perceiving the traffic congestion, concentration, and duration.
			[18]	In this paper, authors have proposed an improved traffic control and observing model for transferring information quickly. The mobile-based sensors run a congestion control algorithm under a vehicular ad-hoc network (VANET) to evenly establish the traffic movement by evading the congestion at specific area. It can prevent accidents, crimes, can provide driver flexibility and also make the travelers safe and secure.

(*Continued*)

Table 10.1 Present state of art in different dimension of smart cities. (*Continued*)

Sl. no.	Application area	Problem domain	Reference	Solution/Methodology
10	Energy Consumption monitoring	The huge rise in urbanization in previous years demands sustainable, competent, and intelligent solutions for environment, conveyance, supremacy, standard of life, etc. The IoT bids various complex and universal applications for smart cities. IoT devices expanding in both numbers and need, so the requirement of energy is also increasing. Managing the energy in effective way is the extremely vital component of smart city.	[19]	The authors have proposed a genuine and novel idea to integrate MANET over WSNs, after studying the existing WSN inter-operability After surveying the existing WSN interoperability efforts given for urban sensing. It can push city data collection in IoT. Overlays are utilized to dynamically distinguish and speed-up the distribution of crucial sensed data over low-latency MANET tracks by integrating with latest emergent standards for WSN data gathering.
11			[20]	Authors gave a model for energy effective arrangement and optimization of smart cities that are IoT-based. They discussed about energy conserving in smart cities that can be a great solution for distribution of the generation of low-power devices. They also did case studies on energy-efficient algorithm for smart homes as well as transfer of power in wireless fashion for IoT devices in smart cities.

(*Continued*)

Table 10.1 Present state of art in different dimension of smart cities. (*Continued*)

Sl. no.	Application area	Problem domain	Reference	Solution/Methodology
12	Automated and Intelligent Parking Management	Identifying a parking spot can be a tedious task especially when a person does not know the ending destination of the drive and the parking space is complex with numerous spots. It is expensive to find the exact parking location because it leads to increase in vehicle traffic which further leads to pollution.	[21]	Authors proposed the idea of using a blend of magnetic and ultrasonic sensors for exact and dependable recognition of automobiles in a parking lot. They explained an improved variety of the minimax algorithm for finding of automobiles using magnetometers, and an algorithm for ultrasonic sensors. They got very good results using these two sensory system.
13			[22]	The author describes the energy-efficient algorithm for smart homes and transfer of power wirelessly for IoT devices to be used in the smart cities. According to the results obtained from the simulations, there is considerable effect in the performance of IoTs in the smart city operation due to energy-efficient algorithm optimization and wireless power transfer. The author has emphasized on the challenges associated with energy management along with significance of energy harvesting in smart cities.

(*Continued*)

Table 10.1 Present state of art in different dimension of smart cities. (*Continued*)

Sl. no.	Application area	Problem domain	Reference	Solution/Methodology
14			[23]	The author has explored the benefits associated with cheap Wireless sensor networks for traffic planning and parking ease. Different types of sensors, ultrasonic, and magnetic type have been used to accurately detect the parking area for correct and reliable recognition of vehicles in a parking lot. For vehicle detection using magnetometers, a revised version of minimax algorithm has been proposed and separate algorithm to give the output using ultrasonic sensors has been proposed. Several experiments conducted in the multi-floor building parking space have shown the benefits associated with the usage ultrasonic sensors with magnetometers for correct vehicle information for accurate vehicle detections.

(Continued)

Table 10.1 Present state of art in different dimension of smart cities. (*Continued*)

Sl. no.	Application area	Problem domain	Reference	Solution/Methodology
15	Smart Lighting System	The lighting system of a city consumes one of the greatest parts of total energy produced. So, it is one of the most important areas that must be taken care of with high priority by implementing IoT, hence energy or electricity could be conserved.	[24]	The author discusses on the importance of smart systems associated with vehicle parking. The automated system has significantly helped in reducing time, energy and money by assigning the correct parking space. These IoT-based systems can be integrated with each other to provide real-time data to the user to properly plan the route conditions. It can also prove beneficial toward traffic planning and suggest suitable directions for important vehicle movements like ambulances. The author has used micro-controller-based system along with wireless communication system (Zigbee) integrated with the smart phone application. Comparison of the performance of Zigbee with other conventional wireless technologies shows significantly better results in providing real-time data to access the parking in busy city areas like malls and offices. Notification of the empty parking space is communicated through GSM module by delivering SMS from the software application to the user. The IR sensors put in the parking areas also helps in giving real-time information of the vacant spaces for proper space allocation. This greatly reduces the human interventions and reduces the efforts involved.

(*Continued*)

Table 10.1 Present state of art in different dimension of smart cities. (*Continued*)

Sl. no.	Application area	Problem domain	Reference	Solution/Methodology
16			[25]	The author has proposed a search optimization methodology for faster access to the free parking zone by involving multi-layer hierarchical model in which the algorithm first lays importance to nearest car parking area. Once the nearest car parking area has been identified the second layer of search involves the searching of an empty spot for car parking. The proposed methodology reduces the time involved toward finding suitable parking spot in the space constraint environment associated with congested city parking. Several rounds of simulation have resulted in assessing the hierarchical approach and have proved it to be time saving as well as energy saving option.

(*Continued*)

Table 10.1 Present state of art in different dimension of smart cities. (*Continued*)

Sl. no.	Application area	Problem domain	Reference	Solution/Methodology
17	Home Automation	In today's time, the natural resources must be preserved. Conserving the natural resources, security of the people, convenience, comfort, and power to control the home appliances must be given high priority. This can be achieved by using Home Automation.	[26]	The author has brought in the study of energy scavengers and their usage for low-power systems. The study covers the energy scavenging circuits for wireless body area networks (WBAN). The battery charging associated with these WBAN limits its onboard capabilities as well as the communication range. As a result of these limitations, it becomes quite impractical to draw energy from batteries which are a conventional practice toward sourcing of power to WBANs. The study revolves around the possibility to eliminate the dependency on batteries by utilizing the ambient energy sources. Energy scavenging studies has evolved as an important research area toward this direction. Different interface circuits in energy scavenging along with different efficiency level have been suggested to get rid of the limitations of batteries in WBANs.

(*Continued*)

Table 10.1 Present state of art in different dimension of smart cities. (*Continued*)

Sl. no.	Application area	Problem domain	Reference	Solution/Methodology
18			[27]	The author in this paper describes the importance and benefits associated with the smart lighting system (SLS) in substantially reducing the power consumption to a level of 33.33% for indoor/outdoor lighting atmosphere. Different IoT-enabled communication protocols have been discussed by the author pertaining to its usage for the SLS toward building a smart city. The author has also analyzed different environmental conditions pertaining to the usage and consumption with the perspective of indoor/outdoor lighting. The author has also put a road map for future research works for a better SLS.

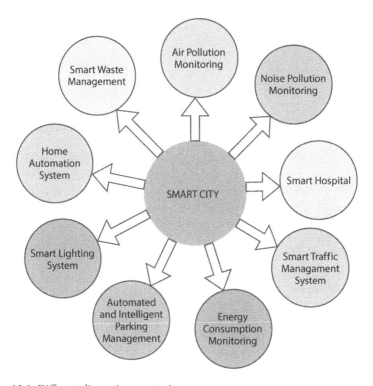

Figure 10.1 Different dimension smart city.

Out of all the issues related to smart city, privacy and security of information is the biggest challenge. Information security takes care of this aspect. Huge amount of data is generated when IoT devices are used and are communicating with each other. The confidential information needs to be protected from attack of viruses and malicious attacks from hackers. There can be various kind security issue related to use of technology like abuse of RFID tags, denial of service attack, spoofing, eavesdropping, jamming, tag killing, jamming attacks on authentication, and botnets [28].

10.5   Conclusion

Development of smart cities would impact each and every field of life and would make life easier. But along with the positive, there are a number of challenges which need to be taken care for the successful implementation of Smart Cities. Thus, more research work needs to be done in the area related to system interoperability, cost-efficient technology, and most importantly the security aspect of it.

References

1. Lemayian, J.P. and Al-Turjman, F., Intelligent IoT Communication in Smart Environments: An Overview. Artificial Intelligence in IoT Transactions on Computational Science and Computational Intelligence, pp. 207–221, 2019.
2. Winkowska, J., Szpilko, D., Pejic, S., Smart city concept in the light of the literature review. *Eng. Manage. Prod. Serv.*, 11, 2, 70–86, 2019.
3. Roychansyah, M.S. and Felasari, S., Measuring level of friendliness of smart city: a perceptual study. *IOP Conf. Ser.: Earth Environ. Sci.*, 126, 1, 1–9, 2018.
4. Guo, J., Ma, J., Li, X., Zhang, J., Zhang, T., An attribute-based trust negotiation protocol for D2D communication in smart city balancing trust and privacy. *J. Inf. Sci. Eng.*, 33, 4, 1007–1023, 2017.
5. Aletà, N.B., Alonso, C.M., Ruiz, R.M.A., Smart mobility and smart environment in the spanish cities. *Transp. Res. Proc.*, 24, 163–170, 2017.
6. Hameed, A.A., Smart city planning and sustainable development. *IOP Conf. Ser.: Mater. Sci. Eng.*, 518, 2, 1–12, 2019.
7. Duan, W., Nasiri, R., Karamizadeh, S., Smart city concepts and dimensions. *ACM International Conference Proceeding Series*, pp. 488–492, 2019.
8. Skouby, K.E., Lynggaard, P., Windekilde, I., Henten, A., How IoT, AAI can contribute to smart home and smart cities services: The role of innovation. *25th European Regional ITS Conference*, International, Telecommunications Society (ITS), Brussels, pp. 1–13, 2014.
9. Nuortio, T., Kytöjoki, J., Niska, H., Bräysy, O., Improved route planning and scheduling of waste collection and transport. *Expert Syst. Appl.*, 30, 2, 223–232, 2006.
10. Tambare, P. and Venkatachalam, P., IoT Based Waste Management for Smart City. *Int. J. Innov. Res. Comput. Commun. Eng.*, 4, 10, 1267–1274, 2016.
11. Al-Ali, R., Zualkernan, I., Aloul, F., A mobile GPRS-sensors array for air pollution monitoring. *IEEE Sens. J.*, 10, 10, 1666–1671, 2010.
12. Toma, C., Alexandru, A., Popa, M., Zamfiroiu, A., IoT solution for smart cities' pollution monitoring and the security challenges. *Sensors (Switzerland)*, 19, 15, 74–80, 2019.
13. Maisonneuve, N., Stevens, M., Niessen, M.E., Hanappe, P., Steels, L., Citizen noise pollution monitoring, in: *Proceeding of 10th Annual International Conference on Digital Government Research: Social Networks: Making Connections between Citizens, Data and Government*, pp. 96–103, 2009.
14. Almehmadi, A., Smart City Architecture for Noise Pollution Mitigation through the Internet of Things. *Int. J. Comput. Sci. Netw. Secur.*, 18, 7, 128–133, 2018.

15. Li, X., Shu, W., Li, M., Huang, H.-Y., Luo, P.-E., Wu, M.-Y., Performance evaluation of vehicle-based mobile sensor networks for traffic monitoring. *IEEE Trans. Veh. Technol.*, 58, 4, 7–1653, 2009.

16. Reddy, R.M., Rao, K.N., Prasad, S.V.S., Traffic Congestion Monitoring and Management by using IoT. *Int. J. Innov. Technol. Explor. Eng. (IJITEE)*, 8, 9S2, pp. 688–689, 2019.

17. Ramon, B., Gozalvez, J., Sanchez-Soriano, J., Road traffic congestion detection through cooperative vehicle-to-vehicle communications. *Proceeding of Local Computer Networks (LCN), IEEE 35th Conference on*, pp. 606–612, 2010.

18. Rath, M., Smart Traffic Management System for Traffic Control using Automated Mechanical and Electronic Devices. *IOP Conf. Ser.: Mater. Sci. Eng.*, 377, 1, 1–11, 2018.

19. Bellavista, P., Cardone, G., Corradi, A., Foschini, L., Convergence of MANET and WSN in IoT urban scenarios. *IEEE Sens. J.*, 13, 10, 3558–3567, 2013.

20. Ejaz, W., Naeem, M., Shahid, A., Anpalagan, A., Jo, M., Efficient Energy Management for the Internet of Things in Smart Cities. *IEEE Commun. Mag.*, 55, 1, 84–91, 2017.

21. Lee, S., Yoon, D., Ghosh, A., Intelligent parking lot application using wireless sensor networks. *Proceeding of International Collaborative Technologies and Systems, 19–23*, pp. 48–57, Chicago, 2008.

22. Qadir, Z., Al-Turjman, F., Nesimoglu, T., ZIGBEE based time and energy efficient smart parking system using IoT, in: *International Conference on Research in Education and Science (ICRES)*, Marmaris, Turkey, April 2018.

23. Kizilkaya, B., Caglar, M., Al-Turjman, F., Ever, E., An Intelligent Car Park Management System : Hierarchical Placement Algorithm Based on Nearest Location. *32nd International Conference on Advanced Information Networking and Applications Workshops (WAINA)*, pp. 597–602, Krakow, 2018.

24. Demir, S. and Al-Turjman, F., Energy scavenging methods for WBAN applications: A review. *IEEE Sens. J.*, 18, 16, 6477–6488, 2018.

25. Sikder, K., Acar, A., Aksu, H., Uluagac, A.S., Akkaya, K., Conti, M., IoT-enabled smart lighting systems for smart cities. *IEEE 8th Annual Computing and Communication Workshop and Conference, CCWC*, 2018.

26. Kastner, W., Neugschwandtner, G., Soucek, S., Newmann, H.M., Communication systems for building automation and control. *Proc. IEEE*, 93, 6, 1178–1203, 2005.

27. Alam, T., Salem, A.A., Alsharif, A.O., Alhejaili, A.M., Smart Home Automation Towards the Development of Smart Cities. *APTIKOM J. Comput. Sci. Inf. Technol.*, 5, 1, 13–20, 2020.

28. Ijaz, S., Ali, M., Khan, A., Ahmed, M., Smart Cities: A Survey on Security Concerns. *Int. J. Adv. Comput. Sci. Appl.*, 7, 2, 612–625, 2016.

29. Pichler, M., *Smart City Vienna: System Dynamics Modelling as a Tool for Understanding Feedbacks and Supporting Smart City, Strategies*, Universidade nova de Lisboa, Lisbon, Portugal, 2017.

30. Liu, J. and Tong, W., Dynamic Service Model Based on Context Resources in the Internet of Things. *6th International Conference on Wireless Communications Networking and Mobile Computing (WiCOM)*, Chengdu, pp. 1–4, 2010.

31. Kumar, A., M., Payal, P., Dixit, J.M., Chatterjee, Framework for Realization of Green Smart Cities Through the Internet of Things (IoT), in: *Trends in Cloud-based IoT*, pp. 85–111, 2020.

Blockchain—Does It Unleash the Hitched Chains of Contemporary Technologies

Abigail Christina Fernandez[1]* and Thamarai Selvi Rajukannu[2]

[1]*Knackcrow, Trichy, Tamil Nadu, India*
[2]*Department of Computer Applications, Bishop Heber College, Trichy, Tamil Nadu, India*

Abstract

Technology hysteria coupled with novelty is the apt combo in today's contemporary world. A technological solicitation intended for diversified practical utility, equipped with reiterated smartness and unceasing innovation, amidst its circumference of efficacy, would undoubtedly prove to be a top notch in the digital arena of revolution. The ever evolving and exhilarating blockchain has made its way in instilling incitement and exploration all around and has also ushered the amalgamation of itself, with the peer technologies in the upfront like Artificial Intelligence, Big Data Analytics, Internet of Things, and Cloud Computing. Blockchain poses astounding challenges of superseding the surviving technologies with the daunting concept of a Decentralized Autonomous Organization (DAO), immutability, resilience, and integrity, making it optimally infallible. This chapter focuses on the new hysteria of blockchain that would enrich the whole digital world of revolution, hand in hand with peers, or would it transcend the trending technologies, posing a threat of making them go either archaic or market restraining. The adorned decorum of blockchain alongside its precision in terms of security and reliability will be further apprehended to aid the cause. The keys in making blockchain a debatable benchmark rather than a debacle in the technical podium is elaborated upon.

Keywords: Blockchain, smart technology, consensus algorithms, mining, cryptocurrency, smart contracts, smart infrastructure, convergence of blockchain

Corresponding author: abszarun@gmail.com

Vishal Kumar, Vishal Jain, Bharti Sharma, Jyotir Moy Chatterjee and Rakesh Shrestha (eds.) Smart City Infrastructure: The Blockchain Perspective, (269–292) © 2022 Scrivener Publishing LLC

11.1   Introduction

Smart and Tact go hand in glove when it refers to the point of responsibility, contribution, and involvement to society in varied hemispheres of indulgence. This could be a decisive action that needs to be taken in a business venture, or a money indulgence in a financial transaction, or a health service rendered to a community of people, or the maintenance of legitimate assets or a smart city infrastructure that needs to be accentuated or the need to be immutably resilient and secure and the list goes on. In business practicality, all these shades of business were earlier maintained in a physical record referred to as a ledger, which actually holds proof of the undertakings that have been pursued over a period of time. This ledger entry was a bulky book that was again made as a replicated entry of information all around the process by the many parties involved in the business transaction. This posed a subtle and yet serious issue of a default factor that was liable to make an incorrect entry in a ledger, due to the negligence of the staff concerned. This retracted the legitimacy of the accountability aka responsibility.

Apparently, the entire process involved in a business deal, needed to make rounds from start to end both from person to person and ledger to ledger encompassing a considerable amount of error, stipulated time, and a consumable amount of money involved. Under this scenario, researchers came up with ideas of maintaining the same ledger records that were earlier done physically into a virtually maintained database, which is decentralized. Each entity involved in a business routine possessed an updated ledger entry record. Whenever there was a change made in the ledger entry, the same would be reflected in all the ledger entries of all the entities holding individual ledgers. This ruled out the dominion and centrifugal focus of authority of a single head in the business arena thereby led to the birth of blockchain.

The distributed framework was further extended in terms of application in different pitches of business undertaking. It started off with the simple record maintenance of asset records and money transferences and later expounded its diaphragm to a wider spectrum. With the umpteen of technologies that keep sprouting in today's digitalization, blockchain has managed to coordinate and culminate with technologies such as Artificial Intelligence (AI), Cloud Computing, Internet of Things (IoT), Analytics, and many more. This has catapulted its footprints in the many business domains prevalent in the market. Innovative and exciting technologies have been come up in vogue and have stirred up the urge to quest for more sensational useful expertise and know-hows.

Blockchain has gained the potential of attracting attention from long-standing enterprises, new start-up firms, and media due to its subtle democratic, transparent, and reliable process flow. Despite the fact that blockchain is still in its nascent stage, financial players from different arenas are flocking to capitalize in its technology. The swift, seamless, and cost-effective transaction of operations provides ushers its undertaking at all spheres. The immutable tact of blockchain is the key that makes blockchain robust in terms of data integrity, inhibiting fraud and irreversible in nature.

The use cases of blockchain seem to be multiplying manifold in a short span of time due to its intriguing incorporation with the existing technologies at relevant areas of expertise and need. The core of blockchain, the consensus algorithm, which is a consent in accordance is a sophisticated cryptographic authorization to verify the trust among the participants in a blockchain in any business undertaking. This is enhanced by effective tamper proof timestamping of events, security, authenticity, B2B ownership, resilience, and data loss protection in any transaction of business operation. The latest trends in blockchain amalgamated technologies will be featured in this chapter.

11.2   Historic Culmination of Blockchain

Blockchain has been building up its stature for the last three decades, from theories, models, and principle works of many researchers in the germane field, to this technologically sapid structure of utilization it has attained today. The concept of blockchain was being adapted since the early 1990s and has made a more definitive presence in the expertise arena, after it has been coined with the name, alongside the cryptocurrency Bitcoin in 2008. Indisputably since then, many researchers and techno experts have been trying to build up the blockchain with a protracted list of cryptocurrencies, accentuating different consensus algorithms that work their way up nattily.

As the very first step, the need for a well-maintained accountable ledger was felt in the business world. In the 1990s, the data structural ideology was handed down from Stuart Haber and Scott Stornetta, who came up with the timestamped document maintenance. This was further elaborated with the inclusion of hash pointers, tagging the referred documents and later the linking of documents, onto a single strand through the concept of Merkle tree, from Josh Benolah and Michael de Mare. The Byzantine Fault Tolerance (BFT) caused a daunting adversary in terms of misconceived nodes identity leading to disturbance in the operational functionality of the distributed ledger. Lamport, Robert Shostak, and Marshal Pease addressed this as state replication and forks resolution. Miguel Castro and Barbara Liskov in 1999 made a benchmark in suggesting multifaceted variants and other related protocols and optimizations to the practical BFT (PBFT). POW referred to as Proof of Work, (PoW) the first in the line of consensus algorithms originated in 1992, by Cynthia Dwork and Moni Naor. It also covered the featuring of effective treatment of Spam, Denial of Service, and Sybil Attacks. A somewhat similar instance of the guessing of the nonce was derived from Adam Back in 1997, before the actual utility of PoW in Blockchain or Bitcoin Mining, Markus Jakobsson, and Ari Juels in 1999.

All the above concepts and technics existed as just individual practices in different cases of functionality, until Satoshi Nakamoto in the 2008 gave the unabridged process a definitive portrayal and coined the term Bitcoin-Blockchain [1]. Blockchain professed the electronic exchange of cash system with peers in a business transaction, with an augmented monetary value through a cryptocurrency named Bitcoin, coupled with the seamless transparent decentralized deputation of operation.

Bitcoin, the brainchild of blockchain, came as an augmentation to this decentralized electronic exchange of information/cash among peers in a business transaction that worked in unison with a predefined consensus. Apparently, this gained momentum and utility, as this not only focused on the maintenance of documents but also inclined to the tagging facts related to accountability in terms of time, finance, and people involved in a transaction. The affirmative fact behind the effectuation of a web-centric payment system that is secure, robust, and cost-effective encompassing a decentralized stature and functionality is due to the adaption of smart contracts and consensus algorithms. This crisp outline elucidates as to how blockchain has reached its magnanimous stature today, from few bits and pieces of adept techniques that were beaded together effectively to evolve to a cutting edge of a technology, it showcases in current enterprising practices.

11.3   The Hustle About Blockchain—Revealed

Blockchain is a new system of a distributed ledger, which encompasses on storage and maintenance of sensitive information, over a P2P network of blocks, whose nodes are threaded across the chain cryptographically cascaded, following predefined consensus algorithms agreed among the participants of the setup, with no intervention of a third party whatsoever. So, the hushed creation of a block, the addition of nodes, appending of all the blocks, with the new block information that is added, is a crisp one liner behind the implementation of blockchain. The cryptocurrency Bitcoin, top on the list, holds the surety to a secure and tranquilized transfer of funds or documents between parties in a transaction [36].

11.3.1 How Does It Work?

Participants in a blockchain or owners of the blocks in a chain could proceed with the exchange of monetary or notary value in a transaction, with no revelation of identity or trust for peers on chain. The addition of a new block calls for the guessing of a nonce (that is a number used only once), which involves a computational program to reach at the conceived value of the nonce by the miners. The competition at guessing the hashed value of the nonce is the crux, to the Bitcoin mining process. This computation is solved by specifically designed ASIC (Application Specific Integrated Circuit), made for the purpose and the pool of miners at times jointly work in unison at guessing the hashed value and share the mined value among themselves. The approximate time to find a hashed value and to add/update a block is 10 min. The block comprises of a block version number, a timestamp, hash of the previous block in the chain (predecessor), hash of the Merkle tree, the nonce guessed, and the current hash of the block created. The chain keeps expanding when a new instance of transaction is called for, and again, the process of guessing the nonce is instigated and the process goes on. The whole cyclic process is referred to as PoW.

11.3.2 Consent in Accordance—Consensus Algorithm

An unanimity agreed and sufficed prior to the actual addition of a block that maybe required for a new business or management venture, demands for the consensus to be invoked. This is where the dominance of the consensus algorithm stages cast, irrespective of the type of cryptocurrency that chains the blocks alongside - the different consensus algorithms with the conceptualization practiced is enlisted in Table 11.1. The consensus of an algorithm seems to be achieved, provided there is a legitimacy maintained in terms of validity, agreement, liveness, and total order of the nodes of the blockchain as proposed by Wenbo Wang *et al.* [2].

Initially, Nakamoto started it with the consensus algorithm, the PoW, but later, in its years of transcending, many consensuses have been proposed and corresponding cryptocurrencies novelized to utility in recent times. The consensus algorithms intriguing the electronic cash to cash transactions are based on proof, vote, stochastic, alliance, and hybrid methodology that elect the mining of the cryptocurrency involved in the block creation process [3].

Table 11.1 Consensus algorithm alongside the conceptualization.

Consensus algorithms	Concept
Proof of Work (PoW)	Based on the miner who cracks the hash, the reward is decided and blocks appended to the chain
Proof of Stake (PoS)	The coin stack at hand with the miner decides participation of miner in the mining process.
Proof of Activity	The perfect blend of PoW and PoS strategy, to create a block and split the spoil in the rewards of roles such as winner and validators played by the miners.
Proof of Burn	The miner, which a maximum burn or spend of coins from the wallet, gets to mine the block.
Proof of Capacity	The computation power and the storage space in the capacity of the miner prioritize the participation in the mining of a new block.
Proof of Authority	Here, specifically, an admin block decides/authorizes to proceed to decline a transaction.
Proof of Elapsed Time	The randomly distributed waiting time approves the endearing chance of a miner.
Delegated Byzantine Fault Tolerance	Selection of miner is vote based and is ideally targeted a total of 66% of nodes participating in a consensus.
Proof of Importance	Every minor has an importance score that would schedule the miners to stand a chance in mining.

L.M. Bach *et al.* [4], in their research paper, focus on the analysis of steps the consensus algorithms follow, the scalability of the algorithm in varied scenarios of mining, the methodology engaged in the distribution of rewards appropriately to the miners involved, the efficient time pulled into the mining and the security risks underlying in the process. Many professionals in the field of blockchain technology are ardently pent on exploring the varied possibilities and combinations of the consensus algorithm to arrive at a real-time secure and fault-tolerant transaction.

11.4   The Unique Upfront Statuesque of Blockchain

Blockchain has attained the edifice of secure, immutable, transparent, robust, and dynamic manifestation based on the augmented characteristics that actually expound the implementation of the blockchain. The whole enterprise of the functioning of blockchain is an interconnection of a series of concepts that are intertwined for the better effectuation of the blockchain.

11.4.1   Key Elements of Blockchain

Blockchain—the long story told short would be a distributed decentralized peer-to-peer network of operations, adapting cryptography, mathematical and computational algorithm, and economical attributes in multi-field infrastructure construction of an enterprising market value. Housed with reliability to store sensitive content in terms of tracking and maintenance of medical records, document derivation, food traceability, voting or management ventures, and blockchain handles all this and much more incorporating these six elements of maneuvering:

> ➢ Decentralization: no centralized dependency.
> ➢ Transparency: seamless and trustworthy.
> ➢ Open Source: open to publicly valid the authenticity of records maintained.
> ➢ Autonomy: trust shifted from a single source to a multiple verified trust with no intervening.
> ➢ Immutability: records remain reserved forever, until and unless a participant exceeds 51% of undertaking in a nodes involved in a blockchain.
> ➢ Anonymity or secrecy in the data transactions done: business transactions do not require revealing of person's identity, rather the address of nodes interconnected in a chain matters for the blockchain creation and maintenance.

M. Niranjanamurthy *et al.* [5] clarify the essentials of blockchain through SWOT analysis in terms of association in business and commercial projects endeavouring of blockchain. The straightforward listing of the many characteristics blockchain possesses is expressed as strength, weakness, opportunities, and threats.

11.4.2   Adversaries Manoeuvred by Blockchain

Since its inception in the 2009, many novel applications of blockchain have queued up to deployment in the real-time market world, and researchers are trying zestfully to readdress the historic issues such as double spending, eclipse attacks, selfish mining, and superior smart contracts to make the blockchain better than the existing stance.

11.4.2.1   Double Spending Problem

Blockchain entered the stream of utility use cases starting from the financial business arena with the primal aim of solving the double spending problem which was a long pent problem to crack at. The model adopted by Blockchain was the FITS model [6].

F stands for Fraud. This aims at curbing the likelihood of the prevalence and indulgence of fraudulent activities in the business environment.

I stands for Intermediaries. The picture of a mediator in business transaction is ruled out totally, thereby saving cost incurred in that manner as well as increase in the settlement time of a transaction operation at the least of 15 min to 2 days maximum.

T stands for Throughput. The transaction rate per second is paramount higher in comparison to other financial services provided by master card of visa cards. It is approximately 400,000 per second.

S stands for Stable. Data transacted is highly immutable and non-volatile in nature making it exceptionally stable.

11.4.2.2   Selfish Mining and Eclipse Attacks

The core unique feature of a blockchain that makes it abreast amidst the existing technologies is the decentralized, distributed digital property. Information transacted in a business undertaking is made transparent to all the users involved in the blockchain, with the distribution of copies of transactions made, along with timestamps and properly encrypted keys to each and every dedicated node of a block in the blockchain. However, hackers down the line always tend to disrupt this functionality by activities such as selfish mining and eclipse attacks.

A strategy adapted by a quorum of miners to conspire to increase their revenue, thereby toppling the applecart of a decentralized network of transaction in blockchain is referred to as selfish mining. A malicious attack intended to malfunction the operation of the unmatched blockchain network is inferred as an eclipse attack. Gervais Arthur *et al.* [7] articulated a model in their paper, as objectively reach at a trade-off between the security and performance of the blockchain, taking into concern the PoW consensus algorithm.

11.4.2.3 Smart Contracts

Yet another interesting prospective of blockchain is the secure and immutable smart contracts that the blockchain incorporates in its functionality. The simple terms of a treaty/promise agreed upon by the buyer and the seller involved in a business dealing which outlines on prefixed self-executing set of rules/policies which are hard coded in the programming language of the implementation of the blockchain, thereby making it irreversible to modify/amend or to manipulate at a later point of time.

Samudaya Nanayakkara *et al.* [8] in their paper discuss a roundtable of issues related to the sturdiness of the smart contracts, and the list of indispensable features blockchain exhibits in the supply chain aspect of any industry be it healthcare, retail, real estate, identity management, power grids, etc. Their findings reveal a higher end efficiency in terms of trust, fair, security, transparent, accountability, compliance, and standardization in blockchain that marshals the stake holders of all domains of business to get attracted to the predominate perspectives of blockchain.

11.4.3 Breaking the Clutches of Centralized Operations

One may wonder as to how this concept of decentralized could make a niche area in the business world, thereby accelerating trade avenues in terms of economy and value? The usual centralized techniques of maintaining a database, inadvertently spelt the fact aloud that there was a dependency factor involved in any business venture, and that it involved silent intermediaries that were manoeuvring the behind the scenes operations of any business transaction. The FITS model alongside the DAOs (Decentralized Autonomous Organizations) modestly addressed the Fraud, Intermediaries, Throughput, and Stability (FITS) in a blockchain boosting the technological presence of the. The DAO has shifted focus from a centralized perception to the various individual members of importance committed in unison that actually decide on the stipulated building and maintenance of the blockchain. These nodes (individual proprietaries) are the nucleus to the operation of the blockchain. In other words, the decentralized figure of a consensus followed smart contractual policy of the blockchain is similar to a democratic nation that is run automatically with distributed power and equivalent leadership.

Table 11.2 Transaction latency.

Read Latency Read Latency = Time when response received – submit time	Read latency is the time between when the read request is submitted and when the reply is received.
Read Throughput Read Throughput = Total read operations/total time in seconds	Read throughput is a measure of how many read operations are completed in a defined time period, expressed as reads per second (RPS).
Transaction Latency Transaction Latency = (Confirmation time @ network threshold) – submit time	Transaction latency is a network-wide view of the amount of time taken for a transaction's effect to be usable across the network.

Max Nijland *et al.* [9] have analyzed the influential trail of blockchain in the real estate sector and have researched a breakdown structure that details the varied queries in terms of what is the hype in regard to blockchain? What are the characteristics, values incorporated, buying processes, costs involved, experience felt, misalignments/threats and challenged described and predicted, etc.? While many experts keep rummaging at the existing and the evolving characteristics and key elements and constraints of the blockchain, let us not forget to mention the key metrics that the blockchain follows as a standard policy and uses them during the transactions. The metrics that catch our interest are as shown in the Table 11.2, that unravels the terminology related to transaction and latency involved.

11.5 Blockchain Compeers Complexity

A paranoid hype stance taking rounds in the current digital Cosmos of revolution is that blockchain is very austere and rigid. Primarily, understanding the premonition of the functionality of the blockchain consortium is a bit hard to digest. But, on careful speculation of the immutable secure mechanisms and speedy transactions deployed in any business arena, with no middleman posing a viable commission in the commercial vocation, takes blockchain to the stature of strength and dynamism. The ultimate trade-off in blockchain is that there lies an open liability to eliminate the need of auditors in the trail. The integrity of blockchain combats money laundering through transparent yet fool proof record keeping. Arguably, this removes the incidence of a false claim and streamlines compliance requirements.

The disintermediation of third parties, user empowerment, high quality and durability of sensitive data keeping, integrity in terms of processes involved, transparency amidst anonymity, lower cost, swifter transaction time, and simplified ecosystem of the blockchain are the crème of what blockchain professes and channelizes. These adept concepts may be a total sphere of newness at the initial stages of adaptation, but then the clarity, business benefits, underlying traceability of records, and auditability are remarkably definite attributes to speculate upon and embark gradually.

11.6   Paradigm Shift to Deciphering Technologies Adjoining Blockchain

The world is currently dwelling in the fourth industrial revolution that coincides with a period of unprecedented innovation, technical change and global connectivity. This era is reinforced by the overwhelming advancements in technologies such as AI, robotics, cloud computing, autonomous vehicles, biotechnology, nanotechnology, IoT, quantum computing, and not forgetting the blockchain. The impeccable amalgamation of the technologies in varied peripherals such as physical, biological, and digitalization cumulatively propels the speed, intelligence, and efficiency of enterprise and societal indulgences.

Technology is all about being in the vogue. It spins around the fact of intensifying the scientific and intricate details, rather than contemplating on value transacted in the technology ecosystem. Less values in terms breach of trust, tampered security, lower friction, and governance rules are what the conventional technologies follow. Blockchain, a breakthrough in recent times, has slowly catapulted itself in all the business arenas such as financial services, industrial products and manufacturing, energy and utilities, healthcare, government, retail, and entertainment media. Blockchain has multifarious benefits pertinent to each domain of utility in terms of building trust among the blocks (parties) involved in a transaction, by sharing identity, verifying records, promoting transparency and immutability, and fostering resilience in a distributed topology.

The current phase of digital revolution focuses on blockchain-enabled innovation coupled with the existing technologies at hand. It does not stop with the business or finance, but for the betterment of people and the planet. Opportunities in terms of addressing environmental challenges, such as climate change, biosphere integrity, and water scarcity, are a few game-changing solutions to be explored and incentivize behavioral change thereby. This ensures the inclusion, safety, interoperability, and scalability of applications. Zibin Zeng *et al.* [10] addressed the issues of safety in terms of privacy leakage, interoperability in terms of ruling out centralization of networks, and scalability concentrated in storage optimization and redesigning of blockchain if required to suit the current need of the hour.

In yet another research on blockchain, Shaoan Xie *et al.* [11] emphasized on the advancements in the consensus algorithm of blockchain in terms of node identity management, energy saving, and tolerated power of the adversary, to enhance the consensus speed, stability, security, and retrievability of block processes. Toqeer Ali Syed *et al.* [12] discussed in details the prospective in the conversion rates toward blockchain in terms of the blockchain supporting platforms, consensus models used and the areas of application they span across. They further visualize the effects of coordination and overlapping of the platforms, consensus, and smart contracts to enhance the utility in IoT-enabled technologies thereby.

A few standard features that help motivate the invocation of blockchain with peer technologies with the aim of building smart homes at local point of view and smart cities and infrastructures at a wider angle reveals the inadvertent feature of blockchain such as flexibility, resilience, and distributed collaborative interfacing of technologies in terms of utility extents.

11.7   Convergence of Blockchain and AI Toward a Sustainable Smart City

Smart work is preferred to hard work. Synonymously, smart cities that enhance a better comfortable and sophisticated living standard and practice are the much sought after digitalizing revolution. As blockchain articulates, security and resilience coupled with decentralization and interoperability, the competing technologies have opted to join hands toward the building of a smarter environment. The whole globe has shrunk to the size of one's palm due to the predominant presence of the Internet. Elaborated with this comes, the IoT which idealizes a fool proof integration of internet connected devices that in a smart network that has data transparency, transaction automation, end-to-end process tracking, and a stress-free cloud-based scalability [34, 35].

Saurabh Singh *et al.* [13] discussed the formation of a smart city with blockchain and AI bringing benefits in terms of the following:

- Widen the touch base of experience of smart vehicles driven by Blockchain-AI.

- Effective in terms of cost, time, and effort.
- Enhances the modularity approach of grasping the concepts intrigued with in it.
- Reduces immensely the training of vehicles.

This thereby provides a resilient, decision supportive, smart, and intelligent infrastructure that is safe, scalable, and distributed.

To quote an example of how blockchain benefits with the partnering of AI, Tshilidzi Marwala *et al.* [14] come up with the proposal of bug free smart contracts in blockchain. This overcomes a few underlying vulnerabilities of Blockchain in terms of smart contracts, thereby making it more efficient and dynamic in its usage in a smart environment. Automated troubleshooting, debugging, and root cause analysis are a few application areas of how AI would uphold blockchain, making it error free from error prone.

Cloud computing is yet another nascent but concretely critical technology, especially during this pandemic period. This plays a crucial role at synchronizing remote operations over long distances, different geographical hemispheres, seamlessly in stipulated time frames, maintaining security, and immutability of information exchanged. Sukhpal Singh Gill *et al.* [15] examine the involvement of blockchain, IoT, and AI to propagate the cloud futurology. Cloud computing has been challenged with the constraints of security and privacy in real-time scenarios. They are taken up by blockchain, to service mission critical applications in terms of healthcare, smart cities, transport, surveillance, and system tolerance.

When the wind is high, the tide is also higher. The same goes with the congestion of the network due to the growing expanse of the cloud computing arena of users all over the globe. In order to overcome, the heavy load due to high network traffic at the cloud, technologies such as fog computing and augmented techniques such as edge computing, alongside IoT are making the rounds these days. A secure blockchain based on traffic load balancing using reinforcement learning and IoT (edge computing) has been devised by Kevin Tiba *et al.* [16]. The importance of this is derived from the fact that urban planning is the fast emerging in terms of shaping and building the environment, by overcoming traffic clogging. This answers vehicle detection, identification, count, prediction, and anticipation of traffic congestion through reinforced learning. The smart nodes in a blockchain network captures the images of the traffic in cities and forecasts suggestions, thereby improving uninterrupted flow of traffic.

The society flourishes if the people in it are healthy and abreast with the latest technological means of diagnosis and treatment. Polina Mamoshina *et al.* [17] have come up with the convergent thought of using AI with blockchain, to maintain secure exchange of health records of the patients, adjoined with the techniques of AI, such as deep learning and machine learning that actually transforms simplified medical images scanned to relevant pieces of diagnostic and predictive medical prescriptions.

Robotics and automation are extended tributaries of actual utility of the in-depth features, concepts, and implementations of AI. This is aimed at pampering and providing a comfort zone iterated with smartness and security for the mankind at large. Vasco Lopes *et al.* [18] unscramble the power of blockchain and present the same in robotics and AI to increase the capabilities of all technologies complimenting each other. The information in regard to the robots purchased from the different manufacturers is maintained by the blockchain and using the timestamp, the blockchain could anticipate definitive action such as maintenance, version update, or licensing issues in regard to the robot.

Big Data Analytics is also a blossoming trendsetter that predicts supportive market practices and business avenues in recent times. The efficient incorporation of the data at hand and the subsequent way to reach at more scalable and accurate AI model solutions, including the standardizations and interoperability features of blockchain are elucidated by McConaghy *et al.* [19] within multiple contexts, enhancing the possibilities of data analytics.

Innovation keeps revolutionizing itself in wide arenas of expertise and utilization. Likewise, the emergent technologies get cohesive for the betterment of a wider comprehensive provision to the earth at large. Thang N. Dinh *et al.* [20] discuss the impacts of AI and Blockchain hand in hand, instilling the key properties they portray, and how the marriage between the two would actually make up for the betterment of the other and aid in a more sophisticated digital generation.

11.8 Business Manifestations of Blockchain

The in exhaustive list of industries and technologies benefited by the incorporation of blockchain are manifold. The blockchain has slowly and steadily made its predominance in the commercial and client value market and has brought amusement to the business hub. The speedy operational movements with the consolidated audit streams enhance the potential of blockchain in the capital markets. This heightens the synchronized management of equity swap transactions throughout the lifecycle of the business connections.

Let us go into a detail foot trail of blockchain in diversified areas of application such as the following:

- Financial and banking
- Privacy and security
- Integrity verification
- Data management
- Supply chain management
- Healthcare
- Education
- Real estate
- Media
- Energy

Fran Casino *et al.* [21] have made a mind map abstraction of the multifaceted domains of applications. Blockchain could dynamically be a contributing part of. Blockchain as predicted will play a sustainable role in the global economy, thereby facilitating customers in terms current finance and banking operations and the whole society in general. The securities and derivatives, digital payments, loan management, diversified banking schemes, and tracking audit trails are a few to mention about the role of blockchain in capital marketing and investment. Another sought after characteristic, scalability, and interoperability enables payments and money exchanges globally.

Prateek Goorha [22] in his research paper briefs on the smart contracting solution provided by smart institutional intermediation of the blockchain. This covers off-chain and on-chain statement and settlement in terms of financial transaction.

Blockchain has been considered to fill in the gaps caused in centralized networking of transactions, targeted to enhance the privacy and security constraints of the big data repositories at hand, integrating top notch data storage and data mining methods to obtain useful insights in business practices. The ultimate aim of a decentralized blockchain network in this case would be security, censorship resistance, efficiency, and privacy maintenance.

Another sought after application of blockchain in terms of integrity verification of the information stored at hand, to materialize to lifetime products and services, is to achieve high level of provenance and counterfeit overcoming, Insurance policy tracking and Intellectual Property management. Blockchain links digital content to the owners or creators of data and policy making, paving way to store metadata to recovery and querying of digital assets and digital rights. Insurance management has a list of application areas in connection to blockchain in means of sales, customer onboard, claims processing, payments track, assets transference, etc.

One of the most indubitable properties of blockchain is the ability of data management. Data is unquestionably the fuel that keeps the ball rolling in terms of any business venture. The legitimacy and reliability of the data at hand and proper manoeuvring of the data in applied arenas is all that makes the data auditable and trackable. Blockchain adopts a cross workflow kind of management of information (data), preserving the privacy, intermediating computation, and overcoming human error prone laybacks.

The whole world operates on compromises at situations which organizations globally dread to take up. False records and disruption of processes by compromised human behavior is a definite standby in global business laundering. Blockchain gives no heed to the compromised machines due to the sturdy infractions it holds for security reasons, thereby promoting uncompromised business processes. This is a desired aspect when it comes to the stage of a supply chain management. The supply chain could cater to human resources in terms of commodities or machinery, medicine, or manpower itself. All should be retrospect in advance and rolled out at appropriate time stamped periods at the varied delivery points. The shared consensus marks the legitimacy of operations in blockchain transactions. This steers the ship of the supply chain seamlessly to go undisrupted.

Sara Saberi *et al.* [23] talk about the globalization of supply chains through blockchain. It elaborates on sustainability of the supply chain by the critical examining and applying the smart contracts potential of blockchain to oversee pressures in terms of local and global, consumer, and community. Barriers such as technical and external, inter and intra organizational are analyzed for different use cases at different points of the supply chain process and registers insights for future overcoming of debacles in this arena.

An application perspective of how the blockchain key features such as transparency, validation, tokenization, and automation is inducted into the supply chain process as analyzed by Gregor Blossey *et al.* [24], in their research paper. These aspects pave the way to efficiency in use case clusters of supply chain visibility, integrity, orchestration, virtualization, and finance. Blockchain unlocks the values held in logistics, providing faster and leaner options in the global trade, thereby improvising transparency and traceability in supply chains through the automated commercial processes that stream unbroken.

Looking at the other side of the coin, to non-financial areas of importance, blockchain scrupulously turns focus in industries such as healthcare and education. Cornelius C. Agbo *et al.* [24] have based a study of the PRISMA (Preferred Reporting Items for Systematic- Reviews and Meta-Analysis) to identify, extract, and analyze scientific databases meticulously for purposed use cases. The potential of the blockchain to concentrate on patient-centric approach to foster connection and accuracy of healthcare records in disparate systems has been researched by Marko Holbl *et al.* [25]. With the EHR and EMR at hand, the direction of the functionality of blockchain in terms of health records track and maintenance is predicted. This would gain momentum by yet many more research aimed in the view to present and novelize robust structural designs and frameworks in the blockchain to solve the cause quality data sharing and secure management of health records.

Academic institutions world-wide have made a sustenance through undisrupted online stream of education that has been provided by the many virtual classrooms gratified by the different cloud vendors like Google, Amazon, and Microsoft. As discussed earlier, cloud computing seems to gain extra vigor in zones of security when its coordinates a perfect mix of the blockchain technology side by side. Guang Chen *et al.* [26] discuss the learning outcomes in education to be much more extensive by the inculcation of the blockchain. Blockchain offers support in degree management and summative evaluation of learning outcomes that could be accessed from anywhere using a unique user identification that is verified. It also covers the micro academic project experience coupled with the macro educational background and behavioral modes in the class environment.

Real estate was the primal example portrayed to explain the efficient process of blockchain working. In this line, Sabarish Krishna D *et al.* [27] factualize the encompassing security aspect of undertaking real estate operations through blockchain, managing effortlessly the many challenges that the real estate industry. The asset management, assurance of cost, track of history of assets, faster monitoring, and transference of properties in prescribed timestamps with disintermediation are the key elements that aid the cause of real estate flourishing through blockchain. Somi S. Thota [28], in his paper, rambles on the possible benefits real estate industry could derive from blockchain and also highlights how the limitations in this area could be solved by careful retrospection.

Enormous power consumption was a down standing inhibition that was posed on Blockchain technology in its apparels of usage. This very same aspect has taken a different prospective dimension and has put blockchain to use in the sustainable energy sectors. Merlinda Andoni *et al.* [29] open up the opportunity of the blockchain, systematically classified into varied clusters of activity and implementation of the platform and consensus of blockchain. They have analyzed 140 research projects and have come up with insights that prove commercial viability and adoption in terms of energy sustenance.

Blockchain has also stimulated dimensions of utility in the government sector as well, such as the following:

- Record management
- Identity management
- Voting
- Tax filings
- Trust to non-profit agencies
- Compliance to regulatory audit trail
- Money transfer/micro payments
- Content consumption
- Certify a supply chain
- Share sustainable energy resources
- Household application/gadgets make payments
- Track ownership of assets/legal contract/health records
- Market prediction
- Trade cryptocurrencies

Governance comprehends management and immutability of citizens and governing bodies of specific place, country or globe at large. Blockchain has stepped into the governance sector, to relief the trauma of traditional centralized transactions and record keeping, infringing the participation of intermediaries and ruling out inhibited bias of the system and the persons involved in the government legislation. The public authority service in terms of legalizing documents, attestation, identification, taxes, and voting are by-products that are handled under this umbrella. Karl Wust *et al.* [30] discuss on the e-voting problem in recent times. Privacy and accountability was the lagging aspects to be addressed. Blockchain with its resilience and immutable nature has brought about public verifiability and security at the same time.

Blockchain, nascent in nature, is leniently open to upgradation and development in ways of creating prototype models that would mimic the real cause of utility of blockchain in the real-time scenario. Jorg Weking *et al.* [31], synonymous to this thought, explicate five archetypal patterns from the many blockchain ventures and open vision of the inert capabilities blockchain has, and how these could be transformed into effective innovative business models.

11.9 Constraints to Adapt to the Resilient Blockchain

Blockchain may highlight a number of key characteristics and qualities that tend the investors and business magnums to invest in it, but there are underlying factors that actually pull the reins of the Blockchain to a definite standby. A major constraint in the technology of Blockchain would be the complexity in the adoption of practiced policies of blockchain and mining processes. Julija Golosova *et al.* [32], on a serious note, mention the second hindering block, as high consumption of computation power and electrical energy to keep the sustenance of the chain fault tolerant, censorship resistant, and establishing zero downtime in data storage. The high computation power comes in the scenario while mining of the coin and in the signature verification process by the cryptographic scheme.

Another viable fork as they refer to is the treatment and addressing of the older versions and latest versions intertwining in a single chain, which is a major challenge and constraint. For this, it could probably split the chain, disrupting the special chain feature of the technology.

Any technology that is burgeoning will undoubtedly face a lot of challenges and unexpected constraints and debacles that speak louder than the profound benefits that the scheme would imbibe. In this line, a few attacks such as user identity theft, fraudulence of sender and receiver, impersonation of identities, malicious codes in the distributed ledger, target reconnaissance, and reputational risk of firms to adapt to blockchain try to make this P2P network a projected mayhem.

Kaspars Zile *et al.* [33] are prejudiced with the fact, that any decentralized mode of technology would unquestionably incur a huge cost of capital investment and that the mining that actually happens could be faked or unrealistic at times, unless the blockchain is permissioned.

11.10 Conclusion

The sphere of impingement of blockchain has penetrated deep through the widespread anatomy of the digital revolution, allotting no affiliate to third party services with security as its top notch attributes. The capabilities of the blockchain are fathomless at the moment. Many veterans with expertise in blockchain, on careful analysis of the complete framework of blockchain, provide a justification to the adaptability of this technology to arrive at an idealized sophistication of smart and intelligent architecture.

The cohesion of blockchain with the existing technologies would depict and idyllic base for the beget of many more technologies to come by.

The research with the notion of resilience of technologies and business applications for the betterment, down the business lane functioning, is the need of the hour. Making use of this spectrum of enhanced protocols and standards of blockchain, the modern digital terrain invention would definitely elevate the scalability, security, reliability, and accessibility options of business and research instances. The unbiased intent toward the actualization of blockchain will accentuate the smartness of digitalization in an elegant manner toward stupendous levels. The magnanimous decorum of blockchain, adorned with the dexterity in optimal swiftness of transactions and precision tagged along with security, are the keys that make blockchain a debatable benchmark of prominence that bifurcates the underlying technical podium to astounding stratums.

References

1. Nakamoto, S., *Bitcoin: A Peer-to-Peer Electronic Cash System Cryptography*, 2009, www.bitcoin.org, Mailing list at https://metzdowd.com.
2. Wang, W. *et al.*, A Survey on Consensus Mechanisms and Mining Strategy Management in Blockchain Networks. *IEEE Access*, 7, 22328–22370, 2019.
3. Thamarai Selvi, R. and Fernandez, A.C., A Modified Consensus Algorithm with a Diminutive of Proof of Longevity - Augmenting the Effectuation of Blockchain. *Int. J. Comp. Sci. Eng.*, Open Access Res. Paper, 7, 9, 60–65, Sept 2019.
4. Bach, L.M., Mihaljevic, B., Zagar, M., Comparative analysis of blockchain consensus algorithms. *2018 41st International Convention on Information and Communication Technology, Electronics and Microelectronics (MIPRO)*, Opatija, pp. 1545–1550, 2018.
5. Niranjanamurthy, M., Nithya, B., Jagannatha, S., Analysis of Blockchain technology: pros, cons and SWOT. *Cluster Comput.*, 22, 14743–14757, 2019.
6. Fernandez, A.C. and Thamarai Selvi, R., A Comprehensive Overview of the Constructive Minutiae of the Bitcoin – Blockchain. *IOSR J. Eng. (IOSRJEN)*, 9, 8, 2278–8719, August. 2019.
7. Gervais, A., Karame, G.O., Wüst, K., Glykantzis, V., Ritzdorf, H., Capkun, S., On the security and performance of proof of work blockchains, in: *Proceedings of the 2016 ACM SIGSAC conference on computer and communications security*, pp. 3–16, 2016.
8. Nanayakkara, S., Perera, S., Senaratne, S., Perspective on Blockchain and Smart Contracts Solutions for Construction Supply Chains. *The CIB World Building Congress 2019 at Hong Kong*, June 2019.

9. Nijland, M. and Veuger, J., Influence of Blockchain in the Real Estate Sector in Which Stage of the Buying Process of Commercial Real Estate can Blockchain Provide Added Value for the Stakeholders Involved? *Int. J. Appl. Sci.*, 2, 22, 22–4, 2019, https://doi.org/10.30560/ijas.v2n2p22.

10. Zheng, Z., Xie, S., Dai, H., Chen, X., Wang, H., An overview of blockchain technology: Architecture, consensus, and future trends, in: *2017 IEEE international congress on big data (BigData congress)*, IEEE, pp. 557–564, 2017.

11. Zheng, Z., Xie, S., Dai, H.-N., Chen, X., Wang, H., Blockchain challenges and opportunities: A survey. October 2018. *Int. J. Web Grid Serv.*, 14, 4, 352–375, 2018.

12. Ali Syed, T., Alzahrani, A., Jan, S., Siddiqui, M.S., Nadeem, A., Alghamdi, T., A Comparative Analysis of Blockchain Architecture and its Applications: Problems and Recommendations. *IEEE Access*, vol. 7, 176838–176869, 2019.

13. Singh, S., Sharma, P.K., Yoon, B., Shojafar, M., Cho, G.H., I-Ho, R.a. Convergence of Blockchain and Artificial Intelligence in IoT Network for the Sustainable Smart City. *Sustain. Cities Soc.*, 63, 102364, 2020, https://doi.org/10.1016/j.scs.2020.102364.

14. Marwala, T. and Xing, Blockchain and Artificial Intelligence. *ArXiv*, abs/1802.04451, 2018.

15. Gill, S.S., Tuli, S., Xu, M., Singh, I., Singh, K.V., Lindsay, D., Tuli, S., Smirnova, D., Singh, M., Jain, U., Pervaiz, H., Sehgal, B., Kaila, S.S., Mishra, S., Aslanpour, M.S., Mehta, H., Stankovski, V., Garraghan, P., Transformative Effects of IoT, Blockchain and Artificial Intelligence on Cloud Computing: Evolution, Vision, Trends and Open Challenges. *Internet of Things*, 8, 100118, 2019, https://doi.org/10.1016/j.iot.2019.100118.

16. Tiba, K., Parizi, R.M., Zhang, Q., Dehghantanha, A., Karimipour, H., Choo, K.-K.R., Secure blockchain-based traffic load balancing using edge computing and reinforcement learning, in: *Blockchain Cybersecurity, Trust and Privacy*, pp. 99–128, Springer, Cham, 2020.

17. Mamoshina, P., Ojomoko, L., Yanovich, Y., Ostrovski, A., Botezatu, A., Prikhodko, P., Izumchenko, E., Aliper, A., Romantsov, K., Zhebrak, A., Ogu, I.O., Zhavoronkov, A., Converging blockchain and next-generation artificial intelligence technologies to decentralize and accelerate biomedical research and healthcare. *Oncotarget*, 9, 5, 5665–5690, 2018.

18. Lopes, V. and Alexandre, L.A., An Overview of Blockchain Integration with Robotics and Artificial Intelligence. arXiv:1810.00329, 1, 1–15, 2018.

19. McConaghy, M., McMullen, G., Parry, G., McConaghy, T., Holtzman, D., How blockchains could transform artificial intelligence, 2017, http://dataconomy.com/2016/12/blockchains-for-artificial-intelligence/, Visibility and digital art: blockchain as an ownership layer on the Internet. *Strateg. Change*, 26, 5, 461–470.

20. Dinh, T.N. and Thai, M.T., AI and Blockchain: A Disruptive Integration. *Computer*, Strategic Change, published by IEEE, 51, 9, 48–53, September 2018.

21. Casinoa, F., Dasaklisb, T.K., Patsakisa, C., A systematic literature review of blockchain-based applications: Current status, classification and open issues. Elsevier, *Telemat. Inform.*, 36, 55–81, March 2019.

22. Prateek, G., A Comprehensive Contracting Solution using Blockchains, June 15, 2018. https://ssrn.com/abstract=3237076 or http://dx.doi.org/10.2139/ssrn.3237076.

23. Saberi, S., Kouhizadeh, M., Sarkis, J., Shen, L., Blockchain technology and its relationships to sustainable supply chain management. *Int. J. Prod. Res.*, 57, 7, 2117–2135, 2019.

24. Agbo, C.C., Mahmoud, Q.H., Eklund, J.M., Blockchain Technology in Healthcare: A Systematic Review. *Healthcare (Basel)*, 7, 2, 56, 2019.

25. Hölbl, M., Kompara, M., Kamišalić, A., Nemec Zlatolas, L., A Systematic Review of the Use of Blockchain in Healthcare. *Symmetry*, 20, 470, 2018.

26. Chen, G., Xu, B., Lu, M., Chen, N.-S., Exploring blockchain technology and its potential applications for education. *Smart Learn. Environ.*, 5, 1, 1, 2018.

27. Sabarish Krishna, D., Soumi Aakash, V., Sivaprakash, M., Madhumathi, C.S., Secured Real Estate Transactions using Blockchain Technology. *Int. Res. J. Eng. Technol. (IRJET)*, 06, 03, 1173–1176, Mar 2019.

28. Thota, S.S., Blockchain for Real Estate Industry. Academic Research Publishing Group. 5, 2, 53–56, 2018.

29. Andoni, M., Robu, V., Flynn, D., Abram, S., Geach, D., Jenkins, D., McCallum, P., Peacock, Blockchain technology in the energy sector: A systematic review of challenges and opportunities. *Renew. Sustain. Energy Rev.*, 100, 143–174, 2019, https://doi.org/10.1016/j.rser.2018.10.014.

30. Wüst, K. and Gervais, A., Do you need a Blockchain? *2018 Crypto Valley Conference on Blockchain Technology (CVCBT).*

31. Weking, J., Mandalenakis, M., Hein, A., Hermes, S., Böhm, M., Krcmar, H., *The impact of blockchain technology on business models – a taxonomy and archetypal patterns*, vol. 30, pp. 285–305, Springer, Electronic Market, 2019, https://doi.org/10.1007/s12525-019-00386-3.

32. Golosova, J. and Romanovs, A., The Advantages and Disadvantages of the Blockchain Technology. *2018 IEEE 6th Workshop on Advances in Information, Electronic and Electrical Engineering (AIEEE)*, pp. 1–6, Vilnius, Lithuania, 2018.

33. Zīle, K. and Strazdiņa, R., Blockchain Use Cases and Their Feasibility. *Appl. Comput. Syst.*, 23, 1, 12–20, May 2018.

34. Kumar, A., Payal, M., Dixit, P., Chatterjee, J.M., Framework for Realization of Green Smart Cities Through the Internet of Things (IoT), in: *Trends in Cloud-based IoT*, pp. 85–111, 2020.

35. Jha, S., Kumar, R., Chatterjee, J.M., Khari, M., Collaborative handshaking approaches between internet of computing and internet of things towards a smart world: a review from 2009–2017. *Telecommun. Syst.*, 70, 4, 617–634, 2019.

36. Agrawal, R., Chatterjee, J.M., Kumar, A., Rathore, P.S. (Eds.), *Blockchain Technology and the Internet of Things: Challenges and Applications in Bitcoin and Security*, CRC Press, Boca Raton, FL, USA, 2020.

An Overview of Blockchain Technology: Architecture and Consensus Protocols

Himanshu Rastogi

Department of Computer Science and Engineering, Mangalmay Institute of Engineering and Technology, Delhi, NCR, India

Abstract

A digital ledger, or blockchain, is one of today's most innovative and emerging technologies. Blockchain technology has evolved in the last decade to address the ambiguity and safety issues that come with using distributed networks. Due to its potential in business development for businesses and the increasingly emerging implementations of a distributed smart city system, government, and healthcare, the perception of blockchain has changed significantly over time. Many networks have been developed, each with its own architecture and consensus protocol. Primarily, everybody in the world thought Bitcoin was cryptocurrency, although there were also misconceptions of what the system was and how it might be used in company. Later, the impact of the Bitcoin central technology on industrialists and academicians in various realms such as banking, healthcare, and government has changed the perspective of researchers, industrialists, and academicians in various domains such as banking, healthcare, and government. A blockchain is made up of a series of transaction blocks that are linked together. Client/server (C/S) architecture is used in traditional C/S applications, which are managed by many administrators. However, blockchain is a distributed, open, and peer-to-peer network. Any network participant has the ability to monitor the network. All nodes work as an administrator to monitor and control the network. A blockchain network is made up of several nodes that are linked with each other, and the block, or data container, in the network cannot be modified without permission of the network.

The fundamental understanding of blockchain technology principles and keywords will be discussed in this chapter, so that a thorough understanding of the technology can be gain. The chapter is started from the brief introduction about

Email: himanshu_ras@yahoo.com

Vishal Kumar, Vishal Jain, Bharti Sharma, Jyotir Moy Chatterjee and Rakesh Shrestha (eds.) Smart City Infrastructure: The Blockchain Perspective, (293–316) © 2022 Scrivener Publishing LLC

the blockchain technology and then explained the blockchain architecture. In this architecture, we have explained how the blocks are linked with each other the how tempering of a block can be identified. As blockchain technology is a concept of chain of blocks, we have discussed the block structure. To understand the security in the blockchain, concept of hashing and digital signature is also discussed. The consensus protocol is at the heart of the blockchain, determining how it will work. Different types of consensus protocol, *viz.*, Compute-Intensive–Based Consensus (CIBC) Protocols, Capability-Based Consensus Protocols, and Voting-Based Consensus Protocols, with their respective sub types, are well explained in this chapter.

Keywords: Client server, Bitcoin, blockchain, Compute-Intensive–Based Consensus

12.1   Introduction

These days in various organizations and academics, cryptocurrency has become a jargon. Bitcoin is one of the best cryptocurrencies that has appreciated. Throughout the globe, more than 1,600 cryptocurrencies are available but major share by Bitcoin with 191 billion dollar and then Ethereum with 105 billion dollar. A survey was done by Paxful, with 500 Indian people who are the users of cryptocurrency. In this survey, it is found that largest percentage of Bitcoin adaptation was 90.6 7%. The reasons were as follows:

1. Transfer of cryptocurrency is easy
2. Security
3. Easy available

The price of Bitcoin is rupees 829966.20 INR (October, 2020) and the size of blockchain is 285.06 GB (June, 2020) (statistica.com). Due to unique design, its data storage structure and also transaction in Bitcoin network makes it independent to third-party. Blockchain was implemented in the year 2009 while it was initially proposed in the year of 2008. Blockchain is a public ledger responsible to maintain all transaction in the form of blocks. To maintain the consistency and security of the ledger, various consensus algorithm and asymmetric cryptography are implemented. The main features of blockchain are decentralization, persistency, anonymity, and availability. These features improve the efficiency of blockchain.

Bitcoin block size is 4 MB (theoretically), but in reality, it is 2 MB. The size of Bitcoin depends on the all the transaction included in the blockchain.

To mining a block total 10 minutes are required. The size of block cannot be increased as it will require more time and larger space; this may result in the reduction of Bitcoin user.

12.2 Blockchain Architecture

Nowadays, blockchain is increasingly popular. In the blockchain, blocks containing information are linked with each other and they form a chain. A group of researchers illustrated this technique in the year 1991. The main objective was to timestamp the original document, like a notary, so that document cannot be tampered or forged. For the creation of a new digital currency—"cryptocurrency", blockchain technique was adopted in 2009 by Satoshi Nakamoto [1]. Blockchain is a ledger which is distributed in the blockchain network and completely opens to everyone. An important feature is implemented in the blockchain that once the data has been inserted into the blockchain; no one can modify that data.

Blockchain consists of a series of blocks that contains the list of transactions just like a ledger, which is publically accessible as shown in Figure 12.1. All blocks are interconnected with each other by holding the reference of the parent or previous block as shown in Figure 12.2.

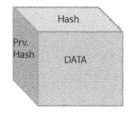

Figure 12.1 A block of blockchain.

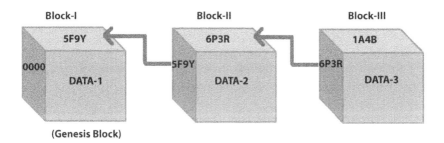

Figure 12.2 Chain of blocks.

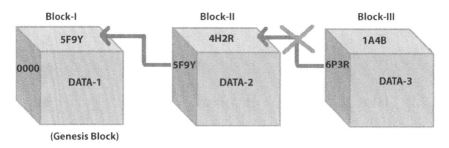

Figure 12.3 Chain of blocks with invalid reference.

Block-I does not contain any value in the previous hash but block-II contains the hash value of the previous block-I in the previous hash. Similarly, block-III is also containing the hash value of a block-II in its previous hash and so on. Since block-I is the super parent of this blockchain as not containing the reference of the previous block it is known as Genesis block.

As shown in Figure 12.3, the reference stored in previous hash of the block-III is different from the reference of hash in block-II. Therefore, it is considered that block-II is not a part of the blockchain. So, further blocks will not be considered as a part of the same blockchain.

12.2.1   Block Structure

A block comprises of the headers and body of the block as shown in Figure 12.4. Specifically, the block header incorporates the following [40]:

    A.   **Block Version:** specify the set of rules to adopt for block validation.

    B.   **Markley Tree Root Hash:** the hash estimation of the afferent multitude of transaction in the block.

    C.   **Timestamp:** current time in second.

    D.   **nBits:** target limit of a substantial block.

    E.   **Nonce:** a 4-byte field that, for any hash measurement, typically begins with 0 and increases.

    F.   **Parent Block Hash:** a 256 digit that focus to the previous block.

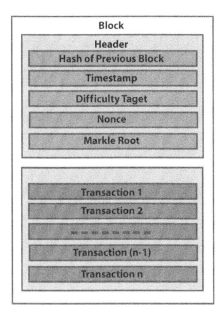

Figure 12.4 Block structure.

A transaction counter and transactions form the body of the block. The largest number of transactions which can be found in a block is dependent on the size of the block and each transaction size. To test transaction authentication, blockchain utilizes an unbalanced Asymmetric Cryptography Method. In an insecure environment, Digital Signature relies on asymmetric cryptography.

12.2.2   Hashing and Digital Signature

Hashing refers to a technique in taking arbitrary data in applying and hash algorithm to produce output data in the form of output hash. Data could be of any type, for example, text, image, audio, and video. Hashing can be implemented depending upon users need or available hashing algorithm. Hashing is used to prevent the data to be tempered or modified. Hashing used in blockchain is to represent the present situation of the block. Therefore, the input is the complete position of block in blockchain, which contains all the records of the transaction, and after applying hash algorithm, it returns the present position of the blockchain utilized for the agreement between parties.

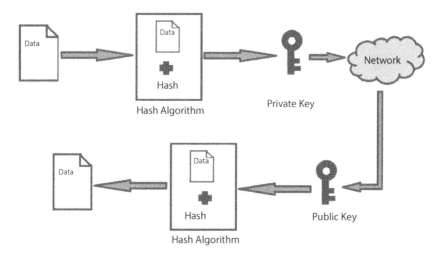

Figure 12.5 Hashing and digital signature.

This system assures that any transaction stored in the record can be tampered by altering any single part of the transaction. So, if it is found that there is any fall short or fail in the block hash, then it is easy to find the tempering by comparing hash values.

Digital signature, as shown in Figure 12.5, shows that the message originates by the specific person not by the hacker. In Asymmetric Encryption Method, a security key is generated by the user which is a grouping of public and private key. With the help of some algorithm, public key is created to be distributed publicly to provide an address to receive messages from other users. The private key is meant as a secret key and used to digitally signed messages sent to the other. With the message the digital signature of the actual user is included so that recipient can verify by using the sender's public key. With this method receiver can be assured that the authenticated user sent the message. In the blockchain, every transaction executed is digitally signed by the sender by using their private key. This digital signature proves the ownership of the account holder and so he is authorized to make money transaction from his account.

12.3 Consensus Algorithm

Principal issue in distributing computing with multiple agents is to manage overall system trustworthiness while some systems are working malfunctioning.

This regulatory expects process to allow on some data which is required at the time of processing. In distributed computing, it is very challenging task to reach a consensus blockchain in a centralized system and all users working on the basis of the incentives plus to the information provided to them. When the information in the blockchain network is broadcasted, this is up to the nodes whether they want to receive or ignore it. At the point when majority of such node wants to work on a single point, a consciousness is accomplished.

In blockchain technology, consciousness can be achieved among the node by the conversion of Byzantine General Problem. This Byzantine General Problem was brought up in ACM Digital Library in the year 2006, see Figure 12.6. In this problem, a group of generals who order a group of Byzantine Armed Force, a few dislike armed force wants to hit, whereas the other generals want to withdraw or retreat. Yet this attack may not be successful, if less number of generals attacked the city. In this manner, they need to agree to retreat or attack. In this distributed network of blockchain technology, none of the nodes works as centralized which can guarantees that ledgers are same on this network. For the consistency of the ledger, at different node, some protocols must be required. In blockchain technology, distributed system and smart contract to be driven adequately for cryptocurrency which ought to be certified by the blockchain. These certifications rely upon, what is employed as consensus algorithm. This consciousness algorithm enables the framework to keep working whether the part of its member are missing. The following are the consensus algorithms.

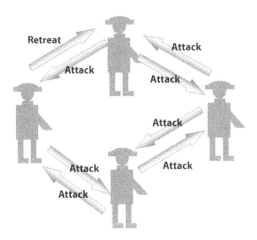

Figure 12.6 Byzantine general problem.

12.3.1   Compute-Intensive–Based Consensus (CIBC) Protocols

CIBC protocols are dedicated for calculations regarding energy mining. In this section, various CIBC protocols utilized in the blockchain are explained.

12.3.1.1   Pure Proof of Work (PoW)

Nakamoto *et al.* [1] implemented the Proof of Work (PoW) calculations in Bitcoin network using blockchain technology in 2008. Bitcoin is the most popular cryptocurrency which uses the PoW consensus algorithm to ensure the performance of records during transaction. During such arrangement, digital computers, ordinarily called minors, associated with a distributed network, carry out the function to approve the transactions for the expansion of total records of current validate transactions. The age of a block is attached in blockchain—to validate all transactions included in the record. This requires clear understanding of cryptographic method to be finished by Brute-Force Technique. In PoW, when a minor mines another block, it relies upon the proportion between the computational power it commits to this work and the absolute computational power by all minors associated with the network. In particular, minors must discover an answer for a single direction hash work by computing new hash dependent on the preceding hash values, which is included with in the message, the new transactions in the block they make a nonce.

12.3.1.2   Prime Number Proof of Work (Prime Number PoW)

Prime Number PoW was proposed by King S., to channelize the high energy utilization of PoW for double use, in the year 2013 [6]. Like the nonce in PoW, Prime Number PoW contains a computational count of prime number's Cunningham Chain [7] which can be utilized to execute self-recoverable, self-authentic cryptosystem to empower a protected, powerful, and recovery proficient document system [8]. Subsequently, the high measure of energy utilization provides the protection of the network of blockchain similar to the advancement of cryptography techniques. The registered chains are distributed in the record. The prime numbers chain must fulfill following necessities:

(1) The chain should have a definite series of prime numbers, as Cunningham chain, which could be of any kind like first kind [9], second kind [9], or bi-twin [10].

(2) The length of the chain supposed not to be lesser than or equal to the target length.

For the assurance, the count is made block explicit to determine every individual block for prime chain. This can be done by distinguishing the hash of the header of the block with the main component of the chain. The prime number PoW is just utilized by the digital money Primecoin [11].

12.3.1.3   Delayed Proof of Work (DPoW)

To secure Bitcoin network, energy consensus protocol is used. Delayed PoW (DPoW) recommends compute intensive security of PoW to make sure about other networks of blockchain which utilizes an energy-efficient consensus protocol. Thus, DPoW is a combination of consensus technique which ensures a network of blockchain utilizing PoW blockchain's mining power.

In DPoW, 64 legal official nodes, called a group, which is selected by the network's partners, are to create a block. The transactions done in the network are approved by every public node and makes a block in a cooperative design not including the register concentrated and eager for energy estimation of the mining confirmation. However, for the assurance of the safety of the network, PoW blockchain is appended with last made block's hash in the DPoW blockchain, at whatever point a block is made in the last mentioned. In DPoW, before sending the block hash to the blockchain network based on PoW [39].

On the basis of the area and network availability, it may be possible that the portion of the network gets a block from one minor (say block P) and the next part gets a block from another minor (say block Q). In the network, all the nodes keep up a duplicate of the blockchain record (let us consider it as a masterchain). A node approves the block P after getting it and annexes the block P to its duplicate of the masterchain and a node approves the block Q after getting it and adds it to its duplicate of the masterchain. At the point while a node containing block P in its masterchain gets block Q, this node checks the authenticity of block Q. Nonetheless, the two blocks P and Q have a similar parent block. In this manner, the node starts another chain. Let us consider this chain, the auxiliary chain. This auxiliary chain split from the masterchain and annexes the block Q in that optional chain.

Thus, node containing block Q will be attached next to the block P in its masterchain, after it has been approved. In a blockchain, if the chain is splitted into two sections, then it is called as forking [3]. The blockchain network, to determine forking, utilizes the standard of that longest chain which contains maximum number of blocks.

This standard expresses that, in the network, if the next block mined will contains parent block, block P, at that point, the blockchain with block P in the masterchain will be viewed as **validate**. If the new block has block Q as its parent block, then the masterchain's blockchain with block Q would be considered as **authenticate**. The blocks in the side chain are then deleted, and the masterchain chain keeps on growing.

12.3.2   Capability-Based Consensus Protocols

Because of its technique, the high energy consumption of networks uses the CIBC protocol, where computing power are used by all minors, to obtain the option to mine the next block. The capacity of a minor can be determined dependent on different factors, for example, the amount of cryptocurrency possessed by that minor, the commitment of the minor to the network, the expectation on the network has on the minor, or the measure of capacity claimed by the minor.

12.3.2.1   Proof of Stake (PoS)

PoS joins block creation with the authentication of a certain amount of digital assets (such as cryptocurrency) linked with the blockchain. For the testing of the next block inside the scheme, the probability of a given prover is selected The fundamental consideration will be that the clients with a big portion of the system's assets are more likely to have authenticated data, making them a more accurate validator. There have been two proposed PoS methods. The first is based on randomized block determination (utilized, for example, in Blockcoin); it uses an estimate to find the minimum hash and stake value. The other strategy is coin-age-based decision (used by Peercoin, for example), which combines randomization and coin-age. PoS is motivated by the "nothing at stack" problem, rather than the fact that it has the ability to address two problems with PoW. Since there is no cost in a few chains, it is possible to mismanage the protocol by opting for many blockchain-narratives, preventing the consensus from ever settling (two fold spending). The coin age can be calculated as follows:

Coin age = Total marked coins * Holding time of the coin (in days)

12.3.2.2   Delegated Proof of Stake (DPoS)

Larimer proposed delegated proof of stake (DPoS) to resolve the problem of rich getting richer in the Proof of Stack [12]. This is by finding the forger based on the selection process instead of the number of coins held. In this protocol, on the basis of the voting system, a group of nodes named as witnesses (additionally known as delegates) are selected where each network node carrying cryptocurrency takes an interest during the time spent in the voting process. The weighting of the vote for a node is proportional to the total number of coins contained by the node. With a single decision in favor of each witness, a node will cast a vote for several witnesses. For mining all the blocks, it is important to secure an observer. This can be done by the selection of first N witness having greatest votes. With the final objective that half of the nodes have determined in support of these multiple witnesses, the quantity of witnesses (N) is selected.

For example, if a significant portion of the nodes have agreed in favor of 10 witnesses at any time, these 10 witnesses containing the largest nodes will be chosen at that point. A block is mined in a round robin manner by the observer in a group. The witnesses list is altered after a set time. If the witness is unable to provide a block, then the next witness will be chosen from the same category within a specified time allotment. When all the witnesses in Tern have been selected, the number of witnesses is rearranged and the round robin begins. The cryptocurrency exchange phases of Bitshares [13], Nano [14], and Cardano [15] use this algorithm.

12.3.2.3   Proof of Stake Velocity (PoSV)

In 2014, Ren suggested Proof of Stake Velocity (PoSV) [16] to resolve economical problem in PoS. In this problem, no transaction is done by the node to create the probability of being chosen as the succeeding forger. The goal was to protect the financial flow in the scheme that is important to grow the economy. PoSV is an initiative to facilitate cash transfers on the network. Even, if the nodes just make cryptocurrency transfers with each other with the intention of re-initializing the coin age, this financial revolution will not help the economy at that point. In comparison, the protocol only benefits the richest and not evaluated for its performance and safety from unwanted threats. The crypto-currency Reddcoin uses PoSV [17].

12.3.2.4   Proof of Burn (PoB)

In 2014, Proof of Burn (PoB) was suggested by Ian Stewart [18] to fix the problem of high energy usage in PoW and the issue of recoverable coins enabling malicious clients in PoS. In PoB, by sending them to an unrecoverable address, called as the Eater Address, the minors had to "burn" the coins. The eater address contains a public key which is not linked with any private key. From that account, retrieval of the coins is very difficult. When transfer from this eater address, the coins are withdrawn from the network and cannot be utilized again. When a minor spends coins to extract a block this prohibits malicious minors to mine an incorrect block. Much like PoW, the underlying idea behind PoB is that the minors invest coin into mining processing in order to maximize their chance of mining the next block and the minors spend more coins in PoB that are equivalent to buying virtual mining.

12.3.2.5   Proof of Space (PoSpace)

Proof of Space (PoSpace) was suggested by Dziembowski *et al.*, which is also called as proof of capacity. The idea was to address the issue of rich getting the richer and the problem of high energy consumption in computing-based protocol. In this protocol, minor having the sufficient disk space wins option to produce the succeeding block in the chain [19]. It is a two-step procedure:
(1) Plotting and (2) Mining.

1. **Plotting Step:** In this step, minor's hard disk is plotted by utilizing hash which guarantees the extra space devoted by the minor. It is a one-time process. The plot uses the hash function of Shabal 256 [20], which produces a hash value output of size 32-byte. The plotting started from producing a value, with size 16-byte, in which the minor account ID is 8-byte and the nonce number is 8-byte.
2. **Mining Step:** Every time it is required to mine a new block, to carried out the mining phase. In the mining stage, the network calculates a generation hash that relies on the preceding block in the chain.

A minor is referred to as a "forger" in PoSpace and is paid with mining fees along with transaction costs. PoSpace's key benefit is that it uses fewer resources as compare to the compute-intensive protocols and will not support the rich, similar to the capability-based protocols mentioned earlier.

12.3.2.6   Proof of History (PoH)

To highlight the issues in CIBC Protocols, Yakovenko proposed Proof of History (PoH) in 2017 [21]. In this protocol, the validators and the mining nodes are pointed as the verifiers and the leader or PoH generators respectively. SHA-256 (Secure Hash Algorithm processed with 32 digit words) algorithm was used in PoH that continually runs over itself, with the next input being the output. For a random initial value, the leader (mining nodes) executes the hash function and gets the output which will forward it again as the input for same hash function. The output received from the function is recorded every time by the leader and the appropriate counter value denotes the iteration. In the network, at the time changing the transaction, the leader is responsible to authenticate the transaction and append the same with the hash output, which is further used as the input for next transaction and the counter value. Again, the transaction done and the output of the hash are mentioned in the ledger. In this way, the transaction is registered as having taken place before and after a specific counter value. The verifiers received the ledger to authenticate the transaction whether it is valid or invalid by calculating it again the out of the hash and all counter values [39].

12.3.2.7   Proof of Importance (PoI)

To highlight the matter of reduction in the transaction flow NEM [4], cryptocurrency platform, proposed the Proof of Importance (PoI). This is due to the minor which they do not show their performance in the transaction so that the chances of the mining will be increased. In this protocol, the mining process is called the harvesting and minors are called as harvesters.

The selection criteria to select a minor which will mine the subsequently block are chosen if the minor will have the greatest score of Importance. This score is determined on basis of the following factors:

(1) The amount or quantity of crypto-tokens allocated by a minor or harvester.
(2) Performance, for making the transaction, done by the members of the minor or harvester.
(3) The amount or quantity and size of a minor's transactions.

To be qualified for the process of mining or harvesting, a minor or harvester is required to have a basic limit of the vested or allocated tokens, and this number is known as vesting amount. To hold the vested token for a specific number of days, it is required to vest 10% of the vesting amount is vested every day [22]. The miner Importance score is directly proportional to the number of the vested coin. Higher the Importance score, higher will be the vested number of coins. Miners, who have vested tokens, are rewarded after performing transactions in PoI with respect to the Importance score. Miners take care of the decrease in transaction flow and the holding period of the coin, if any [22]. At last, the Importance score too relies on the amount of transactions done over the last 30 days by the minor, with each transaction size reaching the threshold value.

12.3.2.8   Proof of Believability (PoBelievability)

To highlight the problems of rich getting richer in PoS, Proof of Believability was suggested in 2017 [23]. In PoBelievability, validator performs the activities of a minor and the validator is chosen for the creation of a block on the basis of the higher believable score. The credibility score is evaluated as per the validator's crypto token, its quantity of recently accepted transactions, and its quantity of service tokens (an incentive given to the validator for willful work) [23]. Providing extra storage space, devoting computational resources, and inspecting third-party applications are part of the willing job. The service tokens cannot be moved from one validator to another, but if a validator makes a block, its value becomes null.

The validators are divided into two groups by PoBelievability, within the network; first is a believable group and other is a natural group. This normal group is further broken into small subgroups, and each subgroup is assigned to a believable group validator. Transactions are disseminated at random between groups, here the transaction's validity is verified and then a block is created by each believable validator. After this, the block is added within the chain in a network. This is achieved to increase the network's transaction throughput by organizing several transactions at similar time. In addition to the transaction fee, trustworthy validators are honored with mining expenditure. The block is then confirmed by the individuals allocated to that believable validator from the usual group. If the believable validator is determined to be harmful, then it will lose all of its crypto tokens, and the believable score will be zero.

12.3.2.9   Proof of Authority (PoAuthority)

In 2015, a reputation-based consensus protocol was introduced as evidence of authority where the minor's reputation is stacked rather than coins [24, 25]. A validator performs the portion of a minor in PoAuthority. In this algorithm, validators (known as experts or authorities) are officially approved, the identification of which is checked by an approved public notary system and is publicly approved. The authority must have a great reputation in order to be a validator, keeping them far from behaving maliciously. A block will be generated by each validator in a round-robin way. If a validator acts maliciously and proposes an incorrect block, then it is associated with a negative reputation. PoAuthority is utilized by PoA network [26] and Vechain crptocurrency exchange phases. Incentive is not given in terms of fee with PoAuthority, but it enhances the authorities by adding reputation to their name. Proof of Reputation (PoR) is a variety of PoAuthority, where a reputed affiliation is used as validator instead of an accepted identity [27].

When an object passes through a notary for authentication, it is delegated to the network's approved nodes, and agreement is maintained in a similar way to PoAuthority. Using market estimation, brand vitality, and whether the company is public or private, an organization's credibility is measured. Nowadays, PoR is utilized by the Gochain [27] and Menlo One [28] trading platforms. Because mining is carried out by the fixed validator party, the blockchain network is less decentralized by the PoAuthority and PoR algorithm.

12.3.2.10   Proof of Elapsed Time (PoET)

Proof of Elapsed Time (PoET) was developed in 2016 by Intel [29] as a cost-effective consensus protocol to resolve the problems of the rich getting richer and centralizing the network. After a random waiting period is generated, each authenticating network node in PoET sleeps, and the main node is given the option of creating the next block to finish the waiting period. By executing code in the Trusted Executive Environment (TEE) utilizing Software Guard eXtensions (SGX) developed by Intel, the random waiting time is provided by a marked verification that confirms the code transaction in a confidential environment. While using the code implemented in TEE, every node in PoET generates a marked random waiting period/time and then sleeps throughout that timeframe [30].

12.3.2.11   Proof of Activity (PoA)

In PoW, in addition to the transaction costs, the minors obtain a mining fee to encourage the minors to take part during the mining process and thereby secure the network. In additon, 12.5 Bitcoins are the new mining incentive and it is split after every 210,000 mined blocks. When the mining incentive is expired, the PoW turns out to be less important, and the minors only depend on the transaction fee. The minors who devote their processing power will also require a high transaction fee to discourage the utilization of the network. This is due to the cost of mining would be much greater than the benefits due to low transaction fees. This problem is known as the Commons tragedy [31], where everyone is looking for their own benefit without adding protection to the network. The transaction validators often not received any reward for their function in the majority of the consensus protocols.

Initiated in 2014, Proof of Authority (PoA) [32] solves these problems by utilizing PoS and PoW algorithms in a single algorithm. This is done by the minor and the validators sharing transaction fees, allowing the nodes to cooperate more dynamically.

PoA serves as the PoW in its first point, where all minors contend to build a block with a specific nonce. So, an empty block is created by a minor in PoA. The minor transmits the block made to the network. In the next step, PoA chooses to refer to N validators as partners based on the number of coins utilizing the PoS algorithm. The block was approved and signed by that partner and transmitted to the network.

All the identified N-1 partners mark or sign the block before it reaches the Nth partner who remembers the block transactions. The Nth partner hashes the block and shares it with all the network nodes. The transactions are split between the minor who made the block and the N partners for the transactions included by the Nth partner. As in PoW, PoA encounters the problem of high energy usage and it benefits the rich as in PoS. In reference to execution and security risks, PoA was not confirmed. It is utilized by Decred [33], a cryptocurrency.

12.3.3   Voting-Based Consensus Protocols

This consensus protocol employs a voting process to choose a miner to build a block. The issue of high energy consumption of compute intensive dependent protocols has been eliminated thanks to the selection of a miner based on a competitive approach. As the option is focused on wealth superiority, they also discuss the issue of the rich getting richer in capacity-based protocols.

Such protocols are projected to tolerate Byzantine problems by considering free node crashes or that malicious nodes may be carried on by a portion of the nodes in the network. With regard to distributed networks, Byzantine fault tolerance refers to the blockchain network's ability to reach optimum consensus rather than shortening or maliciously carrying on a portion of the system's nodes [34].

Furthermore, voting-based protocols are categorized into two protocols, *viz.*, Byzantine Fault Tolerance (BFT)–based and Crash Fault Tolerance (CFT)–based protocols. The instances of the failure node and the malicious node are protected by BFT-based consensus. BFT is extracted from the concern of the Byzantine general [35], a distributed computer network name for a condition when the nodes have to keep away from entire failure in a single, by knowing that some of the nodes might not be accurate.

12.3.3.1   Practical Byzantine Fault Tolerance (PBFT)

Castro *et al.* suggested Realistic Byzantine Fault Tolerance in 1999 [36]. Oracle, Hyperledger Iroha, Hyperledger Fabric, etc., use PBFT. A central authority chooses one node in the PBFT protocol as the leader and the others as the backup nodes. In order to reach an agreement, all the nodes in the network exchange data with each other by considering that all the actual nodes contain the similar ledger copy. The total number of nodes which are malicious, must be lesser than n/3 for the PBFT protocol to operate properly (n is the number of nodes in the system).

With a growing number of nodes, the network is stronger; since it is more unlikely that 1/3 of the total number of nodes in a network is malicious. In comparison to the blockchain, every single round to build a block in this protocol is known as a view. This can be divided into four different steps.

(1) A leader node receives a request form the client for the execution of the transaction.
(2) All the transaction records will be collected by the leader node which they grouped in a block.
(3) The transactions of the block are authenticated by every backup node in the network and create an authentic block of transaction. The node processes the block's hash and broadcasts it to various nodes.
(4) To respond with a similar hash, a node keeps two-thirds of the nodes. If the node receives a common response, then the block is appended to that node's record.

12.3.3.2   Delegated Byzantine Fault Tolerance (DBFT)

This protocol was suggested in order to ignore the centralized elect of a leader and also back up node in Practical Byzantine Fault Tolerance [37]. In DBFT protocol, by using a voting method, the nodes are chosen and leader node is termed as a speaker while the delegate node is termed as the backup node in the network.

The delegates are elected through a voting method in which the participants of the network holding the cryptocurrency engage during the voting era. The weighting of the vote is relative to the total of currency owned by the member. The selection of the speaker is randomly from the agent. Yet, on the basis of the voting system, the nodes are elected, there is a chance that every member votes for himself to be a delegate. During this time, the network faces the problem of overhead contact when all the participants are chosen as delegates.

12.3.3.3   Federated Byzantine Arrangement (FBA)

In 2014, the Federated Byzantine Arrangement (FBA) was proposed by Schwartz *et al.* [38] to preserve the decentralized feature of the blockchain and the overhead of communication can be ignore. In comparison to PBFT, for the authentication and handling of transactions, this protocol does not need elected nodes list from the authority. Within the network any node will take part in the process of consensus. In case of 80% of the nodes stick to the transaction status, another transaction is included in the network. The network will encounter the poor communication with all the nodes that participate in the consensus and relay the status of the transaction to each other to receive 80% of the confirmation. Each node in the network interacts with a group of nodes and this node is referred to as the Unique Node List [2], to solve this problem. The convergence of the Unique Node List by any two nodes in separate Unique Node Lists should not be less than 1/5th of all nodes connected in the network, as per the ripple network. This ensures that transaction will be accepted by all of the connected nodes. A node from the Unique Node List accepts a transaction while receiving a transaction and updates the client list. From all the nodes in the Unique Node List, each node interacts with its candidates. If 80% of the nodes agree that it is genuine, then a transaction is said to be validated [39].

12.3.3.4   Combined Delegated Proof of Stake and Byzantine Fault Tolerance (DPoS+BFT)

To select the node from within consensus process DPoS consensus algorithm was used and for the updation of ledger during protection against malicious attack, another algorithm, BFT algorithm was used. Combination of these two algorithms (DPoS+BFT) was created by the Credits blockchain stage [5] in 2018. The (DPoS+PBFT) algorithm can be splitted into two phases: (1) nodes identification and (2) ledger updation.

During initial phase, i.e., at the nodes identification, the algorithm chooses the head and trusted nodes to take an interest in the consensus process. The approval of transaction is given by the head nodes and makes a block, whereas a list of validate transactions to include the block utilizing BFT is created by the trusted nodes. Every node in the network will engage in the selection process in the form of a head node or a trusted node at any round of block formation. In the ledger, hash of the last block should be provided by the current node to the preceding head node that has generated it within a predefined time period in order to get selected. The nodes that have been unable to submit the hash value are excluded from the participation after this point. All nodes in the valid list are allocated a random number and the list is prepared sequentially. The head node will be the first node of the list and a specific node from among the rest nodes are chosen as the trusted nodes.

In next stage, head node produced a list of transactions and forwarded it to all the connected trusted nodes. All these transactions are approved by trusted nodes and prepare a list of approved transactions. The selection of nodes is done on the basis of the transactions having the highest validations in the lists by utilizing BFT algorithm. These lists are received from every trusted node. Every node forwards its list of validated transactions to the next trusted nodes. If a node does not matched with the other node is viewed as malicious or faulty, then it is terminated from the network. To build the transaction's block in the list, this validated list is transferred to the head node. For the authentication of the node, block is forwarded to other nodes within the network. This will starts the initial phase for another round. The DPoS+BFT protocol raises the overhead of communication immensely. In comparison with the PBFT, the level of data transmission between the trustworthy nodes is double the amount of data move between the backup nodes.

12.4   Conclusion

About a decade ago, blockchain technology was developed to transfer digital currency over peer-to-peer groups of unreliable network users without the involvement of a third party. Blockchain has developed over time to create an open decentralized technique in a variety of areas other than financial transfers. As a result, a number of blockchain architectures and consensus protocols also emerged. This is because of the ever-changing application criteria for improved services in a large-scale shared environment such as governance, social networking, smart cities, and healthcare, which are aiming for reduction in cost and time. Scalability, protection, energy use, and privacy risks were all big challenges in the blockchain network when it was first deployed on a decentralized network with open participation by no access control for data. After that, blockchain architectures and consensus protocols were created to allow for the application on a shared network while addressing protection and privacy concerns. Transitions in the blockchain network take longer time to complete as the number of users on the network grows. Therefore, transactions over the network are more expensive than average and so this reduces the number of users. The entire transaction takes hours or days to finish. So, the technology is becoming less and less profitable as a result of this blockchain implementation issue.

Consequently, the high energy usage needed to ensure protection is one of the major challenges in such architectures and protocols. With an increase in the number of members, the energy demand of CIBC protocols rises, having a negative impact on the environment. As a result, alternative ways to minimize energy consumption have been suggested, such as capability-based or voting-based protocols. However, these efforts to address the problem of high energy consumption resulted in architectures and consensus protocols that were less modular and decentralized.

References

1. Nakamoto, S., *Bitcoin: A Peer-To-Peer Electronic Cash System*, 2008, Available online: https://bitcoin.org/bitcoin.pdf.
2. Nguyen, T. and Kim, K., A survey about consensus algorithms used in Blockchain. *J. Inf. Process. Syst.*, 14, 101–128, 2018. [CrossRef].
3. Antonopoulos, A.M., *Mastering Bitcoin: Unlocking Digital Cryptocurrencies*, O'Reilly Media, Inc., Newton, MA, USA, 2014.

4. NEM White Paper, Available online: https://nemplatform.com/wp-content/uploads/2020/05/NEM_techRef.pdf. Symmetry 2019.

5. Credits White Paper, Available online: https://cryptorating.eu/whitepapers/CREDITS/TechnicalWhitePaperCREDITSEng.pdf

6. King, S., *Primecoin: Cryptocurrency with prime number proof-of-work*, July 7th 2013. Available online at https://primecoin.io/bin/primecoin-paper.pdf.

7. Ingham, A.E. and Ingham, A.E., *The Distribution of Prime Numbers*, Number 30, Cambridge University Press, Cambridge, UK, 1990.

8. Young, A. and Yung, M., Finding length-3 positive cunningham chains and their cryptographic significance. *International Algorithmic Number Theory Symposium*, Portland, OR, USA, 21–25 June 1998, Springer, Berlin/Heidelberg, Germany, pp. 289–298, 1998.

9. Forbes, T., Prime clusters and Cunningham chains. *Math. Comput. Am. Math. Soc.*, 68, 1739–1747, 1999, [CrossRef].

10. Ribenboim, P., *The New Book of Prime Number Records*, Springer Science & Business Media, Berlin/Heidelberg, Germany, 2012.

11. Primecoin, Available online: http://primecoin.io/about.php#what-xpm.

12. Delegated Proof of Stake With Downgrade: A Secure and Efficient Blockchain Consensus Algorithm With Downgrade Mechanism, Available online: https://ieeexplore.ieee.org/stamp/stamp.jsp?arnumber=8798621

13. bitshares.foundation/BitSharesBlockchain.pdf at master_bitshares-foundation/bitshares.foundation_GitHub. Available online: https://github.com/bitshares-foundation/bitshares.foundation/blob/master/download/articles/BitShares Blockchain.pdf (accessed on 23 January 2019).

14. Nano: A Feeless Distributed Cryptocurrency Network, Available online: https://content.nano.org/whitepaper/Nano_Whitepaper_en.pdf

15. Cardano—Home of the Ada Cryptocurrency and Technological Platform, Available online: https://docs.cardano.org/new-to-cardano/proof-of-stake.

16. Ren, L., *Proof of Stake Velocity: Building the Social Currency of the Digital Age*, 2014, Available online: http://cryptochainuni.com/wp-content/uploads/Reddcoin-Proof-of-Stake-Velocity.pdf

17. Reddcoin Social Currency—Official, Website. Available online: https://red-dcoin.com/reddcoin.html

18. Proof of Burn—BitcoinWiki, Available online: https://en.bitcoin.it/wiki/proof_of_burn

19. Dziembowski, S., Faust, S., Kolmogorov, V., Pietrzak, K., Proofs of space, in: *Proceedings of the Annual Cryptology Conference*, Santa Barbara, CA, USA, 16–20 August 2015, Springer, Berlin/Heidelberg, Germany, pp. 585–605, 2015.

20. Bresson, E., Canteaut, A., Chevallier-Mames, B., Clavier, C., Fuhr, T., Gouget, A., Icart, T., Misarsky, J.F., Naya-Plasencia, M., Paillier, P. *et al.*, *Shabal, a Submission to NIST's Cryptographic Hash Algorithm Competition*, 2008, Available online: https://www.cs.rit.edu/~ark/20090927/Round2Candidates/Shabal.pdf

21. *Solana: A New Architecture for a High Performance Blockchain*, Available online: https://solana.com/solana-whitepaper.pdf

22. Proof of Importance, Available online:https://docs.nem.io/en/gen-info/what-is-poi

23. Proof of Believability, Available online: hhttps://github.com/iost-official/Documents/blob/master/Technical_White_Paper/EN/Tech_white_paper_EN.md#proof-of-believability

24. Proof-of-Authority—Wikipedia, Available online: https://en.wikipedia.org/wiki/Proof-of-authority

25. Wiki/Proof-of-Authority-Chains.md at Master_paritytech/wiki_GitHub, Available online: https://github.com/shihao-guo/parity/wiki/Proof-of-Authority-Chains

26. *POA Network: Public Ethereum Sidechain with Proof of Autonomy Consensus by Independent Validators*, Available online: https://poa.network/

27. Gochain-Whitepaper, Available online: https://www.allcryptowhitepapers.com/wp-content/uploads/2018/11/gochain-whitepaper-v2.1.2.pdf

28. Menlo One—Tools that Make BlockchainWork for Business, Available online: https://www.menlo.one/

29. The Second Coming of Blockchain|IntelR Software, Available online: https://software.intel.com/en-us/blogs/2017/02/14/the-second-coming-of-blockchain, (accessed on 18 December 2018).

30. Chen, L., Xu, L., Shah, N., Gao, Z., Lu, Y., Shi, W., *On Security Analysis of Proof-of-Elapsed-Time (PoET)*, Springer, Cham, Switzerland, 2017.

31. Hardin, G., The tragedy of the commons. *Science*, 162, 1243–1248, 1968, [PubMed].

32. Bentov, I., Lee, C., Mizrahi, A., Rosenfeld, M., Proof of activity: Extending bitcoin's proof of work via proofof stake [extended abstract] y. *ACM Sigmetrics Perform. Eval. Rev.*, 42, 34–37, 2014.

33. Decred—Autonomous Digital Currency, Available online: https://www.decred.org/

34. Driscoll, K., Hall, B., Sivencrona, H., Zumsteg, P., Byzantine fault tolerance, from theory to reality, in: *Proceedings of the International Conference on Computer Safety, Reliability, and Security*, Edinburgh, UK, 23–26 September 2003, Springer, Piscataway, NJ, USA, pp. 235–248, 2003.

35. Lamport, L., Shostak, R., Pease, M., The Byzantine generals problem. *ACM Trans. Program. Lang. Syst.(TOPLAS)*, 4, 382–401, 1982, [CrossRef].

36. Castro, M. and Liskov, B., Practical Byzantine fault tolerance, in: *Proceedings of the 3rd Symposium on Operating System Design and Implementation (OSDI)*, New Orleans, LA, USA, February 1999, Unisex Association, Berkeley, CA, USA, pp. 173–186, 1999.

37. NEO White Paper, Available online: https://docs.neo.org/en-us/whitepaper.html

38. Schwartz, D., Youngs, N., Britto, A., *The Ripple protocol consensus algorithm*, p. 8, Ripple Labs Inc White Pap., 5, 2014. Available online at https://ripple.com/files/ripple_consensus_whitepaper.pdf

39. Ismail, L. and Materwala, H., A Review of Blockchain Architecture and Consensus Protocols: Use Cases, Challenges, and Solutions. *Symmetry*, 11, 10, 1198, 2019.

40. Kibet, A. and Karume, S.M., A Synopsis of Blockchain Technology. *Int. J. Adv. Res. Comput. Eng. Technol. (IJARCET)*, 7, 11, 789–795, 2018.

Applicability of Utilizing Blockchain Technology in Smart Cities Development

Auwal Alhassan Musa[1,2]*, Shashivendra Dulawat[1], Kabeer Tijjani Saleh[3]
and Isyaku Auwalu Alhassan[2]

[1]Civil Engineering Department, Mewar University, Chittorgarh, Rajasthan, India
[2]Civil Engineering Department, Kano University of Science and Technology, Wudil,
Kano, Nigeria
[3]Regional Planning Department, Mersin University, Mersin, Turkey

Abstract

The focus of this work is to highlight general overview of reliability and resiliencies of smart cities and their devastating challenges which includes security, energy consumption, and need for controlling huge amount of data that can be done by the use of blockchain technology through the integration of smart sensors, Internet of Things (IoT), artificial intelligence, cloud computing, and powerful software. Its benefits are to both dwellers and managers involved in the smart cities development. Apart from the problems and solutions of smart cities that are related to technology, other related challenges hindering its development are lack of intervention from policy-makers, funding, skilled workforce, and existing gap between industries and academia. Therefore, there is an urgent need to invest hugely to the sector, equipped it with enough skilled manpower, as well as special fund package to support both small- and medium-scaled industries. Hence, proper implementation of proposed recommendations made, the future of smart cities especially in developed countries can safely be guaranteed.

Keywords: Resilience, smart city, intervention, system, Internet of Things, blockchain

Corresponding author: auwalalhassanmusa@gmail.com
Auwal Alhassan Musa: ORCID: https://orcd.org/0000-0002-2216-1062
Shashivendra Dulawat: ORCID: https://orcd.org/0000-0002-2948-9546
Kabeer Tijjani Saleh: ORCID: https://orcd.org/0000-0001-7118-0596
Isyaku Auwalu Alhassan: ORCID: https://orcd.org/0000-0001-7999-8010

Vishal Kumar, Vishal Jain, Bharti Sharma, Jyotir Moy Chatterjee and Rakesh Shrestha (eds.) Smart City Infrastructure: The Blockchain Perspective, (317–340) © 2022 Scrivener Publishing LLC

13.1   Introduction

Over the past few years, smart infrastructural development is among the top topics of discussion between professionals and experts in the industrial sector especially the technology industries as well in academia. This trend seems to be the most competitive scenario in the near future of the technological revolution around the world. The world competition in smart infrastructural development transformation is taking new shape among technological industries in Europe, USA and Asia. This competitive move between these industries in recent time has brought about a rapid change toward their activities and help industries to smartly transform and change their entire systems of production, construction, and manufacturing into digitized one using the blockchain technology [1]. An industrial revolution for implementing smart and artificial intelligence (AI) would bring about progress in economic development, meeting costumers demand, time reduction, improved quality, as well as the flexibility to suit the demanding market through an integrated human-machine interaction. This recent innovation would drastically minimize the manpower requirement, increased product quality, and cyclic, undisrupted, and connected supply chain of production in the manufacturing process. This has brought about transparency in the industrial hierarchy thereby increasing the effectiveness of productivity. However, up to now, very few industries have been able to rapidly adopt these technologies.

Since the beginning of the 21st century, the need for shelter especially in urban has been intensified due to the high rise of migration from rural areas to urban areas across the world especially in Africa, Latin America, and some countries in Asia, unlike before the 18th century where only 5% of the world population living in cities. This was aligned with the prediction of the United Nation which was made in the last decade that the urban population would rise by almost 63% from 3.9 to 6.3 billion between 2015 and 2050 [2]. Among these countries, India which may hit 1.7 billion and Nigeria might reach up to a population of 399 million. The reasons behind these migrations are search for stability of living which includes jobs, education, medicals care, while other reasons are due to political and conflict reasons.

Long ago the migration phenomenon keeps occurring due to these aforementioned reasons while cities keep becoming crowded. The services they offered which ranges from the safer and efficient transportation systems, non-polluted environments, improved health facilities, a sustained educational system to strengthen security of life and properties, but due

Figure 13.1 Conventional developed city [3].

to the concurrent migration processes to the current existing cities will hardly cater to those needs efficiently. In addition, urban development and cities contribute immensely toward the problems involved in the natural and man-built environment and socio-economic activities. However, it is necessary to provide a progressive service efficiently while at the same time maintaining the goal of sustainable socio-economic growth (Figure 13.1). Therefore, it is necessary to initiate new means to which these rapid changes in the world population due to migration can be managed smartly as the world is becoming more urbanized. The need to create an innovative technology that will reduce the social, political, and administrative complexity due to high population, energy consumption resource, and environmental problems such as air and land pollution is perhaps necessary.

13.2   Smart Cities Concept

The main objective of resilience in smart cities is to have a sustainable, enhanced and innovative infrastructure by using state-of-the-art technology that will be incorporated with the utilization of energy, manpower, cost, and other resources. An intended aim of satisfying customer needs without compromising the construction processes and causing disturbance to the environment and remain capable of considering economic, political, and social demand of the society. While also capable of resisting future possible disruption from unforeseen circumstances such a natural pandemic. This can be achieved by ongoing competition and initiation of innovative ideas of world-leading technologies companies in developed and developing countries such as China USA, and India. Smart cities' implementation aimed in enhancing the peace and welfare of the urban community in different ways and it is being created with the maximum consideration to the sustainable diplomatic in modern urbanization. Smart cities focused to exploit technology and resources, land uses, and infrastructures to achieve a harmonious environment. However, it is also associated with some setbacks that disturb the human environment. These effects exist in different elevated forms ranging from air pollution, water, heat, noise, and land which are relatively known as a distress to the urban environment.

13.3   Definition of Smart Cities

No single definition that is generally acceptable and formally to be used as the universal definition of the smart cities. Nonetheless, different scholars and experts in the field tried to give a more specific definition that will suit the basic characteristics of the smart cities. Though some terms are used interchangeably to replace the names of the smart cities, these terminologies include cities for future, digital cities, intelligent cities, resilient cities, and sustainable cities; however, these terms were used in the late 90s, while the term smart cities are fully used nowadays which suits and comprises the most features of the above terms, such as rapid technological advancement, the term also suits the current political, economic, and environmental views. The smart city has to fulfill the six dimensions namely economy, people, governance, mobility, environment, and living. Some of the few definitions of the smart city were cited below.

The smart city is the city that integrates the application of ICT for sustaining life improvement to its inhabitants [4]. The smart cities are geographically occupied spaces that optimized the combination of tangible and non-tangible resources and maximize their usage to its inhabitants [5]. It is an integrated process of combining effort of physical infrastructures, digital systems, and human activities within the already build environment to ensure full deliverance of services to its inhabitants and provide means of neutralizing the expected challenges [6]. The smart city is the city that transforms its elements such as infrastructures into ICT compatible. These infrastructures can be roads, tunnels, subways, buildings, waterways, pipelines, seaports, and airport; these compatibilities can be in terms of security, maintenance, and maximizing the service of the Infrastructures to the inhabitants [7].

Any physical city that can be able to optimize the use of its human and non-human resources including infrastructures and equipment to maximize their usage to the inhabitants without causing any hazardous and

Figure 13.2 The proposed future smart city adapted from [11].

degradable effect to the environment [8]. It is also an innovation designed to offer sustained services and growth to the quality of life of the inhabitants thereby reducing any other environmentally related problems. The smart city is the city designed with aim in applying information and technology architecture to all elements forming the city such as roads, buildings, health care services, educational institutions, markets, and any other element that build up the city and transforming those elements to offer better services to the citizen smartly [9], and organizational structures that encourage collaboration, innovation, and the application of that information to solve public problems [10] (Figure 13.2).

The smartness of the cities is ensured by the proper and seamless integration of the higher powered digital telecommunication networks which include 5G network (nerves), digital sensors, and other physical organs for assisting sensing and transmitting the information. Highly powered software capable of running large data in lesser time and huge data storage for such complex computation are also prerequisites. In addition, data capturing, computing, transmitting, storing, retrieving, as well as security are of paramount importance. This can be achieved by using the Internet of Things (IoT) [9].

13.4 Legal Framework by EU/AIOTI of Smart Cities

The legal benchmark with regards to the security of the IoT was fully developed and financed stably to address the issue of security of intensive usage of IoT in smart cities; these benchmarks were set by Alliance for the Internet of Things Innovation (AIOTI) which was established and funded by EU in the year 2015. The legal framework recommended by two-sided principles privacy by design which include a strong inclusion of security measures at the initial stage of designing technology and the privacy by default. This term refers to the need of collecting only basic and essential data, while any other irrelevant data collection should be avoided at all level by the cities managers. The activities of the forum were channeled and shared by different organizations, telecom companies, professional bodies, and academic institutions for proper implementations. EU believes that data security in the IoT is of paramount importance for the progressive growth of the smart cities.

13.5   The Characteristics of Smart Cities

The current inconsistency and scarcity of essential services offered by the nowadays cities to the increasing inhabitants amplify the need for further timely innovation which will identify and solve the problem that classical approach fails to solve. The smart cities work based on incorporating day-to-day activities of these build cities with the application of advanced technology in providing the solution to the problems of citizens of the cities and also maximize the yielded benefits to the life of the inhabitants. The following characteristics of the smart cities were mentioned [12].

13.5.1   Climate and Environmentally Friendly

With regard to the environment, the smart city has the potentials of managing and sustaining the environment; these include the ability to locate disposed waste and recycle it, minimize the pollution, clean and healthy water supply, and regulate other related issues to the environment. Climate-friendly, another challenging task in developed cities is complete control of pollution being it air, water, and land pollution due to industrial, transportation, and other human activities. While in smart cities, greenhouse gas emissions and other pollution-related activities will be drastically reduced.

13.5.2   Livability

One of the most interesting features of the smart cities, it offers its inhabitants the most compatible and improved basic and secured living services such as digital protection of lives and properties, improved health services, and sustainable education system.

13.5.3   Sustainability

The sustainability of the smart cities is increased and managed by the use of technology; this sustainability includes management and protection of natural resources related to the infrastructures.

13.5.4   Efficient Resources Management

The smart city has the capability of managing, tracking, and detecting the level of resources used by its inhabitants, so that the level of consumption and rate of supply will not be disrupted.

13.5.5   Resilient

These cities were designed to offer resistance toward most forecasted challenges by providing disease control response teams, tie security against fraudsters and hackers, earthquake detection and resistivity, etc. Conventional cities are facing specific problems related to safety and security, including crime and violence, shooting, and terrorism; these problems are threat to the safety of citizens and cause a vast challenge to governments and cities alike.

13.5.6   Dynamism

Flexibility in adjusting the level of service they offer to the inhabitants is one of the most important features of a smart city. This dynamism enables the city to detect and make decisions about the citizen's needs.

13.5.7   Mobility

The smart cities are incomplete without resilient and consistent smart transportation systems; the smart mobility infrastructures aimed and focused on maximizing the efficiency and performance of the transportation systems thereby saving energy, reducing carbon emission and reducing the cost of travel, as well as increasing the comfortability offered by the system to the users. The relevant terms related to smart mobility includes intelligent transport systems, smart taxi, improved metro lines, smart logistics, smart parking, electric vehicles, and the smart traffic management. The classical system of transportation system is full of problems ranging from the accident occurrence, congestion problems, and release of harmful gases to the environment.

13.6   Challenges Faced by Smart Cities

It was confirmed by [13] that more than 75% of activities involved in the IoT failed to adhere with lengthy and complex secured passwords of access. This gives the fraudsters and hackers access to almost 70% of the data stored by the enumeration process.

13.6.1   Security Challenge

The majority of the activities in the smart cities are not secured personally rather they are controlled by a third party. Because, for a smart city to exist, we must have smart space, and that smart space needs to know almost if not anything about the citizen living in those cities for it to smoothly offer the basic services without hindrance. These integrated systems need to know exact personal identifiable information about the household data of every citizen living in those cities, compile these data, and use them to generate new flexible profile to these citizens. Therefore, various services can be offered to them and make a real-time decision about them. For example, let us look at the smart vehicles which can be a cars, drones, space vehicles, etc., they were designed with an inbuilt GPS device, full ranged wireless connections and sensors which can detect passenger's location and condition such as exact home and workplace address, time of his movement, and duration of time spent within particular smart city infrastructures by using radars installed in these infrastructures. Also, these vehicles' behavior in relation to smart road activities such as speed, flow, travel time, route origin and destination, and driver identity can actively be detected and controlled using sophisticated installed softwares and other technological detecting devices on the road. Therefore, the citizen's activities in smart cities are no longer privates in all perspectives as a result of highly interconnected network activities which are prerequisite to the smooth running of the cities activities, failure to have such data the smartness behavior of the city would not be attained and may lead to the breakdown or total shutdown of the system. The smart city infrastructure, which combines the IoT, Big Data, and Energy Internet, is one of the most effective solutions [14].

13.6.2   Generation of Huge Data

All the activities in smart cities, which include water supply system, energy generation and transmission process, transportation and logistics activities, waste generation and disposal processes, e-learning system, and many more, generate a continuous huge amount of data progressively. This data is stored cloudly using IoT infrastructures. The weakness features of the IoT are the data security problem as it was mentioned by [15]; these problems include unsecured web interface, weak mobile interface, unencrypted network usage, and lack of privacy of personal data. In addition, data generated from the interaction of tangible and non-tangible objects is difficult to be controlled using traditional means.

13.6.3 Concurrent Information Update

All the integrated functions of the smart infrastructures were developed in order to suit the need of the citizen living in the smart cities as all the activities has turned to merely virtual unless necessary, all the relevant data of each and every citizen should be updated time to time by the third party in managing the activities of the smart cities; this includes exact contact information, family-related issue, health condition, and emergency conditions. However, the riskiest condition about this information recorded is the fear by the inhabitants that they do not have knowledge about the data processing and transmission. What they might actually know is the process of collecting all this information.

13.6.4 Energy Consumption Challenge

It has been mentioned before that the smart city needs reliable and uninterrupted power supply, which most of the technological infrastructures use for their smooth running. All these shall be compatible with the real intelligence which is the working brain integrated into the system. All these heavily depend and require a huge amount of smart energy; the smart energy here refers to the uninterrupted electric power supply. Also, the process of smart energy provision helps the cities in providing safer, efficient, and effective means of generating energy of various kinds and, at the same time, helps in managing and controlling the prices and reduce the pollution emitted from these energy sources. Therefore, to have reliable smart power supply, the conditions are as follows: non-polluted energy sources, smart metering, efficient public lighting integration of the electric vehicle, and active involvement of the consumer [16].

13.7 Blockchain Technology at Glance

After its emergence in 2008, blockchain technology is one of the distributed ledger technologies (DLT), a way of recording and sharing data across multiple data stores (also known as ledgers), in which each has the same data records and is collectively maintained and controlled by a distributed network of computer servers, which are called nodes. By a non-identified illusive person called Satoshi Nakamoto. However, no single and universally accepted definition of blockchain technology exists; rather, it is normally based on the perspectives functionality of its implementation. One may assume that it is based on popular cryptocurrency which permits the proper execution, tracking, transaction, and using highly protected and sophisticated security means to protect the records in the distributed ledger as it was initially developed for that purpose. However, the blockchain technology is beyond that as it was used to apply in the IoT to mitigate the security challenges of data in smart cities. Still, the application of blockchain technology in various fields is yet be fully understood [17]. However, many of the best definitions emphasize on public, digital, chronological, and distributed ledger for transactions, where it interferes with most academic and practical specializations. Therefore, the blockchain is a resilient, systematic, traceable, immutable, automated, and peer-to-peer distributed ledger that provides a strong platform for keeping data on the internet. While the security techniques were achieved by the use of cryptographic means and mathematical protocols. Having non-centralized and distributed characteristics make it a perfect flexible system for verifying all transaction occurred [18].

Therefore, on the perspective of the smart cities, the blockchain technology can be redefined as the process of applying advanced automation, control, simulation, and modeling which will result in safer, quicker, efficient, effective, and cheaper products or services that meet the demand of the consumer without causing due effects to the habitants and environment. It also involves the integration of automation, computation, networking, cloud computing (CC), and adoption of advanced information technology for the production of reliable and updated goods and services.

The blockchain developed was categorized based on the functional development as follows [19].

i. **First Category:** This deals with the initial intention of creating the blockchain technology of performing and keeping the financial transaction of cryptocurrency.

ii. **Second Category:** This deals with expanding the initial invention to run the smart contract activities; these include the exchange of digital assets, smart property businesses (property rights), and digital decentralized market. The smart contract is enabled by the blockchain

technology which allows automated exchange and transaction of token which was represented by physical assets
without the interference of any centralized party.

iii. **Third Category:** This includes the application of the first
two categories with an additional infrastructural application which emerges and brings new paradigms of smart
cities.

iv. **Fourth Category:** This is the most recent and is still at the
infant stage of development which deals with the smart
manufacturing and development of 5.0 digital industries.

The most interesting feature of blockchain technology is the mining
process. The mining begins with the transaction verification by the users
through the series of stages. Though these processes involved in the mining need to have a strong and reliable complex computational capability
which needs time and energy consumption. This decentralized property
of blockchain technology is secured by applying strong and reliable cryptographic techniques; these technologies include digital hashes, asymmetric cryptography, and digital signatures. Another important feature
of blockchain technology is that it can be public (*permissioned*) or private (*restricted*) [20]. The former deals with an open environment having
no restriction to users having access to the network, example of this is
Bitcoin platform, while the latter concerns with the limited entity to the
environment, as a decentralized and transparent technology which is able
to provide the security especially to data which is the most critical issue
concerning the smart cities development. The main advantage of using
blockchain in the smart cities is that the hackers need to have an access
to each and every device to get exact information needed because of its
decentralized nature. In short term, the blockchain system has no single
point of failure; rather, it has a decentralized point which is difficult to
manage by a single person.

13.8   Key Drivers to the Implementation of Blockchain Technology for Smart Cities Development

The key technologies/drivers enabling the blockchain technology in smart
cities are sensors, wireless connection, data analysis, generative design,
computer-aided design, and advanced robotics, IoT, CC, and AI.

The emergence of AI gives the breakthrough to the development of the smart manufacturing due to its multipurpose characteristics of capable storing, computing, and sharing huge data which gives the technological manufacturers ability to improve the level of production and increase their competitiveness. AI is a cognitive system which combines the machine learning and its capabilities to detect and interact with the natural language and provide reliable information from a huge amount of data. These systems receive information from humans through the natural language, which allows them to digest it and detect if there is need for additional information. This replaces the existing system of computation as a result of their vast learning and reasoning abilities which help them to solve the ambiguity and general uncertainty to which the user can heavily rely on. These systems will help to have a resilient smart activities especially in transportation. For example, the driverless car uses such system for its services deliverances, and in some of the developed cities in the world, this system was developed to replace the airline pilot with a robotic pilot. Another innovative system included in the AI is the invention of drones; these drones can play a vital role in smart cities' activities.

13.8.1   Internet of Things (IoT)

IoT which sometimes correlated with the CC which serves as the main storage of IoT's data and provides a medium to which the users can interact and retrieve data, the innovation of IoT and CC provides an opportunity for construction industries to save a lot by avoiding them to unnecessarily to create individual sites and communication platforms for their products which can be accessed by other independent service providing companies [21]. The IoT provides a means to which the data can be captured, recorded, identified and transfer without the human intervention. The IoT is the collection of physical devices such as smartphones, personal computers, and other internet-related devices. Even though, the number of connected devices is increased geometrically every year. Currently, the IoT rely heavily on the centralized server-client systems which mostly offer solution through CC. Because of this centralized nature of this system, the attackers and internet hackers utilized to have access to the vulnerable information. Therefore, it is necessary to implement a new approach for protecting individual data through decentralized systems such by using blockchain technology.

13.8.2   Architectural Organization of the Internet of Things

In most cases, the architectural organization of IoT is generally organized based on the three layers [22]. However, considering the current status and field of discussion, it can be broadened to four layers with additional layers; these layers include perception layer, support layer, network layer, and application layer [23, 24].

a) **Perception Layer (Physical Layer):** This is sensing and the layer in the IoT organization, as the name implies, its main application is to collect data from different sophisticated devices, and sensors present in the smart space then send them to the neighboring layer for an immediate processing [25].

b) **Network Layer (Internet Layer):** This sometimes called communication layer as the name implies it usually serves as the heart of the Intent of Things (IoT) as it serves as the receiving and at the same time as transmitting medium of the already collected data from the perception layer for proper connectivity to the network and other server devices.

c) **Support Layer (Interface Layer):** This layer is just an additional layer between the network and application layer, the basic essence of this layer is to provide strong support using advanced computing technologies which include cloud, fog, and edge computing.

d) **Application layer (Database Layer):** After long processing of transfer from the bottom/perception layer, this would provide the intelligent platform for various benefits to the smart city users; this application area includes smart space, smart transportation, smart infrastructure, and smart public services.

13.9 Challenges of Utilizing Blockchain in Smart City Development

The application of blockchain technology varies from city to city, from project to project, depending on economic and social conditions, infrastructure, technical expertise, and other factors so does its problems as well [26]. Like any other successful project development of a city, blockchain technology also experiences some setbacks either in its proposal, implementation, or execution, most especially in developing a smart city which requires consideration of all the utilities of a city from people's movements to their daily routine activities such as commercial activities, educational, agricultural, industrial, and likes. Major metropolitan areas are by this time being faced with the problem of substituting relatively old infrastructures, such as transportation tunnels, steam pipes, underground wiring, and as well as installing their modern kinds. Thus, funding and provision for new infrastructures projects for blockchain technology in smart cities is limited and approval processes can take years. Moreover, complicated and costly infrastructures is involved in installing, operating and maintaining these technologies. Perhaps, questions like: How can these infrastructures be powered? Will they need a hard-wiring, solar energy, or battery operation? Or, in case of power failure, what will be the fate of the technology [27].

These challenges surely affect the nature of the blockchain projects ranging from security and privacy, lack of technical know-how on how to operate blockchain-related technology properly, cost and high energy consumption nature of the technology, infrastructural provision and installation challenge, and lack of government cooperation in executing blockchain related project especially in the case of smart cities development. Below are some of the identified major challenges to blockchain technology based on the smart cities creation perspective.

13.9.1 Security and Privacy as a Challenge to Blockchain Technology

Security and privacy protection grieves and require more attention when it comes to a blockchain kind of technology; this is a result of most its data that are being stored in an open and unsecured network, a global network to be precise that can be accessed from different handlers providing a more simplified access to projects blueprints, process, nature and safety record of contracts, and business documents and transactions. As a decentralized ledger, it records every transaction and stores information in a global network [28]. While blockchain is more secured than traditional computer systems, hackers can still breach apps, systems, and businesses built on a blockchain. With all information being stored in a global network, blockchain technology is capable of simplifying the project collaborations and history as the original design of blockchain technology is made to be publicly visible and accessible. As a result of the simplified access to information, several apprehensions were developed because of project execution companies, firms, and government need to be able to restrict and control access to their data.

In other words, blockchain technology cannot work with sensitive and confidential data. The remedy is not only limited to government protection of privacy. Self-sovereign identities on blockchain will enable us to regulate and control our data. While there is a lot of work on several privacy protocols such as proof of zero-knowledge, to overcome these obstacles and good identity initiatives are ongoing, we are still a long way from a fundamentally welcoming the technology with end to end encrypted data storage in the case of a smart urban center formation. Furthermore, it is possible to customize a blockchain so that the general public can only be able to access parts of the blockchain that are limited and relevant to their tasks. Private or associations blockchain could work here. One might get limited access, and all sensitive information would stay private as it should be. Although it will take relatively some time to strategy and make the adoption of blockchain technology more probable.

13.9.2 Lack of Cooperation

A good number of companies developed their commands of blockchain technology which gives rise to the lack of proper coordination between the organizations to control, tackle, and enhance the blockchain technology methodology, challenges, and operating guidelines. So like in the development of a smart city, the cooperation between architectural companies, engineering firms, urban planning, and design authorities go a long way in partnerships to the standard and meaningful outcome of a developed city. Like should be expected when it comes to using the blockchain technology in the development of the smart cities. Organizations shall develop the concept of working together as a body from every aspect. The approach of standing alone that most of the companies engaged in developing their blockchain and applications to run on top of it should be discouraged.

13.9.3 Lack of Regulatory Clarity and Good Governance

Smart city development using blockchain technology can be considered as a bulk project that requires proper government contribution and intervention to the achievement of its goal. However, in the general case of blockchain technology implementation, it suffers a major negligence from the government also there is a lack of regulatory clarity regarding the primary blockchain technology, which is a substantial barricade for mass adoption of the technology. From the angle of a sharing service, there is a need for governance to protect users of sharing services from fraud, liability, and unskilled service providers [29, 30].

13.9.4   Energy Consumption and Environmental Cost

Smart cities activities include data collected from citizens, devices, buildings, and assets then processed and analyzed to monitor and manage traffic and transportation systems, power plant, utilities, water supply networks, waste, crime detection information systems, schools, libraries, hospitals, and other community services [31]. It is a project that really requires a large energy consumption because smart cities use data and technology to create efficiencies, improve sustainability, create economic development, and improve quality of life standards for people living and working in the city.

The use of smart computing technologies makes the critical infrastructure components and services of a city which include city administration, education, healthcare, public safety, real estate, transportation, and utilities more intelligent, interconnected, efficiency, and effective [32]. It is also important to note that blockchain kind of a technology that predominantly captures data from nook and cranny of the city, from every smaller pinging network source in the city consumes a high percentage of energy beyond expectation which can be considered as a setback to the technology.

Nowadays, most attention paid by various cities in the world focusing on modern technologies as well as aiming to reduce costs, use resources optimally, and create a more livable urban environment [33]. However, in the case of blockchain technology, the amount of energy consumed by computers that compete to receive, store, and manipulate a municipal data can relatively be huge in consideration of the nature of how big a smart city might be. Therefore, it is a project with high cost and energy consumption in its implementation. Backward-looking at the city development, a city encompasses a larger and different branch of land uses at different sectors, whereas the distribution of resources should be relatively considered and optimally distributed as minimal as possible. Hence, due to the nature of the cost of this technology, this can also be considered as a challenge to it.

The list of blockchain adoption challenges mentioned above clearly highlights the need for technological improvement, not only for smart city development but for the technological industries in general.

13.10   Solution Offered by Blockchain to Smart Cities Challenges

Blockchain technology is designed to bring a number of tremendous changes toward the broad ranges from industries, businesses, and other aspects of living. The following are some of the areas where blockchain plays a vital role in smart cities.

13.10.1   Secured Data

Smart cities have special features which enable it to provide reliable and efficient support toward data security which can be difficult for the security threat [34].

13.10.2   Smart Contract

One of the most important features of the blockchain technology is the disappearance of the third party in performing various activities such as financial and legal processes which required linkage and validation of the third party [35]. The emergence of the blockchain gives room for the performance of the smart contract which does not require an intervention of a third party. The transaction of data used is traceable and they give room for verification and negotiation [36].

13.10.3   Easing the Smart Citizen Involvement

The existence of blockchain gives assurance to the citizen for their data security. Other activities perform collectively such as voting can be performed using this improved system of blockchain due to its decentralized identity nature a citizen can also send complaint and receive feedback within shortest period time [37].

13.10.4   Ease of Doing Business

Although there is confusion and disagreement between the experts whether this technological and innovative advancement will cut the employments and jobs opportunity drastically [38]. But in another perspective, the blockchain technology will ease all the ways of doing businesses and initiate transparent means which does not requires any third-party intervention.

13.10.5   Development of Sustainable Infrastructure

With regard to the development of smart infrastructure, many technologies such as CC automation and AI can be used to improve all the processes and develop an integral and transparent system between the leaders and other policy-makers in the building and construction sectors [39]. The blockchain can be deeply implemented especially in the area where different interests are needed to be negotiated by different parties to suit the customers' demands, especially in the area of transport and energy. In addition, using the AI and the IoT will provide smooth means to which successful standard data security, reliability and data manipulations is guaranteed.

13.10.6   Transparency in Protection and Security

The special decentralized special feature of blockchain technology makes it become highly transparent in sharing, processing, and given the expected outcome of information to which the users might rely upon. Also, using the process of track and trace (T&T) functionality can manage, identify, and trace the exact movement or any related activities in the smart processes which include both tangible and non-tangible objects. Another important aspect of data protection is assisting government officials in the smooth running of complex public schemes.

13.10.7   Consistency and Auditability of Data Record

One of the most challenging aspects of the normal traditional means of recording data is comprehensive and assurance of the data recorded especially in government agencies which deal with robust and mismatched cumbersome data. Also, with regard to the private organizations, data exchange might not be fully controlled and secured, which sometimes, it needs a third party agent for actualization processes. All these challenges faced by private and public organizations in our conventional urban areas will drastically reduce if the blockchain technology is implemented [40]. It will provide room for proper means of monitoring, recording, and strong and reliable audible track existing of data.

13.10.8   Effective, Efficient Automation Process

Most of the traditional network systems used nowadays have limited efficiency with regard to the data processing which is associated with substandard security issues and related manual interventions [41]. Relying on the IoT layers (application layer, support layer, network layer, and perception layer) can improve the efficiency usually in transaction, and automated business processes can be controlled, handled, and run smoothly with no or little hindrance.

13.10.9   Secure Authentication

As mentioned before each layer in the IoT serves a different purpose ranging from the data collection, transfer, processing and finally to the consumer for application, therefore during these process there is need of strong authentication of the data between the layers, therefore with the help of the IoT devices installed in the smart cities, the authentication process becomes merely simple and possible with high precision. These authentication processes are implemented by using encryption-based technology because the hackers use the nodes to access information.

13.10.10   Reliability and Continuity of the Basic Services

The constant and continuous supply of the basic humans need which include uninterrupted power supply, clean water supply, strong communication channels, resilient transportation systems, and waste management are some of the essential features of the smart city [42, 43]. Therefore, the city managers and other cities stakeholder have to ensure and prevent the disruption of such services, and in case of the disruption, it has to be recovered speedily.

13.10.11   Crisis and Violence Management

Early detection and tracking criminal activities would be at ease because reliable and all the information needed from the inhabitants is recorded robustly. The blockchain technology can help in providing an instant and real-time location of the criminal activities.

13.11   Conclusion

The hybridization of the digital activities in the construction, production, and manufacturing industries has been the key factor in the revolutionary movement of smart cities which may lead to the fifth edition of the industrial revolution. Also, considering the current challenges and disruption in supply chain and value chain activities, implementing blockchain technology in the construction industries will help in alleviating them. Again, the successful trends of blockchain implementation in smart cities are likely to be the conditional advancement to the change in the current difficulties faced for the development of smart cities. However, most of the industries embarked on this trend are still at the infancy stage crippled with the scarce funding, poor and unavailability of well-trained skilled manpower, as well as lack of proper support from their governments. Lastly, to have a robust, resilient, reliable, less costly, and environmental friendly smart cities, it is necessary for private and public sectors especially in the production sector to work jointly with the provisional guidelines prescribes by the policy-makers.

In general, technological advancements take a long time to be developed, adopted, and to fully reach functional and stable standard needed to be accepted generally in the technological world. Like any technological innovation, blockchain will follow the same, slow trajectory of adoption over the upcoming years. Although there are many possibilities, it will still take time to get free from all the challenges and use it to achieve all the paybacks of it.

References

1. Appio, F.C., Lima, M., Paroutis, S., Understanding Smart Cities: Innovation Ecosystems, Technological Advancements, and Societal Challenges. In press at *Technological Forecasting Social Change*, Technological Advancements, and Societal Challenges, https://doi.org/10.1016/j.techfore.2018.12.018.
2. United Nation World Population Prospects, *The 2015 vision: key findings and advance tables*, 2015.
3. Developed Cities Eedge out towns in the smart city race Smart Cities council, 2014, https://www.indianexpress.com.
4. Georgescu, M., Păvăloaia, V.D., Popescul, D., Tugui, A., The Race for Making up the List of Emergent Smart Cities. An Eastern European Country's Approach. *Transform. Bus. Econ.*, 14, 2A (35A), 529–549, 2015, Available:http://www.trans-formations.khf.vu.lt/35a/article/thera
5. British Standards Institute (BSI).
6. United State of America Office Technical and Scientific Information.
7. Moir, E., Moonem, T., Clark, G., *what are future cities? Origin meaning and uses complied the business of cities for the foresight future of cities project and future cities catapult*, government office of science, UK, June, 2014.
8. Lee, J., Phaal, R., Lee, S., Lee, H., An integrated service-device-technology roadmap for smart city development. *Technol. Forecast. Soc. Change*, 80, 286–306, 2013.
9. National League of Cities, *Blockchain in Cities: Restoring Trust and Transparency Digital.Transactions*, 2016, https://www.nlc.org/sites/default/files/2018/06/CSAR_Blockchain%20Report%20PR INT.pdf.

10. Simpson, P. and Rocque, M., *Smart cities: understanding the challenges and opportunities Smart Cities World in association with Philips 2017*, 2017, www.smartcitiesworld.net.

11. Li, S., Application of Blockchain Technology in Smart City Infrastructure. *2018 IEEE International Conference on Smart Internet of Things (Smart IoT)*, pp. 276–2766, Xi'an, 2018.

12. Transform, Transformation agenda for low carbon cities. online: https://urbantransform.eu/about/smart-energy-city (visited August 2020).

13. Hewlett-Packard Enterprise, Internet of Things research study, 2014, accessed on 4-May-2016 [Online]. Available: http://www8.hp.com/h20195/V2/GetPDF.aspx/4AA5-4759ENW.pdf.

14. Saber Talari, Miadreza Shafie-khan, Pierluigi Siano, Vincenzo Loia, Aurelio Tommasetti and Joao P. S. Catalao., A Review of Smart Cities Based on the Internet of Things Concept, *Energies Review*, 2017, 1-23, 10, 421, 2017. https://dx.doi.org/10.3390/em10040421

15. Jing, Q., Vasilakos, V.A., Wan, J., Lu, J., Qiu, D., Security of the Internet of Things: Perspectives and Challenges. *Wirel. Netw.*, 20, 8, 2481–2501, 2014, Availablehttp://link.springer.com/arti-cle/10.1007%2Fs11276-014-0761-7#/page-1.

16. Yaga, D., Mell, P., Roby, N., Scarfone, K., *Blockchain Technology Overview*, 2018, National Institute of Standards and Technology U.S department of commerce Internal Report 8202 66 pages (October 2018).

17. Sarmah, S.S., Understanding Blockchain Technology. *Comput. Sci. Eng. 2018*, 8, 2, 23–29, 2018.

18. Eremia, M., Toma, L., Sanduleac, M., the smart city concept in the 21st century. *10th international conference interdisciplinary in Engineering, INTER-ENG 2016, Proc. Eng.*, 181, 12–19, 2017.

19. Damianou, A., Angelopoulos, C.M., Katos, V., An Architecture for Blockchain over Edge-enabled IoT for Smart Circular Cities.

20. Liu, Y. and Hou, R., About the Sensing Layer in Internet of Things. *Comput. Study*, 2010, 5, 55, 62, 2010.

21. Selinger, M., *Test: Fitness wristbands reveal data*, pp. 1–7, Test AVTEST GmbH, Klewitzstr, Germany, Jun. 2015.

22. Salha, R.A., El-Hallaq, M.A., Alastal, A.I., Blockchain in Smart Cities: Exploring Possibilities in Terms of Opportunities and Challenges. *J. Data Anal. Inf. Process.*, 7, 118–139, 2019, https://doi.org/10.4236/jdaip.2019.73008.

23. Mittal, S., Khan, M.A., Romero, D., Wuest, T., Smart Manufacturing Characteristics, Technologies and Enabling Factors. *Smart Manufacturing Digital Factory: Proc. IMECHE 2017 Part B: Manuf. Eng.*, 233, 5, 1342–1361, 2019.

24. Tan, L. and Wang, N., Future Internet: The Internet of Things, in: *Proc. 3rd Int. Conf. Adv. Comput. Theory Eng. (ICACTE)*, pp. V5–376_V5–380, Aug. 2010, vol. 5, 2010.

25. Cui, L., Xie, G., Qu, Y., Gao, L., Yang, Y., Security and privacy in smart cities: challenges and opportunities. *IEEE Access*, 6, 46134–4614, 2018, http://www. dx.doi.org/10.1109/ACCESS.2018.2853985.

26. National League of Cities, Trends in Smart City Development, 2016, https://www.nlc.org/sites/default/files/2017-01/Trends%20in%20Smart%20 City%20 Development.pdf.

27. Barzilay, O., 3 ways blockchain is revolutionizing cybersecurity, Forbes, 2017, Available: https://www.forbes.com/sites/omribarzilay/2017/08/21/3-ways-blockchain-is-revolutionizing cybersecurity/5e4b25f82334.

28. Bifulco, F., Tregua, M., Amitrano, C.C., D'Auria, A., ICT and sustainability in smartcities management. *Int. J. Public Sect. Manage.*, 29, 2, 132–147, 2016.

29. Woods, E., *Smart City Challenges & Opportunities innovative energy review*, Navigant Research, 2017, 2017.

30. Ranchordás, S., Does sharing mean caring: Regulating innovation in the sharing economy. *Minn. J. Law Sci. Technol.*, 16, 413, 2015.

31. McLaren, D., Agyeman, J., *Sharing Cities: A Case for Truly Smart and Sustainable Cities*, MIT Press, 2015.

32. Washburn, D., Sindhu, U., Balaouras, S., Dines, R.A., Hayes, N.M., Nelson, L.E., *Helping CIOs Understand "Smart City" Initiatives: Defining the Smart City, Its Drivers, and the Role of the CIO*, Forrester Research, Inc., Cambridge, MA, 2010, http://public.dhe.ibm.com/partnerworld/pub/smb/smarterplan.

33. Barbosa, A.C., Moraes, T.M., Tesima, D.T., Pontes, R.C., de Sá Motta Lima, A., Azevedo, B.Z., Smart Planning: Tools, Concepts, and Approaches for a Sustainable Digital Transformation, in: *Smart and Digital Cities:From Computational Intelligence to Applied Social Sciences*, pp. 221–236, Springer, Cham, Switzerland, 2019, 2019.

34. Biswas, K., Muthukkumarasamy, V., Securing Smart Cities Using Blockchain Technology. *2016 IEEE 14th International Conference on Smart Cities*, pp. 1392–1393, 2016.

35. Pieroni, A., Scarpato, N., Di Nunzio, L., Fallucchi, F., Raso, M., Smarter City: Smart Energy Grid Based on Blockchain Technology. *Int. Adv. Sci. Eng. Inf. Technol.*, 8, 298–306, 2018, https://doi.org/10.18517/ijaseit.8.1.4954.

36. Christidis, K. and Devetsikiotis, M., Blockchains and Smart Contracts for the IoTs. *IEEE Access*, Special section plethora Res. IoT, 2292–2303, 2016, 2016.

37. Lee, J.Y., A decentralized token economy: How blockchain and cryptocurrency can revolutionize business. *Bus. Horizons*, 2019, 62, 773–784, 2019.

38. *The Smart City Revolution Improving Outcomes for Citizens and Businesses by Applying Industry Expertise and Digital Technology*, SAP SE or an SAP affiliate company. Thought Leadership Paper Smart City, 2018.

39. Oliveira, T.A., Oliver, M., Ramalhinho, H., Challenges for Connecting Citizens and Smart Cities: ICT, E-Governance and Blockchain. *Sustainability*, 2020, 12, 2926, 2020.

40. Novotný, R., Kuchta, R., Kadlec, J., Smart City Concept, Applications and Services. *J. Telecommun. Syst. Manag.*, 3, 117, 2014.

41. Gilman, H.R., *Participatory Budgeting and Civic Tech: The Revival of Citizen Engagement*, Georgetown University Press, Washington, DC, USA, 2016, 2016.
42. Jha, S., Kumar, R., Chatterjee, J.M., Khari, M., Collaborative handshaking approaches between internet of computing and internet of things towards a smart world: a review from 2009–2017. *Telecommun. Syst.*, 70, 4, 617–634, 2019.
43. Kumar, A., Payal, M., Dixit, P., Chatterjee, J.M., Framework for Realization of Green Smart Cities Through the Internet of Things (IoT), in: *Trends in Cloud-based IoT*, pp. 85–111, 2020.

About the Editors

Dr. Vishal Kumar is presently working as an assistant professor in the Department of Computer Science and Engineering at Bipin Tripathi Kumaon Institute of Technology, Dwarahat (an Autonomous Institute of Govt. of Uttarakhand). He holds a PhD degree in Computer Science and Engineering from Uttarakhand Technical University, Dehradun, an MTech from the National Institute of Technology, Hamirpur, and a BTech from Kumaon Engineering College (now BTKIT Dwarahat). He is a life member of the Computer Society of India (CSI) and a senior member of IEEE. He has almost 15 years of teaching experience, research and administration.

Dr. Vishal Jain is currently an associate professor at the Department of Computer Science and Engineering, School of Engineering and Technology, Sharda University, Greater Noida, UP India. Before that, he worked for several years as an associate professor at Bharati Vidyapeeth's Institute of Computer Applications and Management (BVICAM), New Delhi. He has more than 14 years of experience in the academics. He obtained a PhD (CSE), MTech (CSE), MBA (HR), MCA, MCP and CCNA. He has more than 450 research citation indices with Google Scholar (h-index score 12 and i-10 index 15).

Dr. Bharti Sharma earned a PhD in Computer Science and Engineering from Uttarakhand Technical University, Dehradun. She is currently serving as an assistant professor and academic head of the MCA department of DIT University, Dehradun. She has 17 years of rich experience in academics and research. Her research work is mainly associated with natural language processing (NLP), intelligent transportation systems (ITS), big data analytics, machine learning and respective application domains. In her research work, her team is mainly engaged in the development of intelligent computational models using machine learning methods to solve various challenging problems related to transportation and other relevant areas.

Jyotir Moy Chatterjee is an assistant professor in the Information Technology Department at Lord Buddha Education Foundation (LBEF), Kathmandu, Nepal. Prior to joining LBEF, he worked as an assistant professor in the Computer Science and Engineering Department at GD Rungta College of Engineering and Technology (CSVTU), Bhilai, India. He received his MTech in Computer Science and Engineering from Kalinga Institute of Industrial Technology, Bhubaneswar, Odisha, and a BTech in Computer Science and Engineering from Dr. MGR Educational and Research Institute, Chennai. He is credited with 59 international research paper publications, 3 conference papers, 3 authored books, 10 edited books, 16 book chapters, 2 Master's theses converted into books and 1 patent.

Dr. Rakesh Shrestha received a BE degree in Electronics and Communication Engineering from Tribhuvan University (TU), Nepal, in 2006, an ME degree in Information and Communication Engineering from Chosun University in 2010, and a PhD degree in Information and Communication Engineering from Yeungnam University in 2018. From 2010 to 2011 he was a security engineer with Honeywell Security Systems; from 2010 to 2012 a core network engineer with Huawei Technologies Company, Ltd., Nepal; and from 2018 to 2019 a postdoctoral researcher at the Department of Information and Communication Engineering, Yeungnam University, South Korea.

Index

Printed and bound by CPI Group (UK) Ltd, Croydon, CR0 4YY